CASS SERIES: STUDIES IN INTELLIGENCE
(Series Editors: Christopher Andrew and Michael I. Handel)

ETERNAL VIGILANCE?
50 YEARS OF THE CIA

Also in this series

ETERNAL VIGILANCE?
50 YEARS OF THE CIA

Edited by

RHODRI JEFFREYS-JONES
CHRISTOPHER ANDREW

FRANK CASS

LONDON • PORTLAND, OR

First published 1997 in Great Britain by
FRANK CASS & COMPANY LTD
2 Park Square, Milton Park,
Abingdon, Oxon, OX14 4RN

and in the United States of America by
FRANK CASS
270 Madison Ave,
New York NY 10016

Transferred to Digital Printing 2006

British Library Cataloguing in Publication Data
A catalogue record for this book is available from the British Library

Library of Congress Cataloging in Publication Data
has been applied for
ISBN 0-7146-4807-8 (cloth)
ISBN 0-7146-4360-2 (paper)

This group of studies first appeared in 'Eternal Vigilance? 50 Years of the CIA',
a Special Issue of the journal *Intelligence and National Security*,
Vol.12, No.1 (January 1997)
published by Frank Cass & Co. Ltd.

Contents

Editor's Preface

The condition upon which God hath given liberty to man is eternal vigilance; which condition if he break, servitude is at once the consequence of his crime, and the punishment of his guilt.

These words, spoken by John Philpot Curran in 1790 in defence of the right of election of the Lord Mayor of Dublin, spring once again to mind in 1997, a year that marks the 50th anniversary of one of America's best-known institutions. In February 1947, the White House submitted to Congress a bill for the unification of the armed forces which, in its 102nd clause, provided for the establishment of a central intelligence agency. After several months of Senate and House hearings, Congress approved the bill on 26 July. the National Security Act came into force on 19 September and, the following day, the modest Central Intelligence Group gave way to the mighty United States Central Intelligence Agency (CIA) – an agency whose destiny came to be synonymous, in the mind of its supporters, with vigilance in the defence of liberty. In the mid-1970s, however, the belief that the defence of liberty also required increased vigilance towards the CIA itself led to the creation of the congressional intelligence committees.

No single volume of essays can hope to cover all, or even most, of the CIA's diverse activities during its first 50 years. *Eternal Vigilance?* seeks, however, both to offer reinterpretations of some of the major established themes in CIA history (the origins and foundation of the Agency, its assessment of the Soviet threat and the Iranian revolution, and the problem of accountability) and to open up new areas of research (foreign liaison, relations with the scientific community and the use of scientific and technical research, covert funding of women's groups, economic intelligence, and the Agency's changing attitude to its own history).

The editors have sought to include in this volume articles by both well-known scholars in the field and young researchers at the beginning of their academic careers. Contributions come almost equally from both sides of the Atlantic. All draw, in varying degrees, on recently declassified documents and newly-available archives. And, as the conclusion seeks to show, all point the way to future research.

1

The American Road to Central Intelligence

BRADLEY F. SMITH

Intelligence changes rained down upon the United States in a great torrent during the 1940s and early 1950s, culminating in the creation of the Central Intelligence Agency in 1947 and the National Security Agency in 1952. This occurred in part because World War II intelligence developments such as those within the US Army (Military Intelligence Division), the US Navy (Office of Naval Intelligence) and in William Donovan's Coordinator of Information and Office of Strategic Services (OSS) organizations, provided the US government with the experienced and skilled personnel to make such postwar intelligence innovation possible.

In addition, unsettled conditions in the postwar era played a part by requiring innovative new political-military arrangements in every corner of the globe. But probably most important, there came the threatening forward pressure of the USSR which manifested itself in the late 1940s. When this 'Soviet threat' was combined with the residual shock and sense of vulnerability that had been engendered by Hitler's *Blitzkrieg* surprises, and especially the Japanese attack on Pearl Harbor, the American public and its leaders were given a new sense of vulnerability and a belief that new and more assertive methods needed to be employed to protect national security.

However, it is important to remember that neither the American intelligence organizations which had been created during World War II such as OSS, nor the CIA and the National Security Agency (NSA) which followed them, arose from a historical vacuum. Men such as Franklin Roosevelt (born 1882) and William Donovan (born 1883), had lived not only through periods in which American intelligence had been weak and backward, but also eras in which the US intelligence system was strong and nearly the equal of those of other great powers.

Therefore to form a realistic picture of how and why OSS/CIA and its intelligence modernizing companions were created in the period 1941–52, one must acknowledge the great changes and challenges which took place in those 11 years. But it is also useful to examine the main phases of American intelligence history from the Civil War era to 1942, in order to gauge whether or not the creations of the 1940s and 1950s were radical departures in American history or were simply new superstructures built on earlier eras in which the US had quite effective intelligence organizations.

It is a reasonable truism that extensive and bitterly fought conflicts tend to produce innovation in all things military, including intelligence. Such developments definitely occurred in the great revolutionary struggles which began with the American Revolution and stretched on through the wars of the French Revolution to the Vienna settlement of 1815. This 40-year period saw warfare energized by new organizations, tactics and strategies, made possible by the ideological enthusiasm which made individuals willing to fight and die, if necessary, to further one cause or another. The spirit of ideological commitment also penetrated into the intelligence realm, and some individuals, including perhaps even General Benedict Arnold, pursued the trade of espionage and treachery out of some idealism as well as greed and resentment.

However, following the Vienna Congress of 1815, the revolutionary fires were dampened and the 'old order' continued to hold on to power for at least half a century. Wars were few and limited in scope and time, so the European governments were primarily concerned to pursue real or imaginary security and subversive dangers at home and abroad. Intelligence modernization was consequently muted in Europe as well as the USA in an era in which 20 per cent of the British Foreign Service budget was spent on secret service activities aimed more at subversive than at foreign military activities.[1]

The two decades following 1850, however, witnessed a series of major wars – the Seven Weeks War (Austro-Prussian), the Franco-Prussian War, and, most important for the USA of course, the American Civil War in which technological change and military innovation determined in large measure who would win and who would lose. The US armed forces on the two sides of the American Civil War did not produce any startling intelligence innovations during that conflict (despite the employment of observation balloons), but they did make a series of important innovations in weaponry, including submarine and torpedo technology, the development of high quality artillery, and a leap ahead regarding military signals. In consequence, throughout the 1860s and 1870s, foreign governments, led by the British, spent considerable time and effort studying US Army and Navy equipment and combat methodology. Most such examinations, including that done by the British Navy, were carried out openly by visiting officers and the British Naval Attaché who made the intelligence rounds between the principal naval powers. The British also used some Secret Service money in America during the 1860s and 1870s, but virtually all of it was to finance secret information on the Fenian Irish.[2]

Much of the detail on weaponry of the Powers was at that time made freely available to foreign governments. After developing new defences on the Potomac river in 1866, Washington promptly revealed the details to the British authorities, even though the only country which had previously launched an attack up the Potomac was Britain (in the War of 1812).[3]

But the dispatch of the first US Naval Attaché to his new post in London in 1882 showed that America was now prepared to play the game, and make use of the prevailing openness to increase the inward flow of information on the armed forces of other countries. In the same era, the US Army, while engaged in the great Indian Wars on the Western Plains, showed itself equally willing to cooperate with British authorities regarding information on the most formidable of Indian challenges, a British intelligence report on Sitting Bull being supplied to the Americans in the late 1870s.[4]

The 1880s was an era of increased tension in Europe with the Austro-German Dual Alliance converted to the Triple Alliance by the adhesion of Italy in 1882. This initiated the struggle of alliance blocs which led to World War I 35 years later. During the 1880s, at a time when the British government began to complain that other countries were becoming secretive, American military and naval intelligence threw off most of the shackles of innocence and timidity, and introduced many of the same organizational innovations being carried out by the other major powers. In 1885, the United States established an Intelligence Group in the War Department and three years later the first US Military Attaché took up his post abroad.[5]

The US Navy, which launched a major modernization and building program in 1885/86, also carried through extensive intelligence reforms. The navy's Office of Naval Intelligence (ONI) was created in 1884, well ahead of the Royal Navy's replacement of its old-fashioned Naval Intelligence Committee by a new Naval Intelligence Division (NID).[6] Most importantly, the US Navy enthusiastically shared in the use of the most important technical intelligence innovation of the age, the application of still photography to the identification and detailing of foreign naval vessels. Although the Royal Navy was collecting photographs of foreign ports and warships at least as early as 1878, the US Navy began to shift from artists' renderings to photographs for ship identification by 1885, the same period in which the Royal Navy introduced its first foreign naval vessel identification-volumes using photographs (1886).

The only aspect of intelligence in which the United States seriously lagged behind the other powers during the mid-1880s was in the realm of secret information in respect to security suspects. In 1880, the British Army's share of the secret budget was £65,000, but most of the secret vote was still not expended on any form of intelligence related to military operations. The bulk of it went to the Home Office and the British authorities in Ireland.[7]

The US remained a wide open country, dependent on local police authorities committed to crime prevention and criminal punishment, with little or no idea of anti-subversive operations. There was also only a rudimentary respect for the application of technology to police work and the identification of suspects. When, for example, in November 1884 the London police requested that the State of Nebraska supply a photograph of a man from that State who was held in London for murder, the Nebraska authorities replied that they had no photograph of the man in question, but they were happily forwarding a photograph of his brother![8]

Such naiveté, and blindness to the minimal requirements of fair play and internal security, underscores that in the 1880s the United States was still a very decentralized country trying to play the international game with widely diffused authority at home. But it is also true that in regard to intelligence on foreign military and naval matters, the US government was in the same league as the major European powers, with ONI in existence, army and navy attachés abroad, and naval cameras recording details of foreign navy units.

The subsequent decade, the last of the nineteenth century, faced American intelligence with a new series of challenges. Again, the stakes were raised, and the game made harsher and faster, by the formation of another alliance bloc. The Franco-Russian Alliance of 1894 left this pair of countries confronting the three members of the Triple Alliance (Germany, Austria-Hungary and Italy), and only three powers remained free agents, Britain, Japan, and the USA. Inevitably, Britain then tried to snuggle closer to both the United States and Japan. Even before the Spanish–American War dramatically raised the US profile in international relations, Britain had elevated its Mission in Washington to the Embassy level in 1893 (over the objections of Queen Victoria), and soon thereafter the two countries were exchanging samples of their basic infantry weapons, and British officers were permitted to make detailed studies of American coastal fortifications.[9]

The Spanish–American War of 1898 revealed the United States for the first time as an assertive military power within, and beyond, the Western Hemisphere. Some intelligence fiascos occurred, such as the discovery after the war began that one major War Department secret report on the Philippines had actually just been copied from the *Encyclopaedia Britannica*, but over all American intelligence, based largely on the work of such secret emissaries as Lieutenant Whitney in Puerto Rico and extensive questioning of merchant ship captains, was adequate to get forces ashore, and improvized combat intelligence operations then helped take the American ground forces on to victory.[10]

Throughout the campaign, American intelligence gathering was greatly aided by US Navy and Army attachés stationed in both Europe and Asia, who provided valuable information (in some cases through running espionage agents) regarding Spanish armament, dispositions and intentions.[11]

But no sooner did the United States complete the leap into something approximating full membership in the modern intelligence club through participation in the Spanish–American War, than great power international relations sharply increased in the ominous complexity and modernity of its weaponry. Although the Americans and the British managed in 1899 to squeeze the Germans out of Samoa, and Britain also strengthened its position in Asia by an alliance with Japan in 1902, Britain was soon absorbed into the system of alliance blocs. The *Entente Cordiale* was signed by Britain and France in 1904, and when supplemented by the Anglo–Russian agreement of 1907, Europe was divided into hostile camps, with Britain, Japan, France and Russia on one side, and Germany, Austria–Hungary and Italy on the other. The USA was therefore the only nation of consequence left out of the alliance bloc system.[12]

Running parallel to the march toward confrontational blocs of great powers in the early twentieth century, there occurred a new, and more deadly arms race. The armies and navies of the European powers and Japan underwent modernization, and the main features of maritime power were transformed, The Royal Navy launched HMS *Dreadnought* in 1906 and ceased attending German Navy maneuvers in order to prevent reciprocal German visits in hopes of slowing the pace of German dreadnought development. But the Germans nonetheless launched a comparable super battleship in 1907, maintaining the balance and raising the risks involved in European conflict.[13]

In the same era local wars, from the Boer War in 1899–1902 to the Russo–Japanese War in 1904–5, and the Balkan Wars (1912–13) which followed, became testing grounds in which new military technology and military techniques were employed.[14]

Although the only power not directly involved in the new alliance structures and the arms race (except for some naval building which paralleled it) was the United States, American shyness about armaments was in some important ways paradoxical. Industrial strength had become the basis of military power, and the era from 1899 to 1905 was precisely the point when American industrial strength took off and established a commanding US lead in nearly all aspects of basic production. So in fact the

United States had the basic strength but only lacked the instruments and the will to assert superpower status even then. But while the US remained on the sidelines, European and Asian tension, conflict and alliance building inevitably led to military expansion and innovations in the intelligence systems of those within the alliances. Britain established a highly-effective army field intelligence system during the South African War, but although the US Army had observers on both sides of that conflict, they do not seem to have grasped the value of British field intelligence, nor did they learn that Britain was using telephoto photography in this struggle, or understand that the War in South Africa had set off such a round of secret agent activity that Britain had reformed its whole secret intelligence apparatus.[15]

Britain spent at least £60,000 on secret intelligence in 1900, including money for agents to check shipment of weaponry to the Boers at a cost of £20,000. Some of this kind of expenditure, which expanded again and again during the tense and threatening first 14 years of the century, may have provided useful bits of information (just as the Russian extensive reading of foreign diplomatic codes in the same period may have strengthened St Petersburg's diplomatic hand).[16] But agents were usually unable to get hard data on the most important matters, such as specific information on other countries' military deployment, technology or strategy. As one British Army official conceded confidentially in this period, one of the Secret Service's most valued agents actually couldn't 'tell one regiment from another'. Masses of British Secret Service money was actually poured into marginal enterprizes such as hidden subsidies to the French newspaper Le Siècle to give it a more pro-British tone, and the engagement of an agent codenamed 'A' who was supposed to gather information on French intentions while running a coal stove business in Paris as a cover. 'A' actually became so mired down in his coal business difficulties that he acquired very little information of value, which led Lord Lansdowne, the British Foreign Secretary, finally to cry out in despair, 'I am heartily sick of A ... let us have done with him completely in God's name.'[17]

Surely not all European secret intelligence activities in the early twentieth century were as appropriate for the comic stage as the saga of A, but that America excluded itself from the running of secret agents in that period probably did not weaken its position as the fantasies of spy fiction writers might suggest. Ignoring other forms of intelligence collection, however, did put the United States at a disadvantage. In 1901, when the French Navy began its first experiments with communication by radio telegraphy, the French carried out the tests in the Mediterranean rather than the Channel, presumably to lessen the possibility of eavesdropping by the Royal Navy. But not only did the British pick up the record of the French tests at a listening station on Gibraltar, HMS Pyramis closely tracked the

French squadron and secured a complete record of the French messages. Apparently this was the first instance of radio intelligence interception, and though the French transmissions had not been in code, the British secured definite intelligence benefit by proving that complete interception was possible, and also because they mastered how the French treated accent marks in the dot, dash system.

Soon thereafter, the Royal Navy went on to establish War Signals stations in the Channel in 1904. Radio installations were then authorized for these stations in 1906, and at least within the next two years, some of the War Signals stations had been equipped with radio apparatus.[18]

Furthermore, by 1907, the internal structure of Admiralty Intelligence had been reorganized, and other branches of the British government were also pushing ahead on intelligence and security matters. The year 1906 saw the first British Army central intelligence organization, and creation of a plan for security control of the press in time of war. Two years later the first British Army intelligence course began and by this time the Admiralty had one secret agent within the German Admiralty and another inside the Krupp works. In addition, the Royal Navy was employing the British Consul in Bremen to photograph German installations, and in 1909 the Admiralty planted a Reuters representative in Kiel to help track German merchant and naval traffic on the Kiel Canal.[19]

Even as the British and other European governments expanded and deepened their intelligence systems in the early twentieth century, their fears of intelligence penetration by real, possible, or imagined opponents grew apace. Panics about the alleged activities of foreign spies and saboteurs swept through the press and chanceries of most European countries in the decade and a half before the outbreak of general war in 1914. Organization and reorganization of intelligence and security service organizations, such as those which produced the British Secret Intelligence Service (SIS) and the Counter Intelligence Section (later MI5) in 1911, then followed in most European countries.

It again must be acknowledged however, that although the various panics about spies and security were heartfelt in every country, and the counter intelligence reforms were also energetically pressed home, most of the espionage threats were imaginary, and most of the controls were extremely lax compared with what would come with World War I. A comprehensive British order issued shortly before the outbreak of war in 1914 required what were seen as stern measures to be taken against foreign sailors and seamen suspected of carrying out espionage, but then added that such a sailor was only 'to be detained' if 'he refuses to give his name and ship.'[20]

So it is obvious that Europeans had stopped well short of the rack and the thumbscrew in dealing with intelligence and subversion up to August 1914. But they had nonetheless moved somewhat closer to modern systems of intelligence collection and security. The United States, on the other hand, while partially keeping on the course of building up its naval power, especially during the Roosevelt and Taft administrations, definitely fell well behind the European powers in all aspects of intelligence and counter intelligence activity between 1909 and 1914. The American government did pursue intelligence information during the Russo-Japanese War, with all US military attachés and observers in the Far East being instructed to grasp every opportunity to gain information on both of the belligerents, and on the details of the conflict itself.[21] The US Navy also continued to exchange some intelligence and technical information with the British, while the armies and navies of Britain and the United States still opened their maneuvers to each other and to observers from other 'friendly' countries.[22] When in 1911 the young Major George C. Marshall was in Britain on a private sightseeing visit, although he was unable to obtain formal British Army permission to observe the maneuvers, he merely dressed in civilian clothes, rented a bicycle, and peddled about examining everything he wished to see. No British official ever stopped or questioned him, or put restrictions in his way; being a young American was apparently enough to guarantee him free passage and virtually free right of observation.[23]

As the other great powers geared up for a general conflict, lurching from one dangerous crisis to another (Algeciras, Agadir, etc.) the US government made a few halting steps in the direction of improved security. In 1908, the Bureau of Investigation, the first modern predecessor of the FBI, was established, and by 1908, ONI instituted a system of moderately tighter security.[24] But American intelligence collection itself failed to expand or improve, although the US Army sent observers to the First Balkan War in 1912, and in the following year US Army officers travelling abroad were instructed to take advantage of their travel opportunities to collect data on foreign armies.[25] In 1910, the Second Division of the War Department was abolished as a separate entity of the US Army Staff,[26] and whatever military intelligence functions remained were lost deep in the quietest eddies of the US Army War College.

Overall, American national security in this era of great peril was left to the traditional defences provided by two oceans and wide open spaces, coupled with American productive and innovative strength. In 1906, the US Navy began yet another new building program, and the United States introduced machine-guns into its Army. In the same year the Wright Brothers' first effective aircraft became operational. The Wrights actually considered selling this plane to the British government for $20,000, but

London thought the asking price much too high – by such threads of chance as this was American security preserved against all comers![27]

It can be argued that American passivity during this, the most dangerous phase of the arms race, was due at least in some measure to the extremely close and warm relations which prevailed between American civil and military authorities on one hand and those of Great Britain on the other. In 1906, an Admiralty memorandum prepared for the Prime Minister declared that Britain was 'on the best of terms' with the United States, and 'a combination between Germany and France, or between either of those countries and the United States against us is inconceivable.'[28] Five years later, the Foreign Secretary Lord Grey told the Committee on Imperial Defence, 'how very sure' he was that 'there can be no serious cause of trouble between the British Empire and the United States.'[29] In the following year, during a Cabinet meeting, fittingly held on 4 July, the then Prime Minister, Herbert Asquith, declared that the 'United States be omitted' from the calculations whereby the British were committed to build a fleet equal to the power of the second and third ranked fleets combined. Ironically, the only Cabinet member who objected to this proposal was the First Lord of the Admiralty, none other than Winston Spencer Churchill, but the Prime Minister would have none of his doubts, and citing 'Lord Fisher and the Board of Admiralty' to support his case, carried the Cabinet with him in excluding the United States from the list of even remotely possible enemies, and Mr Churchill was compelled to follow in his wake.[30]

The details of this development were kept from all foreign governments, including that of the United States. It meant, however, that Britain would put good relations with the Americans above nearly every other consideration, and the USA could rest comparatively easily, even if weak, disarmed, and poorly served in intelligence matters, as long as Great Britain ruled most of the seas.

Consequently, when war began in August 1914, the United States was not merely a poorly and unevenly armed neutral, with only the US Navy in even approximately significant frontline strength; it was also a country subtly, but strongly, tied to Britain, whose own intelligence position was actually comparatively worse than at any time since the middle of the nineteenth century. Since from the beginning of the World War the Central Powers carried on an offensive strategy, it was therefore easy for neutrals to see them as villains, and since German U-boats were the principal threat to American property, life and neutrality, it was also relatively easy for Washington to hold on, smile benignly on the Allies, profit from greatly expanded exports to Britain and France, and do nothing very provocative to either side.

The American armed forces thereby fell even further behind the other powers between the years 1914 and 1917, with military and naval intelligence primarily dependent on attaché reports and newspapers for information about the war. The United States actually only had 14 military attachés abroad in 1914, and though Lord Kitchener invited the American attaché assigned to London to his headquarters, the French consistently refused to allow the American attaché in Paris into the field, even in rear areas. So America slumbered on at a time when intelligence and subversive control was leaping ahead among the warring nations. By the end of 1914, Room 40 was already well along in penetrating German Navy codes, and by 1915, as part of the move of intelligence into the high tech realm, codebreakers began to be recruited from British universities.[31]

The British were also not slow to play out the new, rougher and smarter, intelligence game on American soil. In 1914, the British military attaché in Washington volunteered to live a double life and simultaneously served as a secret agent, and soon thereafter, William Wiseman set up his SIS operation in New York, primarily to check on German 'intrigue.' Soon, however, Wiseman was dabbling in many aspects of American trade and financial activities.

Although the British became more cautious and careful in 1916 in their relations with US officials, because of American hesitation and insecurity, by 1917 the United States Embassy in London was cooperating with Special Branch and other portions of Britain's secret world in the collection of information about subversive dangers. The US Counsellor in charge of this operation, Edward Bell, was ably assisted by George Hurley, who would play a role in secret subversive control and intelligence operations in the United States and France in the later stages of the war, as well as in the early interwar period, (not Patrick Hurley, Herbert Hoover's Secretary of War in the late 1920s, and a special emissary for Franklin Roosevelt in the 1940s).[32]

The increasing American fascination with the counter intelligence and anti-subversive aspects of intelligence (at the expense of secret information gathering) meant that even as a neutral, the US government should have had no difficulty grasping the significance of the great media blitz of hate and fear which had overcome the warring countries. All the belligerent nations waged the secret war with such ferocity that nearly any measure became acceptable as long as it seemed to thwart the enemy and punished those who might weaken national security.

In autumn 1914, one Ernest Waldeman was picked up by the police in northwest London, opposite Belsize Park Underground station. Accused of having communicated with 'a suspect address' (meaning an address that British Security concluded was a German espionage letter drop in the Low Countries), Waldeman had a short morning trial, was quickly convicted,

Countries), Waldeman had a short morning trial, was quickly convicted, then sentenced to death, and immediately shot.[33] The incident was far from earth shaking at the time, and now there seems no way of establishing his guilt or innocence. [It probably sticks in my mind and my craw only because the records of the case have just been released in the Public Record Office, and because once or twice each week I walk past the spot by Belsize Park tube station where Waldeman was swept to his death 80 years ago.]

The Waldeman case is, however, a useful reminder of the dark stains which accompanied Europe's rush into a secret clandestine struggle that recognized few limits and little mercy. It also points up the fact that American reservations in 1914–17 about leaping quickly into full-scale intelligence and anti-subversive operations arose in part out of unease, if not horror, at the great wave of fear, intimidation, repression, and panic which had accompanied Europe's march into war in 1914.

When, therefore, the US finally entered the war in April 1917, awash with Wilsonian idealism, and swept by relatively tame versions of bravado and fear of German subversion, the US military was far behind its Allied colleagues in military and intelligence sophistication. The most recent US Army operation had been the pursuit of bandit bands in northern Mexico, and in that operation the US Army had concluded that Apache scouts were far superior to new fangled things such as aerial reconnaissance in providing useful intelligence. The American Expeditionary Forces (AEF) ground forces sent to France were therefore almost completely dependent on Allied, especially British, operational intelligence sources, and the AEF air staff also received 'British Secret Service' intelligence in France at least as early as December 1917.[34]

In Washington and London, US Army and State Department intelligence cooperation with the British moved into high gear in the spring and early summer of 1917. The American Army's MIS section was established under Major General Ralph Van Deman in May 1917, and a month later, Van Deman began intensive collaboration with the British SIS representative in Washington, Claude Dansey. The same period saw the beginning of receipt by US Navy authorities of secret information from the Admiralty regarding German U-boat and surface operations, much of this information originating from Room 40 codebreaking activities.[35]

Building on this British intelligence support, as well as the American government's recognition that to function effectively in a world war it must conduct serious secret intelligence operations, the US Army turned its attaché offices in sensitive locations such as Denmark and the Netherlands into important sources of secret information.[36] At home, the War Department mobilized semi-official organizations, including the American Protection League, to extend the range of anti-subversive and clandestine information gathering activities into every corner of American society during the 19 months of the US war effort.

The Armistice of November 1918 produced a rapid run-down of the US Army and Navy's emergency intelligence machinery. American military and civil authorities used some secret information collection methods during the Paris Peace Conference of 1919, but all forms of military and naval secret intelligence gathering were sharply reduced with the demobilization at the end of the war. The rise of isolationist sentiment and disillusion which arose from the disappointing results of America's first great crusade in Europe led to a general dismantling of the Great War combative machine and an increase in suspicion regarding the methods and mores of the fractured and battered old world which emerged from the war.[37]

Inevitably, in this era of isolation and suspicion, anti-subversive intelligence remained the central element of American secret intelligence activity. The War, Navy, Justice and State departments were all active in collection of intelligence on alleged subversives in the 1920s. Inter-departmental subversive intelligence exchanges such as those between the War and Justice Departments also continued until at least 1927, while British-American subversive intelligence cooperation went on throughout the 1920s and 1930s.[38]

The US Army and Navy (like the British authorities) also continued codebreaking activities, especially against the Japanese, until 1929, when Henry Stimson ordered that the US Black Chamber be closed. The American military and naval authorities were then left with a weak and limited intelligence gathering apparatus with open sources and attaché reports plus some US Navy code and cipher breaking work again being the main staples of the intelligence diet. Some surveys were made of foreign military exercises, such as the visit of the US Secretary of War to British Army maneuvers in 1927, and throughout the 1920s MID used former MID officers who had returned to civilian life as unpaid sources of foreign intelligence, especially in Latin America and Asia.[39]

No significant changes occurred in the feeble American intelligence arrangements in the early 1930s, but it needs to be emphasized that also in other countries, intelligence rested and rusted in that period. Not until 1935/36 did Britain begin to re-energize its external cryptanalytic activity, and even then the Royal Navy's efforts were aimed at what would soon be seen as literal backwaters, including use of the Suez Canal Company as a hidden center for codebreaking against the French.[40]

Therefore, although American interwar intelligence activity was well behind that of the European powers, it must be noted that until the series of late 1930s crises occurred, beginning with the Italo-Ethiopian War in 1935, the German occupation of the Rhineland (1936) and the Spanish Civil War, followed by the Austrian Anschluss (1938), the intelligence operations of all the great powers were underdeveloped and lacking in systemization. The British were reading a large number of diplomatic codes through much of the interwar period, including most of those of the USA, and carrying out extensive agent and cryptanalytic attacks in which Irish and colonial demons loomed largest in the mind of Whitehall.[41] Britain was also willing to exchange intelligence on subversives with Japan, the USA and various European countries. Not surprisingly, Special Branch even had a secret agent inside the Central Committee of the British Communist Party who, when war broke out on 1 September 1939, permitted Whitehall to track every move of the British CP as it struggled to reconcile its antagonism to the Nazis with Stalin's 1939 non-aggression pact with Hitler.[42]

But the military and naval communications systems of most countries managed to stay ahead of the cryptanalytic activity of others throughout the 1930s, and exchange of visits to maneuvers remained common.[43] Armament innovations, such as Germany's development of Panzer and tactical air force cooperation in the middle and late 1930s, were often shown openly as political intimidation weapons which should have robbed them of tactical and strategic surprise in 1939/40. Overall, the Allied disasters in the first year of World War II were therefore much less due to intelligence failure than to inability (or unwillingness) to grasp the significance of Germany's new *Blitzkrieg* deployment and tactics.

The outbreak of war in September 1939, followed by the smashing German *Blitzkrieg* triumphs, first in Poland and then (May–June 1940) in the West, revealed what excellent German tactical intelligence could do when combined with innovative tactics and state of the art tactical air and armoured deployment. Western defences were shattered, France and the Low Countries quickly fell, and all Western countries, including the USA, were left in a state of shock, while facing a desperate need to mobilize maximum resources, rethink military operational plans and methods, and seize every possible instrument which could assist in stopping the Nazi onslaught.

Intelligence, therefore, was a primary Allied concern, and every effort was made in Britain during 1940/41 to revise and reform the military system. Supplying early warning of German intentions, and providing British forces, especially those at sea and in the air, with secret information, was absolutely vital. But though Ultra showed great promise, the two aspects of Enigma message break-ins which would be most important in 1941–42 – those concerned with North Atlantic U-boat traffic and Luftwaffe operational messages – had not been developed sufficiently soon enough to provide Britain with much of a secret informational shield in the summer of 1940.

Extensive British intelligence reorganization and security reform had to occur in the spring/summer of 1940. Even before the fall of France, the British 'Y' effort (radio traffic analysis) had been reorganized,[44] and amid the disastrous French campaign, Churchill sacked the long-serving head of MI5, Vernon Kell.[45] After the fall of France, the British government nervously reviewed what had gone wrong, reformed the combat intelligence system, and worried about what course the other great powers – Japan, Russia, and especially the United States – would take in the aftermath of the French collapse.

In May 1940, William Stephenson was sent to New York. His mission was to protect British supplies, help detect subversives, and play the anti-subversives intelligence card with the Americans.[46] At this time, the US government was worried about its own security as well as the security of its cash and carry shipments to Britain. But at bottom, the United States was most anxious that Britain remain as an Atlantic shield.

During July 1940 William J. Donovan made his first official visit to Britain. Behind the scenes in official London his visit was viewed with considerable doubt and suspicion,[47] but Donovan was clever, energetic and optimistic, and he was not only wined and dined, but was also taken inside one of the few but new British assets, the secret covert operational world occupied by the Special Operations Executive. Nonetheless, tentative Anglo-American efforts to arrange exchanges of secret intelligence failed in the summer of 1940. By August, the Admiralty had turned cool toward any form of naval liaison, and by 16 October the Royal Navy authorities had concluded that intelligence cooperation with the US fleet in the Pacific was impossible owing to the lack of any US naval intelligence facilities ashore.[48]

Not until winter 1940 did any British and American intelligence organizations get down to the serious business of exchange. The Chief British Censor, E. S. Herbert, visited Washington in October, and then two FBI censorship-intelligence specialists (Agents Clegg and Hine) were sent to Britain.[49] The point of this exchange was to reveal to the American authorities how the British were gaining a significant flow of intelligence as a by-product of censorship, particularly information on enemy agent activities as revealed by the work of the main British censorship organization in Bermuda.

This exchange of visits marked the initial breakthrough into practical Anglo-American intelligence cooperation in World War II. The Americans came into the business through one of its shadiest corners – in depth analysis of other people's mail – but once the Justice Department had bitten into this morsel, the way stood more freely open for other departments to join with the British in more traditional, and perhaps respectable, forms of secret information collection.

Late 1940 and early 1941 also saw more developments which would push the United States and Britain closer together on intelligence matters. Against all odds, Britain was holding, and numerous American visitors were impressed by the country's determination to resist Hitler. William Donovan returned to the UK in December 1940 and again in March 1941, while his efforts in Washington in support of the Lend-Lease Bill earned him special British gratitude, a gratitude expressed in greater British openness regarding Britain's secret assets and activities.[50]

Donovan was not officially taken into the Ultra secret, but anyone with special access in Whitehall could have surmised that London had scored important intelligence successes because the Luftwaffe was beaten over Britain and the Royal Navy was holding its own in the North Atlantic against the U-boat. In the summer of 1941 Bletchley Park had actually scored steady victories against certain important Luftwaffe ciphers, had beaten the Three Wheel Enigma in the North Atlantic and was burrowing away against the new Four Wheel Enigma. By September 1941, Churchill demanded that he be shown 'all Ultra messages daily,' and though he never attained any such complete access to the huge flood of Ultra traffic,[51] he did have at hand enough 'golden eggs' to help make up his mind on many issues and to impress important foreign visitors, especially Americans, by revealing veiled hints and titbits from the golden hoard.

Beginning in June 1941, the United States and Britain took an important step which bound them closer together and laid the basis for what seemed a significant intelligence alliance. The arrival in London of Admiral Robert Ghormley, General George Strong, and General Deles Emmons (constituting a special three-services American liaison mission) appeared to lay the basis for comprehensive intelligence cooperation at a time when Britain's now well honed and Ultra equipped system had much to offer the USA. But three months later the United States refused joint services intelligence cooperation because the American Army–Navy animosity had won out again. By the end of the year, Washington bowed to the inevitable and decided that the three Service observers would not be allowed to interpret the directions they received from the weak and ill coordinated Joint Services Board which preceded the creation of the Joint Chiefs of Staff.[52]

Inevitably, far-sighted people in both the United States and the United Kingdom tried to find ways to remove or sidestep these paralyzing interservice obstacles in Washington. The head of Bletchley, Alistair Denniston, visited Washington in August 1941, seeking to find a way through the American Army–Navy impasse in order to arrange some form of Anglo-American cryptanalytic intelligence procedures, but in the end, he failed.[53] In any event, London was hardly ready for complete openness with the Americans, especially since it continued to read American diplomatic codes until at least 25 October 1941. One positive sign of intelligence cooperation appeared in July 1941 when William Donovan, with the President's support, proposed and had approved, the creation of a new intelligence and propaganda organization for the United States government. The Office of the Coordinator of Information (COI), which aspired to be an American secret intelligence, propaganda, and covert operational organization, was open for business in the last weeks of 1941.

But then, the Japanese attacked Pearl Harbor, which not only vaulted the United States into the war, but as most authors who have dealt with the origins of American central intelligence organization agree, was the most important single event which forced intelligence modernization on the US government.

Pearl Harbor certainly did not stop Army–Navy hostility, however, despite the creation of the Joint Chiefs of Staff in early 1942, for as the Secretary of the British JIC, C. V. W. Cavendish-Bentinck, once remarked, the 'US Army and US Navy would just as soon fight each other as the Japanese.'[54] Nonetheless, in the aftermath of the Japanese attack, 'C' warned the Americans of the vulnerability of their codes, and in January 1942, a secret US-UK censorship and censorship-intelligence sharing arrangement was made. Censorship intelligence thus again led the way toward intimate Anglo-American intelligence cooperation (later in 1942, Churchill even removed the Governor of Bermuda because the Americans had trouble working with him on secret censorship matters).[55]

The establishment of OSS (in June 1942), with British blessing, gave the Joint Chiefs of Staff an intelligence arm for the first time. OSS was created not only because of William Donovan's vision and persistence, but also because America had by then so many clandestine war-making concerns that it was essential to create an agency outside both the Army and the Navy which could work with both services and liaise effectively with foreign secret organizations, especially those of Great Britain.

With the major OSS reform in place, the door was open for other intelligence cooperative arrangements. Between June and December 1942, an Anglo-American naval Ultra deal for the North Atlantic was concluded. In mid-summer 1942, British intelligence censorship specialists were stationed in Washington.[56] During the first six months of 1943, OSS was cut into the British interception of German security service traffic, the Americans and the French were allowed a part in CSDIC (the Combined Services Detention Interrogation Centers that used stool pigeons and buggings to get intelligence from POWs), William Friedman's Ultra Mission went to Bletchley, the Army BRUSA agreement was signed, and British and American army cipher breaking specialists joined together to attack Japanese army codes and ciphers.[57]

It is therefore fair to say that the United States, for the first time in its history, had by then a broad and deep intelligence capability including traditional Army, Navy and State Department collection operations, plus cryptanalysts, photo intelligence, the running of secret agents, and a host of other new intelligence activities. Taken together, these gave the USA a large and sophisticated intelligence system comparable to that of other great powers.

The American intelligence arrangements still had peculiar foibles to be sure. Government officials and press commentators worried publicly about the loss of American innocence, and the American devotion to decentralization and bureaucratic clutter continued in full force. The United States even rejected some forms of three service (army, navy and air corps) intelligence cooperation with the British as late as September 1944, even though the US Army joined with the British and French at this very time in carrying out counter-intelligence operations in Europe, surely one of the most sensitive of intelligence activities for any country at any time.

America thus came of age in intelligence during World War II, even though not all the spirits of innocence and bureaucratic rivalry had been laid to rest. By 1945, the US government had even learned to follow the first, if somewhat distasteful, law of intelligence – 'Thou shalt never jeopardize a valuable source.' When, in 1945, Washington learned through Ultra that the codes of her Nationalist Chinese ally were being read by the Japanese, Washington agreed with London without a whimper, that the Chinese should not be told that their codes had been broken. The Japanese were allowed to go on reading Chinese ciphers to their heart's content, because Washington, like London, believed that the secret of Ultra and Magic had to be preserved at all costs.[58]

Given the long way the United States had come toward intelligence adulthood in a very short time, and the degree to which Washington had cooperated with other powers respecting intelligence between 1940 and 1945, it was virtually inevitable that America would go on to reproduce new intelligence arrangements after the war. The collective memory of Pearl Harbor drove home the importance of intelligence. The value of intelligence cooperation during the war, especially that with Great Britain, proved that the USA could function as a global power within the secret world.

Even before the Cold War fully solidified, US officials were drawing up postwar plans for retention of overseas bases and the retention of agreements with other countries regarding radio interception, as if these arrangements would be eternally useful and necessary. The complications associated with occupation duties in Germany and Japan also meant not only that no complete pullback was possible, but that sophisticated intelligence needs would continue at least for many years to come.[59]

The details of America's march toward a systematic postwar permanent intelligence system, made up of CIA, NSA, and the intelligence organizations of the military services, remain significant elements of American intelligence history. But in the broader sense the central fact remains that after passing through a series of ups and downs between 1861 and 1941, the United States finally came of age in World War II, and that henceforth the only road open to it was one leading to larger, more sophisticated, and better integrated intelligence systems.

NOTES

1. For emphasis on anti-subversive, see HD 3 (new release) in the Public Record Office, Kew (hereafter PRO), Zara S. Steiner, *The Foreign Office and Foreign Policy* (Cambridge: CUP 1969) p.5.
2. See for example, the following British Washington Mission entries, 4 April 1866, FO 115/450, 18 May 1872ff, FO 115/540, 13 Aug. 1872, FO 115/547 and 25 Nov. 1872, FO 115/548, PRO.
3. FO 115/448, 449, and 450, PRO, 17 Jan. 1866ff entries, plus G.J.A. O'Toole, *Honorable Treachery* (NY: Atlantic Monthly 1991) pp.170ff.
4. Jeffery M. Dorwart, *The Office of Naval Intelligence* [hereafter ONI] (Annapolis, MD: Naval Inst. Press 1979) p.31, 26 June 1866, ADM 1/5992, PRO. 15 March 1889 Report and following, FO 115/635, 665, and 666, PRO, plus *Foreign Relations of the United States* (Washington DC: US Govt Printing Office 1879) pp.217, 344–6, and 496.
5. O'Toole, *Honorable Treachery* (note 3) p.177, Bruce W. Bidwell, *History of the Military Intelligence Division of the Army General Staff: 1775-1941* [hereafter *History MID*] (Washington DC: UP of America 1986) p.51.
6. Dorwart, *ONI* (note 4) pp.25-6.
7. HD 3/49, PRO, 1880 Summary.
8. FO 115/739, PRO. Memo, 18 Nov. 1884,
9. Dispatch, 18 Feb. 1897 FO 115/1051 and 15 May 1891 reports, ADM 231/20, PRO.
10. See especially, O'Toole, *Honorable Treachery* (note 3), pp.192ff, Bidwell, *History MID* (note 5), p.65, note 14, and David M. Trask, *The War with Spain in 1898* (NY: Macmillan 1981) *passim*.
11. Dorwart, *ONI* (note 4) pp.56ff.
12. Reports, 17 March 1899 , FO 115/1149 and 31 March 1899 memo, ADM 116/97, PRO.
13. ADM 1/7872, 7874 and 7878, PRO, 20 Jan. 1906 ff.
14. On Anglo-Japanese intelligence, see ADM 116/1231B, 19 May 1902 and 6 Feb. 1905, HD 3/130, PRO.
15. FO 115/1145, 13 Oct. 1899ff; 13 June 1902, WO 108/269 as well as WO 108/270 and 348, PRO.
16. Secret materials, 12 April 1905, HD 3/128 and from 1906, HD 3/ 33, PRO.
17. HD 3/111, pts. 1 and 2, 1900–1906; HD 3/113-115, 117, 122 and 127; Quotation, 3 Aug. 1905, HD 3/131, PRO.
18. ADM 1/7878, 4 Aug. 1906. On wireless security, 3 April and 30 July 1901, ADM 231/34, PRO.
19. ADM 1/7872, 20 Jan. 1906; Nov.–Dec. 1907, HD 3/135, 136, and 138; April 1908, WO 279/19; 14 March 1905, HD 3/130, plus for 19 Oct. 1909, ADM 116/940B, PRO.
20. CAB 16/8 and HD 3/139, 1909–1914, and especially CAB 10/3 for 16 Feb. 1914, all PRO.
21. Bidwell, *History MID* (note 5) p.78.

22. FO 371/160, PRO, 13 July and 14 Aug. 1906 reports.
23. Larry I. Bland (ed.) *The Papers of George C. Marshall*, Vol.I (Baltimore: Johns Hopkins UP 1981) p.53.
24. Rhodri Jeffreys-Jones, *The CIA and American Democracy* (New Haven, ICT: 1989), p.13; Dorwart, *ONI* (note 5) p.87-8.
25. Bidwell, *History MID* (note 5), p.101, note 10.
26. Ibid. p.79-84.
27. FO 115/1397 and 1426 18 Aug. 1906, plus, 20 Aug. 1906, FO 371/160, PRO.
28. Admiralty 1906 preparations for a P.Q., ADM 1/7876, PRO.
29. COID, 111th meeting, 26 May 1911, CAB 2/2, PRO.
30. CAB 2/2, PRO, 4 July 1912, 117th Meeting .
31. Hugh C. Hoy, *40 O.B. or How the War Was Won* (London: Hutchinson 1932) *passim*; Alfred Vagts, *The Military Attaché* (Princeton UP 1967) p.266; Bidwell, *History MID* (note 5) pp.94ff.
32. Sir Arthur Willert, *The Road to Safety* (London: Derek Verschoyle 1952) pp. 15ff; Hugh C. Hoy, *40 O.B.*, pp. 41ff. A volume on US–British cooperation on subversive intelligence 1915–45 is in preparation by Drs Eunan O'Halpin, Keith Jeffrey, and the author.
33. WO 71/1237 (recent release), PRO.
34. *The Diaries of Walter Guinness 1914–1918* (London: Leo Cooper 1987) p.217; Bidwell, *History MID* (note 5) pp.94–5 and 116ff; B. Mauere, *The US Air Service in World War I* (Washington DC: 1978) p.172.
35. Basil Thomson, *Queer People* (London: Hodder & Stoughton 1922) pp.179ff; Bidwell, *History MID* (note 5) pp. 121ff. and 188ff.
36. Bidwell, *History MID* (note 5) pp.162 and 247.
37. Ibid. and Bell memo, 21 Aug. 1919, 123.Bell, RG 59, Diplomatic Branch, National Archives, Washington DC.
38. Bidwell, *History MID* (note 5) pp.203–4 and 275ff, as well as forthcoming work by O'Halpin, Jeffrey, and the author mentioned in note 32.
39. Martin Blumenson (ed.) *The Patton Papers*, Vol.I, 1885–1940 (Boston: Houghton Mifflin 1972).
40. Rear-Admiral John Godfrey's historical papers (new release), ADM 223/284, PRO.
41. For examples see British subversive control cooperation with Portugal during 1930 in FO 371/14936/W7713, and W10805, PRO.
42. HO 45/25521, PRO (new release) Aug. 1939.
43. The HW 1 series in the PRO shows much of the range of what the British were reading early in World War II.
44. ADM 1/26870, PRO, 1 March 1940.
45. Anthony Masters, *The Man Who Was M. the Life of Maxwell Knight* (Oxford: Basil Blackwell 1984) p.119.
46. On British secrecy regarding Stephenson, see PREM 3/463/2B, PRO.
47. Comment by Major Morton, PREM 7/2, PRO.
48. Jeffery Dorwart, *Conflict of Duty, The US Navy's Intelligence Dilemma* (Annapolis, MD: Naval Inst. Press 1983) p.131.
49. DEFE 1/143, PRO, Oct.–Dec. 1940,
50. Air Marshal Slessor Comment, 1940/41, AIR 75/63, PRO.
51. HW 1/1, PRO, Sept. 1941.
52. CAB 122/417, PRO, Sept. 1941.
53. Anyone believing that only Americans were shortsighted and unable to overcome bureaucratic hurdles should read H.G. Wells's scathing account of his failed attempt to convince the Admiralty that helicopters could be of value in anti-submarine war, ADM 1/17073, PRO.
54. Patrick Howarth, *Intelligence Chief Extraordinary. The Life of the Ninth Duke of Portland* (London: Bosley Head 1986) p.161.

55. DEFE 1/104 and 164, Jan. 1942ff, plus CO 967/135, PRO. On US codes, see 22 Jan. 1942, HW 1/362, PRO.
56. Bradley F. Smith, *The Ultra-Magic Deals and the Most Secret Special Relationship, 1940–46* (Novato, CA/Shrewsbury, UK: Presidio/Air Life 1993) pp.131ff and 165.
57. DEFE 1/164. See also ADM 223/296, PRO.
58. ADM 223/298, 7 Feb. 1945. The British had been reading Chinese diplomatic ciphers since at least 1941, HW 1/290, PRO.
59. Smith, *Ultra Magic Deals* (note 56) pp.210ff.

2

Why Was the CIA Established in 1947?

RHODRI JEFFREYS-JONES

Just four days after VE Day in May 1945, Prime Minister Winston Churchill sent President Harry Truman a telegram warning that an 'Iron Curtain' had descended across Europe, and that in light of the Soviet Union's current behaviour it would be foolish for Britain and America to drop their military guard. Truman perceived the gravity of the situation, and began to prepare the United States for what came to be known as the 'Cold War'. He decided that it was essential for the president to be properly informed about national security matters, and, on 22 January 1946, issued an executive order establishing the Central Intelligence Group (CIG). Two days later, he conducted a little ceremony at which he installed his friend and adviser Rear Admiral Sidney Souers as the first director of this interim organization. Playfully dubbing him 'director of centralized snooping', he conferred upon Souers a black coat, black hat, and wooden dagger. Within 18 months of Souers' installation, the Truman administration had completed its blueprint for the reorganization of the national security bureaucracy. The National Security Act of 26 July 1947 established the Central Intelligence Agency (CIA).[1]

According to its admirers, the CIA now embarked on a period of glittering success. In the second, long phase in its history, it fulfilled its mission by contributing to the containment of communist expansionism. Finally, in a triumphant flourish, the agency contributed to the collapse of the Soviet empire and to the discrediting of communist ideas both in the West and throughout the rest of the world.[2] The Intermediate Range Nuclear Forces Treaty of 1987 signalled the end of the nuclear arms race, and by the end of 1989 the fall of the Berlin Wall and collapse of Communism in Eastern Bloc nations had drawn a line under the ideological Cold War.

So, with its mission accompanlished, the stage seemed set for the final phase in the CIA's history, the dismantling of the agency. Why has this not happened? It couldl be argued that new needs for its services suddenly arose just at the moment when logic suggested its extinction. But advocates of the continuation of the US intelligence apparatus suggest that the CIA had never been intended as a purely Cold War institution. This suggestion is of great interest to the intelligence historian, especialy with regard to the motives for establishing the CIA in the first place. Can the pleas of the 1990s apologists be dismissed on the ground that the CIA was first and foremost a product of the Cold War and therefore redundant as soon as it was over? Or is it indeed the case that the agency was an expression of America's determination to be eternally and universally vigilant, regardless of whether the threat came from the Soviets or elsewhere?[3]

Remarkably, no historian has hitherto attempted a balanced and dispassionate answer to the question, why was the CIA established in 1947? One reason for this is that the field is fraught with partisanship, for example over the role of personalities, over the morality and efficacy of the concluded arrangements, and over the issue of original intent – did the agency subsequently stray from its intended course, and was there a hidden agenda amongst its founders that defied the publicly-affirmed definition of the early CIA? The existing literature tends to supply narratives based on a selective reading of the contemporary debate. Although some of it dwells on secret agendas, it does not fully explore the hidden mentalities of the day. Overall, it only partially explains why the CIA was established, and why it was established in 1947.[4] The paucity of documentation has only compounded the problem of partisanship.

Now, however, the declassification programs of the Department of State and the CIA have begun to remedy the latter problem, and it is time for a new look at the problem of causation.[5] It is sensible to begin with three explanations that would immediately occur to anyone reasonably well-informed about American intelligence history. These are that the CIA was established to help counter the Soviet threat, that it was a response to Pearl Harbor, and that it was the outcome of a decision to adopt the least unpopular of several proposed arrangements for the conduct of foreign intelligence.

Before giving automatic ascendency to the argument that the CIA was created as an instrument of the Cold War, certain contra-indications need to be considered. One such contra-indication is that the agency owed its lifeblood and authority to an Act of Congress, yet, in floor debates in the House and Senate in July 1947, no mention whatsoever was made of the Soviet threat. This omission is reflected in the scholarship of Dr Thomas F. Troy. In his capacity as chief historian at the CIA, Troy had privileged access to classified documents. He compiled the most detailed history so far of the agency's origins, a secret official volume that was subsequently

declassified and published in 1975. Troy did not single out anti-Sovietism as a cause of the establishment of the CIA. Soviet Communist Party Leader Josef V. Stalin is mentioned only once and incidentally in the entire 589-page text of his book, and neither Communism nor the USSR are listed in the index.[6] Troy's more recent book, *Wild Bill and Intrepid: Donovan, Stephenson, and the Origin of the CIA* (1996), confirms his earlier judgement in making no reference to the USSR or to Stalin.[7]

How does one explain this disposition to ignore the Cold War dimension of the CIA's origins? In Troy's case, it could be argued that he preferred to put the case for a kind of apostolic succession, emphasizing the influence of the British and their Canadian go-between William Stephenson, and of his chosen hero William J. Donovan. But it is also clear that he was aware of the importance of Congress – and he implicitly recognized the fact that Congress paid little heed to the Soviet threat.

An obvious explanation of congressional and scholarly reticence on the Soviet threat would be that anti-Communism had very little to do with the CIA's formation. However, the historian is now in a position to demonstrate that the *White House*'s motivation in establishing the CIA and its immediate predecessor the Central Intelligence Group (CIG) was about countering the Soviet threat and about little else.

The newly-released documentation confirms the importance of Sovietophobia as a motivating factor in the establishment of the CIA. In February 1946, immediately after the formation of the CIG, Stalin proclaimed that communism and capitalism were incompatible. In March, Churchill made public his 'Iron Curtain' warning in a speech pointedly delivered in Missouri, Truman's home state. Churchill had lost his godlike status and Harvard students protested with a banner inscribed 'Winnie, Winnie, go away, G.I. Joe is here to stay', but the former prime minister still carried weight and his pronouncement had a galvanizing effect. Against this background, Admiral Souers on 29 April issued the CIG's first 'tasking' directive. This was exclusively concerned with the arrangements for gathering intelligence on the Soviet Union: 'There is an urgent need to develop the highest possible quality of intelligence on the USSR in the shortest possible time'. In July, journalist Arthur Krock claimed in the *New York Times* that President Franklin D. Roosevelt had made unnecessary concessions to the Soviet Union because he had been badly informed. Utilizing information leaked to him by presidential special counsel Clark Clifford, Krock implied that such mistakes would no longer occur – the CIG was now briefing Truman.[8]

Thus, a recollection of past weakness as well as a recognition of present imperatives may have motivated the CIG to take the line it did. Of the toughness of that line, there can be no mistake. In July 1946, Truman asked the CIG for information on Soviet foreign and military policy.[9] The CIG's response occasioned some caustic comment. According to James S. Lay Jr, the secretary to the CIG's oversight body the National Intelligence Authority (NIA), the first-ever report by its the Group's Office of Research and Evaluation (ORE) was the fruit of extensive deliberation and consultation amongst intelligence officials in various government departments. But according to an early CIA official Ludwell L. Montague, 'ORE 1 was produced by one man over the weekend to meet an unanticipated and urgent requirement.'[10] Whatever the circumstances of its genesis, ORE 1 set the tone for a certain genre of CIA document right up to the end of the Cold War more than 40 years later. It held that the Soviet Union was bent on the 'undermining . . . of its assumed antagonists'. It would be cautious in the meantime, but would encourage colonial rebellions and engage in other psychological warfare to weaken its enemies; it would 'develop as quickly as possible such special weapons as guided missiles and the atomic bomb.'[11]

On 24 August 1946, General Hoyt S. Vandenberg reinforced the point in a memorandum to the president. Vandenberg had taken over as Director of Central Intelligence (DCI) on 10 June, and would, in his brief stewardship of the CIG, dramatically increase the size and scope of the organization. His memorandum admitted that there were no signs of an imminent Soviet attack – for example, Moscow had issued no warning to its 'shipping throughout the world'. However, he alerted Truman to the facts that Soviet propaganda against Britain and America had intensified since Stalin's speech, and that 'the Soviets might conceivably undertake a concerted offensive through Europe and Northern Asia'.[12]

The preoccupation with the Soviet Union continued without remission. In November 1946, Navy intelligence warned CIG of the need for a 'political-psychological study' of the USSR, and Vandenberg pressed on the NIA the need for 'the timely completion' of such a study.[13] The non-materialization of a Red Army attack in the autumn of 1946 in no way reassured the CIG. In January 1947, ORE delivered a new assessment, 'Revised Soviet Tactics in International Affairs'. According to this, 'the USSR has apparently decided that for the time being more subtle tactics should be employed in implementing its basic foreign and military policy'. It had been dissuaded from military action by various factors, most importantly the firm stand taken by the United States. But it could be relied upon to use every means at its disposal, devious as well as diplomatic and military, to undermine the strength and unity of the West. The Soviets would be opportunistic and would try to catch America off guard with surprise tactics – they would have to be watched carefully.[14]

In the wake of the passage of the National Security Act, the CIA enjoyed its first day as a statutory body on 22 September 1947. The demise of CIG was no more than a paper transition, and the anti-Soviet tone continued. There was concern that the USA had reasonable intelligence on the Near East, the Far East, and Latin America, but too little on Britain, France, Germany and, still the top priority, the USSR. The influential Russian expert and state department official George F. Kennan pushed for an enhancement of the CIA's capabilities.[15] On 17 December, the National Security Council (NSC), NIA's replacement as a supervisory body, issued its chilling directive 4-A:

> The National Security Council, taking cognizance of the vicious psychological efforts of the USSR, its satellite countries and Communist groups to discredit and defeat the aims and activities of the United States and other Western powers, has determined that, in the interests of world peace and national security, the foreign information activities of the US Government must be supplemented by covert psychological operations.[16]

There are some debating points here. Some historians would argue that anti-Sovietism in CIA estimates did not reach the full pitch of its intensity until the late 1940s.[17] Early intelligence officials were not universally regarded as being anti-Soviet. In fact, at the height of the congressional debate the Chicago Tribune even accused the CIG of being a clone of the Soviet secret police.[18] Thus the Truman administration's anti-communism may have been to some extent tactical, an attempt to deflect criticism from the right, or to recruit isolationist support for an interventionist foreign policy. Truman and Souers both maintained, in later years, that they had never intended the CIA to adopt such extreme measures against the communist world. In editorial notes to the State Department's recent compilation of documents on the early CIA, it is even suggested that Truman never officially approved NSC 4-A. But the evidence as a whole points to only one sensible conclusion. The executive, defined as the President and his White House advisers together with CIG and CIA personnel, was in its setting up of the CIA motivated primarily and some of the time even solely by a determination to combat the Soviet Union.[19]

The main evidence for the role of Pearl Harbor in motivating support for the CIA is to be found in congressional hearings and in the floor debate in both houses in July 1947. Although other considerations did matter to the debating congressmen, Pearl Harbor was their pre-eminent concern. Participants in the debate were versed in controversy over what went wrong on 7 December 1941. For example, when quizzing Vice Admiral Forrest Sherman in hearings of the Committee on Armed Services, Senator Millard E. Tydings (Democrat, Maryland) stressed his belief in central coordination

– 'otherwise, we may have another Pearl Harbor controversy, with the question arising, "Who got the information?" And the reply, "It was not transmitted"'. In the same hearings, Hoyt Vandenberg showed himself aware of what worried Congress when he reminded his listeners of the question asked by the recent Joint Congressional Committee to Investigate the Pearl Harbor Attack: 'Why, with some of the finest intelligence available in our history – why was it possible for a Pearl Harbor to occur?' According to Vandenberg, Pearl Harbor had left two legacies: it had demonstrated the need for a central organization to coordinate the great mass of intelligence, and it had shocked the American people into an acceptance of the need for such an organization.[20]

In the House, hearings on the National Security bill fell to the Committee on Expenditures in the Executive Departments. Commenting on its CIA clauses, Congressman William Jennings Bryan Dorn (Democrat, South Carolina) said he had always 'believed that if Admiral [Husband E.] Kimmel at Pearl Harbor was furnished with proper intelligence from Washington that Pearl Harbor would never possibly have occurred'.[21] In the House floor debate Ralph Edwin Church (Rep., Illinois) portrayed the Japanese surprise attack as conclusive evidence of a deficiency that would have to be remedied:

> There is no better proof that we have been extremely backward in our intelligence work than the fact that we were so completely surprised at Pearl Harbor. It is somewhat reassuring to have this emphasis placed on intelligence as part of our national security. Not only is intelligence necessary for the proper functioning of our military machinery, it is indeed of primary importance for the proper conduct of our foreign relations.[22]

Alabama's Carter Manasco (Democrat) emphasized the the overriding need to avoid another Pearl Harbor style fiasco:

> We do not have any man in the United States who has adequate training today to do this kind of work because unfortunately the United States has never gone in for the right kind of intelligence. If we had had a strong central intelligence organization, in all probability we would never have had the attack on Pearl Harbor; there might not have been a World War II.[23]

Intelligence theorists and advocates argued that Pearl Harbor was an intelligence disaster that reflected the weak state of American peacetime intelligence in the 1930s – an argument that carried the clear message that America would need a proper peacetime intelligence agency in the future. In his pioneering book *The Future of American Secret Intelligence* (October

1946), George S. Pettee berated the 'state of recurring unpleasant surprise' that had bedevilled US foreign policy for 30 years and culminated in Pearl Harbor.[24] Influential advocates of the CIA portrayed Pearl Harbor as less the epitome than a symptom of intelligence inadequacy. In his testimony Hoyt Vandenberg had stated that 'before Pearl Harbor we did not have an intelligence service in this country comparable to that of Great Britain or France or Russia or Germany or Japan'. It was not just a matter of avoiding surprise: there was no system of 'national' estimates that transcended departmental parochialism and embraced both military and foreign policy considerations: 'Nowhere was there such an estimate before Pearl Harbor'. Congressman Dorn similarly lamented what he regarded as the generally poor state of American intelligence in the 1930s, when reports on the German and Japanese armed forces had been ludicrously complacent.[25]

In contrasting vein, the philosopher Wilmoore Kendall warned that an obsession with the 'shadow of Pearl Harbor' would be pernicious for the development of American intelligence. In an article published shortly after his service in State Department intelligence and the CIA in 1946–47, he pointed to the dangers inherent in a 'compulsive preoccupation with *prediction*, with the elimination of 'surprises' from foreign affairs'.[26] Although surprise-avoidance remained an important mission for the CIA for both military and political reasons, Kendall's critique and the pleas of Vandenberg and his successors took hold. The CIG had already been committed to national estimates, and its ORE became the CIA's Office of National Estimates (ONE). Not content with this, CIA expansionists successfully campaigned for a 'full service' agency, dealing in intelligence collection as well as analysis, and in counter-espionage, counter-intelligence and political covert action. All this means that Pearl Harbor was not a full, logical justification of the all-singing, all-dancing beast that had emerged by the 1950s.

But, as ever, the historian needs to distinguish between retrospective justification and contemporary motivation. Contemporary motives are historically important, even if they subsequently come under attack for having been based on mistaken premises and false assumptions. Pearl Harbor was an important contemporary motivation for several reasons, not least by default. For Congress was not yet ready for a fully-fledged Cold War. Truman and his allies in the CIG were ready, partly because they were better informed about the Soviet Union and partly because Red scaremongering seemed like a good tactic at the time (later, of course, the tactic backfired in the guise of McCarthyism).[27] In contrast, while Congressmen knew there was a problem east of the Elbe and at least subliminally must have realised that the CIA would be part of the American response, they were not yet ready for the shock of confronting a wartime ally – they preferred the argument that America should prepare itself to anticipate and meet a surprise attack from any quarter.

It suited Truman's Democratic administration to allow Pearl Harbor to be exploited in justification of the CIA. Subjected as it had been to several, high-profile investigations, Pearl Harbor was a kind of political shorthand that needed little further publicity.[28] It helped to protect Truman from attacks by Republican isolationists. For, as part of these attacks, heavy fire had been directed at the Office of Strategic Services (OSS), popularly regarded as the CIA's precursor, on the ground that it was a New Dealers' plot to perpetuate totalitarian/élitist control of the nation – the *Chicago Tribune* reporter Walter Trohan had been particularly prominent in levying such charges.[29] Pearl Harbor was an important, symbolic, rebuttal of all this. To stress Japanese perfidiousness at Pearl Harbor, the surprise nature of the attack, and the inadequacies of American intelligence was by implication to exonerate the governing Democrats of the following charges: that their New Dealers had moved the country toward totalitarianism in the 1930s, that in order to hide their economic inadequacies they had 'manoeuvred' the country into war via the 'back door' by provoking Japan, and that the 1941 attack had been no surprise to them at all. To be sure, it would be a mistake to argue that Truman and his supporters stoked up the Pearl Harbor fires in an overtly partisan, pro-FDR manner. There is no evidence of that, and to have done so would have been to risk alienating essential allies: after all, Senator Arthur H. Vandenberg may have been a pillar of postwar bipartisan foreign policy and Hoyt Vandenberg's uncle to boot, but he was still a Republican, while Tydings, though a Democratic Senator, had been an outright opponent of the New Deal.[30] It suited Truman simply to let the Pearl Harbor rhetoric run, letting others do the talking and allowing the impression to develop that there had been an intelligence disaster in 1941 of an all-encompassing character.

Last and by no means least, the military and particularly naval lobby for central intelligence emphasized Pearl Harbor. Here, emotion fuelled considerations of national security and political expediency. The Navy had borne the brunt of the Pearl Harbor attack, losing 2,008 men out of a total of 2,403 who died, went missing, or expired later from wounds.[31] Secretary of the Navy James V. Forrestal, Rear Admiral Souers, and Truman's Chief of Staff Admiral William D. Leahy were among the senior naval figures pressing for a central intelligence provision. Rear Admiral Roscoe C. Hillenkoetter, director of the CIG from 1 May 1947 and the first director of the CIA, had been wounded in the Japanese attack. Such men inspired special sympathy from some of the legislators who participated in the CIA debate and who themselves had close connections to the military. Congressman Church had two sons in the naval reserve; Congressman Dorn had been a GI in Europe in 1942–45; Senator Tydings was a decorated veteran of the Meuse-Argonne offensive in World War I. These men did not take military casualties lightly, and that was why Pearl Harbor meant a lot to them. It should be added that, in the aftermath of a victorious war, the opinions of military advocates of the CIA naturally carried special weight.[32]

The last of the three main explanations of the creation of the CIA is that the agency was the outcome of a decision to adopt the least unpopular of several proposed arrangements for the conduct of foreign intelligence. This explanation is about the nature and shape of the solution to America's augmented intelligence need, rather than about why people came to accept that augmentation in the first place. But it is still germane in the sense that it explains why America opted for a new agency, instead of developing an existing one.

The decision to set up a new, civilian agency stemmed partly from people's attitude to the military after the war. On the one hand, America's soldiers, sailors and airmen had a heroic status. On the other hand, there was a reaction against wartime priorities, and a feeling that the admirals and generals should be kept firmly in the subordinate position customarily reserved for them in peacetime. Except from Senator Tydings, who wanted them *more* heavily involved, the idea that the Joint Chiefs of Staff should be in charge of a combined intelligence operation produced a chorus of denunciation on the Hill. Congressmen Church and Manasco, for example, had misgivings about military leadership, while the freshman Senator from Wisconsin, Joseph R. McCarthy (Republican), thought that the new law was part of an Army and Navy conspiracy to 'take unto themselves tremendously more power than the other 120,000,000 or 130,000,000 people would care to let them have'. Senator Edward V. Robertson (Republican, Wyoming) thought the 'real intent' of the National Security bill was to 'create a vast military empire', while the proposed CIA had 'all the potentialities of an American Gestapo. Needless to say, it would be an invaluable asset to militarism'.[33]

Earlier rumours that intelligence would be run through the OSS or the Federal Bureau of Investigation (FBI) had stimulated similar distrust and jealousies, while the idea of coordination from Foggy Bottom was unpopular both inside and outside the State Department.[34] From the administration's point of view, it was worth gambling on the proposition that, for once, Americans would prefer the devil they did not know. But it should be remembered that only prior acceptance by most Congressmen of the need for an enhanced intelligence capability made that gamble worth taking.

To explain that prior acceptance more fully, it is necessary to look beyond the major articulations of the need for a central intelligence agency.

Various contemporary considerations and ambient factors help to explain the establishment of the CIA and its timing. Collectively, these formed part of an influential if not always fully articulated discourse. They may be conveniently discussed under the following headings: the impact of the New Deal, the activities of a conspiratorial American élite, the legacy of the Montevideo conference (1933), a dawning awareness of scientific intelligence, and a preoccupation with the problem of sovereignty.

The shadow of the New Deal extended beyond the moribund confines of the Pearl Harbor debate. Large-scale federal activity in World War II and the activities of the Attlee administration in Britain kept the Big Government issue alive. On 6 September 1945 Truman dispelled any illusions about a return to Jeffersonian values when, in his first important domestic message to the Congress, he called for renewed and expanded social-reform initiatives. The New Dealers had typically met a problem by throwing an agency at it – for example, the Agricultural Adjustment Administration (AAA), the National Recovery Administration (NRA) – and the Big Government habit was still ingrained in the postwar years.

An elucidation is necessary here, for a reaction against New Dealism had been gathering momentum ever since the 1930s. Increasing cross-party conservatism as well as the election of Republican majorities in both houses of Congress in the mid-term elections of 1946 inhibited the creation of more reform agencies. However, an exception was made in the case of defence agencies. It proved broadly acceptable, with the proviso of various reductions and modifications, to perpetuate in peace the national security state assembled for the purpose of fighting the war. The higher dictates of national security explain why Senator Tydings, who had raged against the New Deal's 'alphabetical monstrosities', supported the enhancement in government power implicit in the creation of the CIA.[35]

The case of the conservatives' support for the CIA confirms the high expectations invested by many such Americans in the government in which they professed to disbelieve. The paradox is partly explained by their anticipation that the new agency would, through coordination and centralization, achieve greater efficiency. As in the later case of the Defense Intelligence Agency (and with similarly disappointing results), the CIA was meant to eliminate costly duplication and to enable cuts to be made in other parts of the intelligence community – in short, the reform was meant to reduce government, not increase it. Senator Henry Cabot Lodge, Jr (Republican, Massachusetts) told McCarthy that overall military unification 'will certainly produce some economy'.[36] In a prepared statement for the Senate Committee on Armed Services, the lawyer and future CIA director Allen Dulles urged CIA-led central evaluation 'for reasons of economy and efficiency'.[37] In later years, it is true, the failure of the intelligence community to prune itself and the increasing scope and technical costs of its task culminated in a bloated budget. But, once again, the pitfall of wisdom with hindsight should be avoided. When contemporary motives are gauged instead of judged, it seems clear that the CIA was the product both of New Deal instincts, and of a growing sense of financial concern about galloping Big Government.

To contemporary critics like Trohan and McCarthy, the CIA was an undemocratic, élitist conspiracy. Since then, diverse historians have been less repelled than fascinated by the theory that the CIA was the invention and creature of Ivy Leaguers personifying the East Coast Protestant Establishment. Because of the secrecy that still shrouds CIA personnel records, the theory cannot be properly tested, but it seems a reasonable working assumption that Ivy Leaguers were influential at least until the 1960s when the Bay of Pigs débarcle called their wisdom into question. However, the idea that a political and social élite takes a serious interest in an influential branch of government is hardly revolutionary. The question to be examined in relation to the CIA's establishment is whether there were special reasons for the privileged élite to focus on and boost centralized secret intelligence in 1946–47.[38]

Up to a point, there were. The American èlite had been under long-term siege. In the nineteenth century, Andrew Jackson celebrated and Henry Adams lamented its demise. But the élite fought back using a variety of stratagems, such as the building up of the Ivy League universities and the preparatory schools that fed them, and the observance of foreign-service selection norms designed to exclude less-educated, plebeian elements. In World War II, Ivy Leaguers gained a powerful foothold in the OSS, and some of them, for example Allen Dulles, subsequently argued for the CIA, helped to shape it, and provided its early leadership. A collective sense of self-interest and self-perpetuation may have given urgency to this advocacy. For, with the demographic shift to the West, those Harvard, Yale, and Princeton men who were so often the champions of democracy abroad were in danger of becoming its victims at home. It could be argued that in 1946–47 the CIA was one of their last throws, a secret bastion of power that could be shielded from democratic scrutiny on the pretext of national security.

President Roosevelt's undertaking at the Montevideo pan-American conference in 1933 created a situation that gave the CIA a further *raison d'être*. Pursuing his 'Good Neighbor' policy, Roosevelt on this occasion surrendered the self-proclaimed US right to intervene militarily in the internal affairs of other Western hemispheric nations. The problem here was that the *urge* to intervene did not evaporate. At the outset, it was intended that the CIA would take over the FBI's covert networks in Latin America.

The FBI's disgruntled director, J. Edgar Hoover, would not cooperate, but, once it had built up its own assets, the CIA was to conduct covert actions in Guatemala, Guyana, Chile, Cuba and other Latin American nations. By operating in secret, the United States hoped to achieve its ends without incurring opprobrium – an objective of increasing importance in a world which from 1945 had a revitalized forum for international debate, the United Nations, in which the USA had to compete for popularity with the USSR.

Here, it is appropriate to examine a little more carefully the problem of whether its founders originally intended the CIA to engage in political covert action. In the aftermath of the 1961 Bay of Pigs débarcle, both Truman and Souers strenuously denied that they had ever intended such cloak and dagger operations.[39] In March 1946, NIA Directive No. 3 authorized the CIG to collect intelligence, but such clandestine collection is not the same as covert political action designed to influence, not just report on, events in foreign countries.[40] Still, in planning the 1947 enactment, the founders of the CIA may well have had covert action in mind. In cross-examination by Senator Tydings, supporters of the CIA clauses revealed that a separate bill had been prepared to accomplish 'a full and thorough development of the Central Intelligence Agency'.[41] They were trying to reassure Tydings that the armed forces would have a proper say in the running of the new agency, but their tactics can also be understood in a different light. In a later interview, CIG legislative liaison officer Walter L. Pforzheimer recalled that he had withdrawn from the 1947 bill a clause authorizing 'covert and unvouchered funds' because it would have opened up a 'can of worms' and because 'we could come up with the house-keeping provisions later on'.[42] NSC 4-A authorized 'covert psychological operations' (the contemporary euphemism for dirty tricks) soon after the formation of the CIA, and in the Central Intelligence Agency Act of 1949, Congress did make the housekeeping provision:

> The sums made available to the Agency may be expended without regard to the provisions of law and regulations relating to the expenditure of Government funds; and for objects of a confidential, extraordinary, or emergency nature, such expenditures to be accounted for solely on the certificate of the Director and every such certificate shall be deemed a sufficient voucher for the amount therein certified.[43]

Clearly, the housekeeping clause, prudently held over until 1949, had been part of the 1947 plan. Even so, it is not in itself definitive proof that Truman, Souers, Vandenberg, or Pforzheimer had concrete plans for covert action when they created the CIA. However, three further considerations do suggest that covert political action was already on the agenda during the

CIA's 1946–47 gestation period. One is the fact that, in spite of public distaste for such undercover operations, covert political action was deeply embedded in the American foreign-policy tradition.[44] A second indication is that secret plans were afoot, by 1948, to establish the machinery for the implementation of covert political action. Establishing the Office of Special Projects within the CIA in June 1948, NSC Directive 10/2 once again referred to the need to counter the 'vicious covert activities of the USSR'.[45] The 1947 clauses, 4-A, 10/2 and the 1949 Act were part of a planned continuum.

Finally, the CIA did engage in covert operations virtually from the outset: it used secret funds and disinformation techniques to weaken the French and Italian Left, and co-operated with the British in a clandestine operation to overthrow the communist dictatorship in Albania.[46] That is not to say that President Truman planned the whole panoply of 1950s dirty tricks and paramilitary operations in advance, and later lied about his intentions. But it is likely that the executive architects of the agency hoped from the outset that it would enable them to intervene abroad in a hidden manner that would be inoffensive to their friends, and deniable.

A dawning awareness of scientific intelligence undoubtedly contributed to the founding of the CIA as a means of coordinating peacetime vigilance. The deadly quarrels casualty rate had remained a constant proportion of population for thousands of years, but the invention of chemical and nuclear weapons and the means of their delivery, especially rockets and guided missiles, threatened to change this and to bring about human destruction on an unprecedented and even terminal scale.[47] On 31 October 1946, the CIG's scientific advisers had produced ORE 3/1, with 'educated guesswork' about Soviet A-bombs, missiles, aircraft, radar and submarines.[48] Two senior advocates of the CIA stressed the subject in their testimony to the Senate Armed Services Committee, each hinting that there was a link between scientific intelligence and the prevention of surprise attack. Hoyt Vandenberg warned against the dangers of aggression 'in an era of atomic warfare'. Admiral Sherman said 'the power of sudden attack is amplified by further developments in long-range weapons of mass destruction'. In appealing for a 'fluid and flexible' intelligence system and in warning against 'the assumption that science alone could protect us', Navy Secretary Forrestal seemed to confirm the veneration in which science was now held and the pivotal role expected of it in intelligence work.[49]

Finally, the problem of national sovereignty following World War II stimulated a discourse that nurtured the CIA. It may be discussed under two headings, Great Britain and the United Nations. British influence on American intelligence prompted controversy in the 1940s, and led to a demand for a more independent American capability. Even if British influence has sometimes been exaggerated, there can be little doubt that it was important in World War II. The British encouraged the setting up of an American central intelligence service. They trained US secret agents in 'Camp X' on the Canadian side of Lake Ontario. Bonds were formed, and during the CIA hearings there were frank pleas – for example, by Admiral Ernest J. King, who had been US Chief of Naval Operations in the war – for emulation of the British centralized system.[50] The historian Bradley Smith has argued, further, that the wartime sharing of signals intelligence (Sigint) clamped Britain and America together in a permanent manner. Each side was aware that the other side knew its secrets, and could betray them if there were a split.[51]

But this British bond sparked resentment. Some British secret servicemen, for example Ian Fleming of 007 fame, were perhaps tactless in blowing their own trumpets. Fleming, like the Canadian Stephenson, was among those outsiders who laid claim to paternity of the OSS and, ultimately, the CIA, in a way that ruffled American isolationist or patriotic feathers.[52] There was resentment that foreign policy was being forged by what the *Chicago Tribune* called an 'interventionist, Anglophile clique'.[53]

Thus it became good politics to portray the CIA as an assertion of American sovereignty. In any case, there was probably a genuine desire, within the American intelligence community, to come of age and achieve independence from the British who were, after all, a faltering imperial power on the brink of steep decline. That is not the same as saying that the founders of the CIA wanted to be different from their British counterparts. Their behaviour is reminiscent of that of Alexander Hamilton, who had in the 1790s attempted to make US mercantilism the competitive reincarnation of the British model denounced by the American revolutionaries. What sovereignty-minded CIA advocates aimed at was competitive emulation. 'For months', said General Vandenberg reminiscing about World War II, 'we had to rely blindly and trustingly on the superior intelligence system of the British'. But, he continued, 'we should be self-sufficient. The interest of others may not be our interests'.[54]

The second sovereignty issue concerns the United Nations, and here, too, the CIA emerges as the product of contradictory internationalist and nationalist forces. In 1945–47, as in 1919–20, the United States faced the dilemma of how to support an international organization without surrendering power to it. For their part, the founders of the United Nations were conscious of the need to avoid what they regarded as having been the weaknesses of the League. The historian Evan Luard has summed up the thinking on one of these weaknesses:

If the world organisation itself was to become a powerful force in the world, then its chief executive too must become a more powerful figure, able to inject an international viewpoint into the bickerings of national governments; to arouse the conscience of the world when international action was urgently needed; and to act as a watchdog always on the alert for situations where the peace could be threatened.[55]

From the intelligence viewpoint, the question was whether America would tolerate a rival 'watchdog'. In principle, the United States was a keen supporter of the United Nations. Surrender of sovereignty in significant areas was, however, another matter. In October 1945, Senator Tydings commented on the proposed disarmament inspection forces which were intended to deter the spread of nuclear weapons. He insisted that the forces would have to be 'composed largely of Americans'. He explained, 'I'm not so much interested in sovereignty – I want to survive'. But the issue of sovereignty mattered a great deal to some of the most senior senators. In January 1947 Senator Vandenberg agonized, in a letter to Eleanor Roosevelt, over the problem arising now that 'the new system of international peace and security' was beginning to 'mature'. He would withdraw as a UN General Assembly delegate because 'it will always be true that a man cannot serve two masters'.[56]

It is possible to interpret some major foreign-policy initiatives of the Truman era as attempts to extricate America from situations where its sovereignty might be compromised. According to this interpretation, United States negotiators wanted Europe, in the words of Marshall Plan administrator Paul Hoffman, 'on its feet and off our backs'.[57] They hoped NATO would make Western Europe militarily self-sufficient, allowing US forces to withdraw, while the Marshall Plan was designed to free the United States of economic obligations in Europe by encouraging European economic unity and independence. Placed in this context, the CIA was intended to be a defender of America's sovereign right to do things its own way, even if the means of achieving that goal were too internationalist for some of its critics, and even if British Sigint cooperation would have to continue meantime.

In its determination to explain international events in a manner that would defend American interests, the United States would in the future obstruct plans for an independent UN intelligence capability, and has objected even to the use of the word 'intelligence' in connection with UN activities (the phrase 'fact-finding' has had to be deployed instead). To be sure, later Cold War US–UN clashes often reflected new circumstances, and it would be ahistorical to project these problems backwards to 1946–47. Nevertheless, to ignore the implications of the fact that the CIA was formed in the immediate wake of the United Nations and with the support of people conditioned by their own activities in the UN sphere would be to suppress an awareness of an important probability, that the formation of the CIA in 1947 was an assertion of national sovereignty at a time when it could be seen to be under challenge not just from the USSR and Britain, but from the United Nations as well.[58]

The CIA was established in 1947 for several reasons, some of them complex and even contradictory. It is important to consider these reasons in their contemporary context, and to suspend any disbelief occasioned by subsequent developments – otherwise, for example, one might not understand those who conceived of the agency as a cost-cutting measure.[59]

Singling out major causes of the CIA's establishment, it is necessary to distinguish between the executive and Congress. Truman, Vandenberg and their executive colleagues singled out the Soviet menace as a cause for acute concern, and this concern overshadowed all other considerations as their motive in establishing the CIA. They built and shaped the CIG accordingly, and drafted the CIA clauses in the 1947 Act to further the same purpose. However, the CIA owed its essential nature to an Act of Congress, and, on Capitol Hill, fear of the Soviet Union had not yet taken root. Pearl Harbor was the burning issue there, and other justifications of central intelligence received an airing in Congress, too. Curiously the Executive, later accused of intelligence expansionism, originally had a narrow definition of the CIA's role, while Congress, which in later years sometimes demanded a more restricted role for the CIA, showed a broader appreciation of the need for expanded intelligence.

Finally, one needs to take account of the political context of the debate over the CIA's formation. Explicitly in relation to the British and implicitly in the case of the United Nations, the creators of the CIA were seeking to strengthen America's capacity for free thought and independent action. The 1980s expression 'unilateralism' would more closely describe their aspirations than the contemporary term 'isolationism'. To put it another way, in creating the CIA they made a profound and far-reaching statement about American sovereignty.

NOTES

1. The 'snooping' quotation and some of the details are from Rhodri Jeffreys-Jones, *The CIA and American Democracy* (New Haven, Conn.: Yale UP 1989) p.35.
2. Peter Schweizer, *Victory: The Reagan Administration's Secret Strategy that Hastened the Collapse of the Soviet Union* (NY: Atlantic Monthly 1994) p.xvi.
3. The scale of the problem is illustrated by the fact that, at the height of the Cold War, in excess of 60 per cent of America's intelligence resources were directed toward the USSR, whereas, by 1992, less than half that percentage was thus allocated: Loch K. Johnson, 'Smart

Intelligence', *Foreign Policy* (Winter 1992/93, p.54. This and other evidence on the post-Cold War debate is set forth in Todd M. Winterhalt, 'The Debate on the Future of the CIA, 1989-1995, with Particular Reference to the Press' (U. of Edinburgh MSc, 1995).

4. For some reflections on the historiography of the CIA's creation, see B. Nelson MacPherson, 'CIA Origins as Reviewed from Within', *Intelligence and National Security*, 10/12 (April 1995), pp.353–9; John Ferris, 'Coming in from the Cold War: Historiography of American Intelligence, 1945-1990', *Diplomatic History*, 19 (Winter 1995) pp.107–9; Rhodri Jeffreys-Jones, 'Introduction: The Stirrings of a New Revisionism?' in Jeffreys-Jones and Andrew Lownie, *North American Spies: New Revisionist Essays* (Edinburgh UP 1991) pp.5–7, 17–18.

5. Many official papers relating to 1940s intelligence are now available to historians in Archives II, College Park, Maryland, in the Truman Presidential Library, Independence, Missouri, and elsewhere. The papers of most leading officials are also available for scrutiny, although those of Adm. Sidney Souers, rumoured to be in the basement of a private St Louis residence, have not yet come to light. The Historical Office of the CIA over the years produced internal histories narrowly but nevertheless illuminatingly based on CIA documents. Three have now been declassified and pertain to the early years of the CIA: Thomas F. Troy, *Donovan and the CIA: A History of the Establishment of the Central Intelligence Agency* (Frederick, MD.: UP of America 1981); Arthur Darling, B. Darling, *The Central Intelligence Agency: An Instrument of Government to 1950* [hereafter *CIA*] (University Park, Pa.: Penn State Press 1990) and Ludwell Lee Montague, *General Walter Bedell Smith as Director of Central Intelligence, October 1950-February 1953* (ibid. 1991). Recently published documentary compilations of note are Michael Warner (ed.), *CIA Cold War Records: The CIA under Harry Truman* (Washington DC: Center for the Study of Intelligence, CIA 1994) and, in the Foreign Relations of the United States series and ranging beyond CIA archives, *Emergence of the Intelligence Establishment* (Washington, DC: GGPO 1996. Henceforth: FRUS, *Emergence*). A microfiche supplement to the latter volume is due to be published, but has not been seen by the author.

6. Troy, *Donovan and the CIA* (note 5) p.113. An earlier official CIA historian, Arthur B. Darling, did make a few references to the Soviet Union, but not as part of an effort to explain the origins of the CIA: Darling, *CIA* (note 5).

7. Thomas F. Troy, *Wild Bill and Intrepid: Donovan, Stephenson, and the Origin of CIA* (New Haven, CT: Yale UP 1996).

8. Harvard banner quoted in Peter G. Boyle, 'America's Hesitant Road to NATO, 1945–49,' in Joseph Smith (ed.), *The Origins of NATO* (U. of Exeter Press 1990) p.74; Souers memo, 'Development of Intelligence on the USSR,' 29 April 1946, in FRUS, *Emergence* (note 5) p.344; Jeffreys-Jones, *CIA and American Democracy* (note 1) p.37.

9. Clark M. Clifford to William D. Leahy, 18 July 1946, in Michael Warner (ed.), *CIA Cold War Records: The CIA under Harry Truman* (Washington, DC: Center for the Study of Intelligence, CIA 1994) p63. Leahy presided over the National Intelligence Authority, the body that oversaw the activities of the CIG just as later the National Security Council supervised the CIA.

10. Lay paraphrased in Minutes of the Ninth Meeting of the Intelligence Advisory Board, Washington, DC, 31 Oct. 1946 and Memo from the Chief of the Global Survey Group, Central Intelligence Agency (Montague) to the Assistant Director for Reports and Estimates ([Theodore] Babbit), Washington, DC, 12 Nov. 1947, both in FRUS, *Emergence* (note 5) pp. 435, 805. According to Arthur Darling, it was Montague himself who burned the midnight oil to produce the ORE report – with the benefit of background material that included diplomat George F. Kennan's cables from Moscow: Darling, *CIA*, pp.130–31. Like Troy and Darling, Montague became an official CIA historian with a hero. He was to deride DCI Adm. Roscoe H. Hillenkoetter's leadership of the CIA (1 May 1947 – 7 Oct. 1950) in the interest of praising his employer, DCI Gen. Walter Bedell Smith (7 Oct. 1950 – 9 Feb. 1953). For Montague's attack on Darling, who praised DCIs Gen. Hoyt S. Vandenberg (10 June 1946 – 1 May 1947) and Hillenkoetter, see Montague, *Smith*, p.xxvi.

11. CIG, ORE 1, 'Soviet Foreign and Military Policy,' 23 July 1946, in Warner, *CIA under Truman* (note 5), pp.66–9.

12. Memo, Vandenberg for president, 24 Aug. 1946, in ibid., pp.81–3.
13. Minutes of the 11th Meeting of the Intelligence Advisory Board, Washington DC, 26 Nov. 1946, in FRUS, *Emergence*, p.464, n.5
14. CIG, ORE 1/1, 'Revised Soviet Tactics in International Affairs', 6 Jan. 1947, in Warner, *CIA under Truman* (note 5) pp.100–4.
15. Memo. from the Chief of the Global Survey Group, CIA (Montague) to the Assistant Director for Reports and Estimates ([Theodore] Babbit), Washington DC, 12 Nov. 1947, and Memo. form the Director of the Policy Planning Staff (Kennan) to the Under Secretary of State ([Robert A.] Lovett), Washington DC, 18 Nov. 1947, both in FRUS, *Emergence* (note 5) p.805.
16. NSC 4-A, attached to Memo. from the Executive Secretary of the National Security Council (Souers) to DCI Hillenkoetter, Washington DC, 17 Dec. 1947, in ibid. p.650.
17. On the relative mildness of Vandenberg's estimates and the virulence of post-1949 estimates, see, respectively, Phillip S. Meilinger, *Hoyt S. Vandenberg: The Life of a General* (Bloomington: Indiana UP 1989) p.72 and John L. Gaddis, 'Intelligence, Espionage, and Cold War Origins', *Diplomatic History* 13 (Spring 1989), p.200.
18. Walter Trohan writing in the *Chicago Tribune* 15 June 1947.
19. FRUS, *Emergence* (note 5) p.650, n.1. On later denials by Truman and Souers, see Danny D. Jansen and Rhodri Jeffreys-Jones, 'The Missouri Gang and the CIA', in Jeffreys-Jones and Lownie, *North American Spies* (note 4) pp.136–7.
20. Tydings and 'Statement of Lt. Gen. Hoyt S. Vandenberg, Director of Central Intelligence', in Grover S. Williams (ed.), 'Legislative History of the Central Intelligence Agency as Documented in Published Congressional Sources' (Washington DC: Congressional Research Service, Library of Congress 1975) pp.30, 34–5. Troy did not analyze the Pearl Harbor aspect of congressional deliberations in 1947. But he noted that intelligence visionaries had been calling for centralization before 1941, and that the Pearl Harbor attack of that year enhanced their credibility: Troy, *Donovan and the CIA* (note 5) p.409.
21. Dorn in Williams, 'Legislative History', p.123.
22. Ibid. p.141.
23. Ibid. p.144.
24. George S. Pettee, *The Future of American Secret Intelligence* (Washington DC: Infantry Journal Press 1946) pp.1, –7. Pettee's book was symptomatic of contemporary thought rather than a seminal influence on it. The author's own copy, picked up at a secondhand book store not far from CIA headquarters in Virginia, bears the following inscription over Pettee's signature: 'Wiesbaden. 1 Nov. 1947. For [Brig. Gen.] Charles [Y.] Banfill, with all the appreciation that one feels when one is sending, and finds that, thank God, somebody is receiving'.
25. Vandenberg and Dorn in Williams, 'Legislative History', pp.34, 41, 141.
26. Wilmoore Kendall, 'The Function of Intelligence', *World Politics* 1 (1948–49), p.549.
27. See Richard M. Freeland, *The Truman Doctrine and the Origins of McCarthyism: Foreign Policy, Domestic Politics and Internal Security 1946-1948* (NeY: Schocken 1974) [check rebuttal].
28. Examinations of the Pearl Harbor attack were conducted by the Roberts Commission (1941–42), by the Hart Inquiry, Army Pearl Harbor Board, and Navy Court of Inquiry (all 1944), by the Clarke Investigation and the Clausen Investigation (both 1944-45) and the Hewitt Investigation (1945), and by the mammoth Joint Congressional Committee Investigation (1945–46): see Gordon W. Prange, *At Dawn We Slept: The Untold Story of Pearl Harbor* (NY: Penguin 1981), pp.823–5.
29. See Thomas F. Troy, 'Knifing of the OSS', *Int. Jnl of Intelligence and Counterintelligence* 1 (1986), pp.97–100, 102–6.
30. For a political estimate of Millard Evelyn Tydings, see Harvard Sitkoff's entry in the *Dictionary of American Biography*, 7th suppl. (NY: Scribner's 1981).
31. Prange, *At Dawn We Slept* (note 28) p.539.
32. Jeffreys-Jones, *CIA and American Democracy* (note 1) pp.24–5; Darling, *CIA* (note 5) p.194; Rhodri Jeffreys-Jones, 'Roscoe Henry Hillenkoetter', *American National Biography* (American Council of Learned Societies/OUP forthcoming).

33. McCarthy and Robertson in Williams, 'Legislative History' (note 20) pp.43, 132, 141.
34. Jeffreys-Jones, *CIA and American Democracy* v(note 1) pp.28–33.
35. Tydings quoted in Sitkoff, *DAB* (note 30) p.750.
36. Lodge statement (with McCarthy interlocutions) before Senate Committee on Armed Services, in Williams, 'Legislative History' (note 20) p.44. On the failure of the DIA to achieve intended economies, see Patrick N. Mescall, 'A Function of Command: The Defense Intelligence Agency, 1961–1969' (U. of Edinburgh PhD 1995).
37. Dulles memorandum enclosed with letter, Dulles to Chan Gurney, Chairman, Senate Committee on Armed Services, 25 April 1947, in Williams, 'Legislative History' (note 20) p.47.
38. For discussions of the CIA's 'Ivy League élite', see Robin W. Winks, *Cloak and Gown: Scholars in the Secret War, 1939-1961* (NY: Morrow 1987) esp. its discussions of Yale graduates, Burton Hersh, *The Old Boys: The American Elite and the Origins of the CIA* (NY: Scribner's 1992) and Rhodri Jeffreys-Jones, 'The Socio-Educational Composition of the CIA Elite: A Statistical Note', *Jnl of American Studies* 19 (Dec. 1985), pp.421–4.
39. Jansen and Jeffreys-Jones, 'The Missouri Gang and the CIA' (note 19) pp.136--8.
40. A copy of Top Secret NIA Directive No. 3, issued on 21 March 1946, is in the William D. Leahy Papers, Library of Congress, box 20 – cited in Phillip S. Meilinger, *Hoyt S. Vandenberg* (note 17) p.228, n.71.
41. Hoyt Vandenberg and Admiral Forrest Sherman testimony to the Senate Committee on Armed Services, the quotation being from the latter, in Williams, 'Legislative History' (note 20) p.31.
42. Pforzheimer quoted in Tom Braden, 'The Birth of the CIA', *American Heritage* 28 (Feb. 1977), p.11.
43. Section 10 (b). Other key sections of this Act enabled the CIA to post officers abroad under cover (Section 4 (a)) and to disguise its activities by exchanging funds with other branches of the government (Section 6 (a)). The full text of the Act (81 Congress 2 session, 20 June 1949) is to be found in Volume 63, *Statutes-at-Large*, 208–13, and is reproduced in Williams, 'Legislative History' (note 20) pp.275–279A.
44. This is amply demonstrated in Stephen Knott, 'Lifting the Veil: The Roots of American Covert Activity' (Boston College PhD 1990).
45. For the full text of 10/2, see William M. Leary (ed.), *The Central Intelligence Agency: History and Documents* (University: U. of Alabama Press 1984) pp.131–2.
46. See Sallie Pisani, *The CIA and the Marshall Plan* (Edinburgh: Edinburgh UP 1991), and Nicholas Bethell, *The Great Betrayal: The Untold Story of Kim Philby's Biggest Coup* (London: Hodder & Stoughton 1985).
47. On the long-term volume consistency of deadly quarrels, see Lewis Fry Richardson, *Statistics of Deadly Quarrels* (Pittsburg, PA: Boxwood Press 1960) and David Wilkinson, *Deadly Quarrels: Lewis F. Richardson and the Statistical Study of War* (Berkeley, CA: U. of California Press 1980).
48. ORE 3/1 quoted in Darling, *CIA* (note 5) p.163.
49. Vandenberg, Sherman and Forrestal in Williams, 'Legislative History' (note 20) pp.33, 83, 92.
50. David Stafford, *Camp X: SOE and the American Connection* (Harmondsworth: Viking/Penguin 1986); King in Williams, 'Legislative History' (note 20) p.59. For an overview of British influences, see Bradley F. Smith, *The Shadow Warriors: OSS and the Origins of the CIA* (NY: Basic, Books 1983) pp.–54, 62–4, 84–94. On nineteenth century antecedents to British-American intelligence liaison, see Bradley Smith's contribution to this volume.
51. Bradley F. Smith, *The Ultra-Magic Deals and the Most Secret Special Relationship 1940-1946* (Novato, CA/Shrewsbury, UK: Presidio/Air Life 1993), pp.vii, 217, 225–6.
52. On Fleming, see David Stafford, *The Silent Game: The Real World of Imaginary Spies* (Athens: U. of Georgia Press 1991), pp.164–6. On the claims made on behalf of William Stephenson, codenamed 'Intrepid', and on the difficulties they caused, see, respectively, David Stafford, 'A Myth Called Intrepid,' *Saturday Night* (Toronto) (Oct.1989), pp.33–7, and Christopher Andrew, *For the President's Eyes Only: Secret Intelligence and the American*

Presidency from Washingto to Bush (NY: Harper Collins 1995) pp.129–30. For a defence of Stephenson's role, see Troy, *Wild Bill and Intrepid* (note 7).

53. *Chicago Tribune*, 16 Jan. 1948 paraphrased in William L. Langer, *In and Out of the Ivory Tower* (NY: Neale Watson 1977) p.212.

54. Vandenberg in Williams, 'Legislative History' (note 20) p.36.

55. Evan Luard, *A History of the United Nations*, 2 vols. *I: The Years of Western Domination, 1945–1955* (London: Macmillan 1982) pp.12–13.

56. Sitkoff, *DAB* (note 30) p.750; Arthur Vandenberg to Eleanor Roosevelt, 9 Jan. 1947, in Arthur H. Vandenberg Jr, *The Private Papers of Senator Vandenberg* (Boston: Houghton Mifflin 1952), pp.330–1.

57. Paul Hoffman quoted in Peter Foot, 'America and the Origins of the Atlantic Alliance: A Reappraisal', in Smith, *Origins of NATO* (note 8) p.83. For a variety of perspectives, see also: Peter Foot, 'The American Origins of NATO' (U. of Edinburgh PhD 1984); Lawrence S. Kaplan, 'The Cold War and European Revisionism', *Diplomatic History* 11 (Spring 1987), p.155 and *The United States and NATO: The Formative Years* (Lexington: UP of Kentucky 1984) p.5; David P. Calleo, 'Early American Views of NATO: Then and Now', in Lawrence Freedman (ed.), *The Troubled Alliance: Atlantic Relations in the 1980s* (London: Heinemann 1983), pp.7–27 and 'The Founding Cycle: NATO from 1948 to 1960', in Calleo, *Beyond American Hegemony: The Future of the Western Alliance* (NY: Basic Books 1987) pp. 27–43; Michael J. Hogan, 'Revival and Reform: America's Twentieth-Century Search for a New Economic Order Abroad', *Diplomatic History*, 8 (Fall 1984) p.289 and *The Marshall Plan: America, Britain, and the Reconstruction of Western Europe, 1947-1952* (NY: Cambridge UP 1987); Geir Lundestadt, 'Empire by Invitation? The United States and Western Europe, 1945-52', *SHAFR Newsletter*, 15 (Sept. 1984), pp.1–21; Martin H. Folly, 'Breaking the Vicious Circle: Britain, the United States, and the Genesis of the North Atlantic Treaty', *Diplomatic History*, 12 (Winter 1988) p.77; Sallie Pisani, 'Coordinated Intervention', in idem., *CIA and Marshall Plan* (note 46) pp.58–80.

58. Ronnie E. Fry, 'The Uses of Intelligence: The United Nations Confronts the United States in the Lebanon Crisis, 1958', *Intelligence and National Security* (Jan. 1995) pp.60–1, 86; A. Walter Dorn, *Peace-Keeping Satellites: The Case for International Surveillance and Verification* (Dundas, Ontario: Peace Research Inst. 1987), 'U.N. Should Verify Treaties', Bulletin of the Atomic Scientists (July/aug. 1990) pp.12–13, and, courtesy of Dr Dorn, 'Sovereignty, Security and UN Fact-Finding: Developing a Global Watch' (unpub. conference paper, 1995).

59. It is not necessarily absurd to assert that the CIA was a cost-cutting measure. Arguing counter-factually, what would have happened if intelligence empire-building had continued in various parts of the US bureaucracy without a professionally sceptical, central organism?

3

Intelligence and the Cold War behind the Dikes: the Relationship between the American and Dutch Intelligence Communities, 1946–1994

BOB DE GRAAFF and CEES WIEBES

Very little has been published in the Netherlands, and almost nothing in the English language, about the activities of the various intelligence and security services comprising the Dutch Intelligence community.[1] The limited literature on intelligence liaison is chiefly concerned with cooperation between the intelligence communities of the major Western countries. Almost no attention has been paid to the issue of liaison between the bigger and smaller Western intelligence and security agencies. In studies dealing with the activities of the US intelligence community in foreign countries, the Netherlands and its services are almost completely ignored.

This essay looks at three aspects of the intelligence community in the Netherlands: (1) its present structure; (2) American-Dutch cooperation in the field of security, intelligence and counter-intelligence; and (3) some of the activities of the Dutch Foreign Intelligence Service (*de Inlichtingendienst Buitenland*, IDB) and its relations with the US intelligence community for the period 1946–1994.

In 1992 the decision was made by the Dutch government to dissolve the IDB. This made us decide to start writing a full history of our foreign intelligence agency which from 1 January 1994 onwards would no longer exist. Much of the information to be found here is based on our academic study of the IDB in the Dutch language, to be published in the autumn of 1997.

THE PRESENT SITUATION

The present Dutch intelligence community consists of an Internal Security Service (*de Binnenlandse Veiligheidsdienst*, BVD) and a Military Intelligence Service (*de Militaire Inlichtingendienst*, MID) which can be compared with the American Defense Intelligence Agency (DIA). As regards the past, role and activities of the BVD, this Internal Security

Service was formally established in 1949 by confidential royal decree. The decree defined its functions as collecting information about all persons undertaking, or likely to be involved in, activities dangerous to the Netherlands or to friendly countries; gather information about extremist political movements; the furtherance of security measures in all vital and vulnerable government and private institutions and industries; and the maintenance of liaison with friendly foreign security and intelligence services.[2]

The BVD came under the Minister of the Interior despite efforts by the Justice Department to claim the responsibility for the security service. However, in 1949 the memories of World War II were still very fresh. In order not to create the general impression that the BVD would be a kind of 'new Gestapo' it was decided to make a separation between the (counter) intelligence and executive functions. The former was given to the BVD. Investigation, arrest and detention were the responsibility of the police. At present, roughly 500 persons work for the BVD.

The *Military Intelligence Service* (MID) was formally created in 1987 when the separate intelligence services of the three armed forces were integrated into this new organization. The prime task of the MID is to gather intelligence as regards the strength, activities and intentions of foreign armed forces (in the past mostly Soviet and Warsaw Pact nations). In addition it is involved in screening military personnel and safeguarding the security at military bases. The MID also has a close liaison with the Intelligence Division of NATO. In 1996 more than 400 officials were working at the MID.[3]

An important asset of Navy intelligence is the counter-part of the American National Security Agency (NSA), the *Technisch Informatie Verwerkings Centrum* (TIVC), whose headquarters are based in the centre of Amsterdam. Like the NSA and GCHQ, the British Government Communications Headquarters in Cheltenham, it is the most secret member of the Dutch Intelligence Community. It deals with Signals Intelligence (Sigint) and intercepts diplomatic, military, scientific and commercial communications. The intercepted signals may be transmitted by telephone, radio-telephone, radio, cable and satellite. The TIVC cooperates closely as regards Sigint operations with the NSA and the Foreign Intelligence Service in Germany, the *Bundesnachrichtendienst*.

The Dutch intelligence community also has a *Coordinator*, whose prime task is to coordinate the various activities of the services. Usually this official resides at the Cabinet Office and acts as a political advisor to the Prime Minister. In addition, there is the so-called *Comité Verenigde Inlichtingendiensten Nederland* (CVIN) which manages and more or less steers the overall Dutch intelligence effort. Its membership consists of the coordinator, the directors of BVD and MID, and representatives of the ministries of Foreign Affairs and Justice who meet about once a month.

Since September 1976 the *Ministriële Commissie voor Inlichtingen en Veiligheidsdiensten* (MICIV) has also been in existence. This is an official body composed of the prime minister and other ministers, but it hardly meets. Finally, there used to exist in the Netherlands a service called *Intelligence and Operations (I & O)*: a stay-behind organization which would be involved in acts of sabotage and the gathering of military information if the country were occupied by the Red Army and its allies.

DUTCH INTERNAL SECURITY

During the period dealt with (1945–1990) the internal and external enemies were manifest: the Soviet Union, its East European allies and its fifth column, the Communist Party of the Netherlands (CPN). All Dutch security and intelligence agencies concentrated on this communist enemy. At the end of the war several resistance groups were cooperating with the Allied Forces in the field of counter-intelligence. Mainly at the insistence of the Allies, who preferred to cooperate with one single Dutch unit, a *Bureau of National Security* was set up in May 1945. Its main task was to clear up the remnants of the German intelligence and security services: to track down, arrest and hand over to the authorities the agents and collaborators of the Abwehr, Gestapo and Sicherheitsdienst. This Bureau was formally dissolved at the end of 1946.

By confidential royal decree a *Central Security Service* was established in April 1946. This service was expressly modelled on the British security service, MI5, in its mode of operation and on the American FBI in its centralized storage of information. It came directly under the Prime Minister. This small, specialized service was instructed to guard against foreign espionage and sabotage, and against infringements of the democratic order by extremist organizations and persons. As the Cold War started, it started to pay more and more attention to the communists as a potential fifth column for the Red Army. In 1949 the Central Security Service was renamed the BVD and went over to the Department of the Interior.

Dutch membership of the Western European Union and NATO, the stationing of an American air force squadron at Soesterberg, the storage of nuclear weapons, and US military assistance in general, all made Holland an interesting target for the Soviet, and in particular the East German, intelligence services. The BVD appears to have operated successfully in monitoring and neutralising these activities. As regards counter-intelligence, the Dutch service operated closely with other Western intelligence and security services like MI5 and CIA. According to the official historian of the BVD, Dr Dick Engelen,

> Among these allied services the American CIA held a special place. It supplied the BVD with financial and technical assistance in return for generous access to BVD information, concerning not only the Soviet but also the Chinese intelligence organizations.[4]

What amount of financial support was exactly given and in what field did the BVD cooperate with the CIA?

In May 1948 the first CIA representative was stationed in The Hague. This posting had not been an easy affair because the CIA, probably aware of the close and good relationship between the BVD and MI5, wanted to be treated on a basis of exclusivity. The US ambassador even demanded that MI5 should not receive the same information as was handed over to the CIA. The Americans did not want to have anything to do with the British service because, they told the director of the BVD, Louis Einthoven, the British had cheated them severely during the war. However, when the Dutch flatly refused, the Americans gave way, and soon a CIA representative went to The Hague.[5]

LIAISON

Direct liaison with foreign intelligence and security services is a responsibility of the CIA, but this was not explicitly spelled out until an official directive of 21 April 1958. Little has been published about this important topic. For instance, if one looks at the declassified CIA volume *Allan Welsh Dulles as Director of Central Intelligence*, one will quickly discover that in Chapter 3 almost everything about intelligence liaison has been deleted by the American weeders.[6]

Interestingly, liaison is also not explicitly spelled out in the theoretical approaches as regards intelligence. If one looks to the intelligence cycle paradigm, one will even discover that liaison has no fixed location in this cycle because, as Westerfield rightly points out, it is actually a mode of activity at every point in the intelligence cycle. In his view liaison shares this quality with counter-intelligence. The obvious underlying reasons for this are the political sensitivities: internationally and often also domestically.[7]

With respect to the forms of American-Dutch intelligence collaboration, there has never been a fully-fledged American-Dutch liaison authorized formally at governmental level. The classic example of such an arrangement is, of course, the UKUSA Sigint agreement that since 1948 binds the United

States, Britain, Canada, Australia and New Zealand, and has led not only to information-sharing but also often to operations-sharing.[8] However, as Westerfield rightly points out, the sharing of both operations and information can also exist in liaison relationships that lack the whole panoply of fully-fledged liaison.[9] This situation pertained and still pertains to the Netherlands.

There was and is a constant intelligence sharing between the Dutch intelligence and security services and their American, British, German and Israeli counterparts. Information was traded for information. Apart from this sharing, the most common form of liaison collaboration is intelligence support in the form of equipment, training, advice, etc. This also pertained to the Netherlands because from the start the 'Agency' started to back up the BVD. They gave material support like automatic pistols and ammunition but also special equipment destined for illegal technical operations with microphones and for tracking down clandestine radiotransmitters.

This special equipment had an annual value of $25,000 at the beginning of 1950: equivalent at the exchange rate in those days, to more than 10 per cent of the BVD budget. CIA dollars were also used to purchase cars and hire extra staff. Besides the sharing of intelligence there were sometimes also operations sharing in the fields of collection, covert action and counter-intelligence. Sometimes there were 'joint operations' in which a case was being jointly handled. This often happened in the case of Soviet Bloc defectors. In addition, 'allocated operations' took place, during which each agency executed an agreed part of the operation. There were also 'parallel operations' when Dutch and American agencies executed, in collaboration, separate operations against the same target.[10]

An example of CIA-BVD cooperation was Project A, aimed at tapping the telephones of Soviet and communist bloc embassies. The Americans provided the money and technology, and the BVD carried out the operation. The wiretaps were handed over to the CIA which translated the Russian and other conversations. Transcripts of the conversations were then handed to the BVD which examined them for information on Soviet contacts with their agents in the Netherlands. Initially, however, Project A did not run smoothly.

BVD director Einthoven complained to the Director of Central Intelligence (DCI), Allen Dulles, that CIA cooperation in Project A was sluggish. Dulles, who was strongly in favour of extending liaison with friendly services, promised more financial and other support.[11] The wiretaps proved useful in identifying Dutchmen who contacted the Soviet embassy for an appointment. It alerted the BVD, for instance, to the activities of Pavel Petrov, a Soviet 'diplomat' who tried to recruit Dutch informers.

Petrov had to return to Moscow in 1953.

Cooperation between the BVD and CIA led not only to operational successes but also to moments of friction. Some official requests for specific information by the CIA station-chief in The Hague were flatly turned down. The BVD wanted to fight the common Communist enemy in Western Europe but considered that information about political events in the Netherlands was not the business of the CIA. The inquisitive behaviour of the American military attaché in Rotterdam harbour and the contacts between the CIA and the Dutch border police, which took place behind the back of the Dutch security service, also caused resentment in the BVD. The CIA was forced to give way.

Another incident, concerning an American refusal of a visa for a Dutch citizen, made BVD-director Einthoven decide to write a strongly worded letter to the CIA station chief at the American embassy in which he threatened that the BVD 'will be seriously restricted in the future in giving information to your service about supposed activities of Dutch subjects'. He could make this threat because the Dutch government had promised the State Department that the BVD would hand over to the American embassy and consulates all available political background information about those who applied for a visa for entry to the United States.[12]

The letter improved the working relationship and regular BVD-CIA meetings were held once a month from then on. Soon Dutch ambassador J. van Roijen could report from Washington that DCI Dulles was very satisfied with the quality of the BVD work in the field of counter-intelligence in Project A and that the monthly BVD-reports were considered by the CIA of 'high value'.[13] Project A was accordingly continued and led in 1957 to the expulsion of another Soviet diplomat, Vasily D. Drankov, and three officers of the Soviet military intelligence service, GRU.[14]

As the evidence cited above indicates, the Dutch kept the Americans at some distance, and even at the height of the Cold War were not always in favour of joint operations, especially on Dutch territory. The Dutch had far fewer reservations about activities abroad. There were numerous joint CIA-BVD counter-intelligence operations, especially in Germany and in Berlin in particular.

By 1958 about 51 of the then 691 BVD employees were paid with the subsidies from the CIA. In addition to sharing information about Dutch communism and its international links, the BVD also revealed details about operational methods. New BVD employees were trained in Washington by the CIA, and financial support grew year by year. The CIA appears to have been generous in forwarding intelligence about Soviet Bloc diplomats. The Agency also helped the Dutch service with the screening of the more than 400 Hungarian refugees who fled to Holland in 1956.

The BVD, however, was not a 'timid partner' in this intelligence marriage. Certain requests or proposals by the CIA were flatly turned down. For instance, the CIA wanted to buy up a left-wing weekly and subsequently appoint a reliable editor-in-chief. The BVD refused and asked the CIA not to interfere in Dutch internal political affairs. The Dutch displeasure was sometimes frankly expressed. A newly-appointed CIA station chief was, for example, recalled at the beginning of 1956 because the BVD – according to its historian Engelen – was unhappy with his activities in the Netherlands. The real reason, however, was that the director of the BVD and the CIA station chief strongly disliked and distrusted each other. DCI Dulles at Langley considered good relations with the BVD to be the main priority and sacrificed his station chief.[15]

The proposal to make a pornographic film of Indonesian foreign minister Subandrio during his visit to the Netherlands was flatly refused. According to Einthoven, Subandrio could not be blackmailed with this type of operation, and once back in Jakarta would proudly show the photos to his friends and colleagues. The BVD also refused to wiretap the embassy of Egypt in The Hague after Nasser's lengthy visit to Moscow in May 1958. The Dutch were afraid that, if the Egyptians discovered the bugging, this would lead to a serious breakdown in Dutch diplomatic relations with the Middle East.[16] The Dutch had no such inhibitions in conducting a joint operation against the diplomatic mission of the People's Republic of China. Prodded by the CIA, the BVD, which had excellent contact with real estate agents in the Netherlands, bugged the mission. The results were shared with the Americans. Intelligence about the Sino-Soviet split in 1956, difficult to obtain from other sources, turned out to be valuable. Dulles congratulated the BVD for having made a 'substantial contribution to the security of your country and to that of all Western nations'.[17]

Both the legendary Sherman Kent and officers of the CIA Chinese desk regularly travelled to Holland to speak with the BVD officer who ran and reported about this unique operation. In 1958 three BVD employees were sent to Yale to study Chinese. In the same year the CIA drafted a voluminous report primarily based on information received from the Dutch service. This operation continued until December 1963 when it stopped because Chinese diplomats discovered the bugging.[18]

By the end of the 1950s, despite the good relationship between the CIA and BVD, there was increasing concern in The Hague that its security service was partially dependent on a foreign power. After the retirement of Einthoven in 1961, his successor gradually terminated the American subsidies. In 1964 more than 60 BVD employees were still being indirectly paid by the Agency, but a few years later the BVD was no longer receiving funds from the CIA.

INDONESIA

The colonial struggle in the Dutch East Indies worried Washington from July 1947, when the Dutch launched their first military action against the Indonesian nationalist forces. By 1948 the CIA had an agent of its own in Jakarta who recruited Indonesian nationalists in complete secrecy for police training in the United States.[19]

The CIA fired off reports to President Truman criticizing Dutch policy. After the second military action in December 1948, the CIA expressed its concern to Truman by claiming that this step 'has cut the US position to the bone by touching on nearly all basic US security interests simultaneously'.[20] When Indonesia became independent in December 1949 the attention of the CIA changed: in the 1950s the focus was directed much less at Dutch policy towards Indonesia than at developments within Indonesia itself.[21]

After Indonesian independence, however, the main CIA priority in its liaison with the BVD concerned Dutch Communism and the activities of Soviet Bloc agents. The CIA also made numerous recruits among American businessmen who frequently made stop-overs in Amsterdam and The Hague on their way to Moscow and China. This was not liked by the BVD but nonetheless tolerated by the Dutch service as long as the CIA station chief kept the BVD informed about his activities. The BVD was anxious to prevent double recruitment of the same agent by the CIA and by the Dutch.

THE FOREIGN INTELLIGENCE SERVICE

In 1946 the Dutch government decided to establish a foreign intelligence service which was later called the *Inlichtingendienst Buitenland* (IDB).[22] A confidential royal decree tasked the IDB with gathering intelligence concerning developments abroad which were of concern to the Kingdom of the Netherlands. The best way to explain its internal structure is by reference to the well known, albeit oversimplified, concept of the 'intelligence-cycle': the process by which information is required, converted into finished intelligence, and made available to policymakers. The cycle comprises five stages: planning and direction, collection, processing, production and analysis, and dissemination.[23] As regards the first phase of this cycle: the IDB had no overall collection-plan nor any so-called *Key Intelligence Questions* (KIQs) to identify topics of particular interest to national policymakers. The search for intelligence by the IDB was initially conducted somewhat at random.

With respect to steps 2, 3 and 4 of the cycle, the political, military and economic sections of the IDB were individually responsible for the collection, processing, production and analysis. The political section did more analysis than the military section which forwarded the data it acquired immediately to one of the three armed services. In the final step of the cycle, dissemination, the political intelligence product of the IDB was mostly distributed to the Prime Minister's Office and the ministry of Foreign Affairs. Often the IDB analyses were also delivered to the ministries of Defence and Economic Affairs or to the BVD.

From 1946 onwards the Cabinet Office was responsible for the IDB activities. The service had posts in several foreign nations. IDB officers were stationed in Paris, Stockholm, Berne, Bonn, Vienna, Ankara, Madrid, and other capitals. They mostly worked (like CIA personnel) under diplomatic cover with the rank of first or second attaché. In the 1950s the intelligence service employed about 50 persons and it executed operations of its own in the Soviet Union, Warsaw Pact nations and China. The Dutch service recruited informers chiefly among legal travellers such as academics, journalists, sailors and businessmen but also among foreign diplomats who travelled to various destinations behind the Iron Curtain and to China.

On the basis of our analysis of about 200 IDB reports, it can be said that the quality of IDB reports is quite good. Interestingly, in the 1950s the targets of the service were not so much the Soviet Union and its allies but much more NATO partners such as West Germany, France and Great Britain. The service had agents and informers well posted in high places. For instance, the IDB recruited in the 1950s a source very close to Konrad Adenauer in the Chancellor's Office who fired off well-informed and excellent reports on a frequent basis.[24] It also had informers in governmental circles in London and Paris. According to a reliable estimate, about 80 per cent of the IDB informers had a university degree.

As regards the liaison between the CIA and IDB: the most common form of intelligence collaboration is support in the form of supplies, training, advising, etc. This was also offered to the IDB. The CIA was in particular interested in improving the Dutch intercept capabilities and ample funds were provided for that. The Americans wanted to improve the Dutch intercept capabilities with respect to Russian traffic between Moscow and Soviet embassy in The Hague. Apparently there was no explicit role in this venture for the National Security Agency.

IDB staff also received training in Langley, Virginia and in London at MI6. They were trained in the tradecraft but also followed other courses. However, one affair almost caused a breakdown in the American-Dutch intelligence relationship. It turned out that the Dutch had for quite a long time a very well-placed informer at the NSA.

THE PETERSEN AFFAIR

One of the intrinsic risks of liaison with foreign services is being penetrated. Close cooperation between agencies means that some of the intelligence personnel of one agency are identified by the other. This carries with it the risk of direct or indirect recruitment, not only of intelligence personnel but also of officials in other agencies or governmental circles. We now know that the Dutch were not only liaising with, but also spying on, the United States.

The most important case is that of Joseph Sidney Petersen of the NSA, who was arrested by FBI agents on 9 October 1954. He had a long-time cryptologic cooperation with two Dutch experts which had a legal beginning during the war but continued illegally after 1945. Petersen started to give the Dutch copies of top-secret notes and highly classified documents which he smuggled out of the NSA. These documents included details about America's success in breaking Dutch codes. Petersen's generosity lasted almost six years.[25]

The Americans started to work on the Dutch diplomatic and military codes in 1943 with the help of GCHQ. The British gave in August 1943 full information on the Hagelin cipher system used by the Dutch.[26] The American attack on the Dutch system was helped when GCHQ 'pinched' a London-Stockholm key which covered a ten-day period in the summer of 1943. In the summer of 1944 the attack on the Dutch Hagelin traffic proved to be successful and from that moment both the Americans and the British GCHQ were able to read the Dutch diplomatic traffic well into the 1950s.[27]

The fact that Petersen told his Dutch handlers about this infuriated his superiors at the NSA.[28] After Petersen's arrest it was not too difficult for the NSA to track down which papers the Dutch had seen, because the ones they copied were fastened with squared-off Dutch staples of a different colour from the US rounded staples.

The American authorities were outraged and called in the Dutch ambassador in Washington.[29] On 10 October 1954 Dutch ambassador Van Roijen was summoned to see Secretary of State John Foster Dulles. The gravity of the incident was evident from the fact that it was a Sunday and the ambassador had to visit Dulles in his private mansion. Dulles did not hide his anger in his meeting with the ambassador. It does not seem to have occurred to him that the NSA attack on Dutch traffic also gave the Dutch legitimate grounds for complaint. However, both nations decided to minimize the effect this affair would have on their relations. Allen Dulles expressed the same view to Van Roijen: the American response would be low key.

Nevertheless, the legendary James Jesus Angleton was sent by Dulles to The Hague in order to draw up a damage assessment. In a secret cache in his leather belt he carried a one-time pad for direct communications with Langley. In high-level talks an angry Angleton accused the Dutch of 'foul play'. He further wanted to inspect 'files and correspondence' and demanded a full briefing which the Foreign Ministry promised to draft. However, it soon turned out that – according to the Dutch handlers of Petersen – it had been a 'two-way traffic': they had also given cryptologic data to Petersen to forward to the CIA and NSA. At least this is what they claimed. The Netherlands government thereupon decided to take a somewhat tougher attitude and refused to grant Angleton an interview with Petersen's contacts in the Netherlands. Van Roijen told Dulles that the Dutch had done nothing illegal.[30] The whole affair died down to the relief of both governments involved.[31] The British embassy in The Hague reported that the Petersen case had only caused 'a mild stir'.[32]

Nevertheless, after the Petersen case the FBI was reluctant to cooperate with its counterpart in the Netherlands. The relationship of the CIA with the IDB and BVD as regards sharing and exchange of intelligence, joint operations and handling of defectors remained practically unaffected by the case, although Dutch military intelligence had more problems with the fall-out. In particular, the NSA was reluctant to cooperate in the cryptologic field during the 1950s and 1960s.[33]

THE BOTCHED IDB MISSION TO KIEV

The 1950s were a tranquil decade for the IDB: the service was able to work undisturbed and the Petersen case did not affect its work directly. There were no scandals and the service was never mentioned in the press or debated in parliament. However, this would change in the 1960s as the result of a mission by two IDB agents to the Soviet Union. In this period the CIA encountered more and more difficulties with its 'humint' operations behind the Iron Curtain, and was attracted by the opportunities presented by the numerous Dutch ships travelling to Soviet and Chinese ports. The IDB started covert operations in which agents operated from merchant vessels and sometimes penetrated overland into the Soviet Union and China.

These operations were run by the IDB but were planned and coordinated well in advance with the CIA and MI6. The activities by the IDB were mostly confined to taking photographs of ships, quays, buildings, military installations, etc. in harbours such as Murmansk and Archangelsk. Agents also collected water samples and documents and sometimes even carried out incendiary attacks in Chinese ports in order to test the speed and efficiency of the Chinese fire brigades. These agents were trained to work with Leica cameras and were usually debriefed when they returned by the IDB, sometimes in the presence of a CIA representative.[34]

In 1961 two IDB agents, Evert Reydon and Louw de Jager, were selected for an overland mission into the Soviet Union. Their task was to gather intelligence about the sites of ICBM-launchers, airports, bases, military units, transport conditions and other strategically important targets in the southern part of the Soviet Union. It was from the outset 'a mission impossible', more or less doomed to fail. Reydon had already been arrested during a previous visit to the Soviet Union. After months of preparations they travelled as tourists with, on the rear seat of their car, four very expensive cameras with huge lenses, more than 50 rolls of film and two very powerful pairs of binoculars.

From the moment both 'tourists' crossed the border, they were shadowed by the KGB. Even in 1992 Reydon was still puzzled why he and his partner did not immediately return to the Netherlands.[35] Nonetheless, they continued and took many photographs in the Ukraine, at Odessa, Kiev and near Yalta, but when they arrived again at the border they were of course arrested for espionage. Later they were sentenced to 13 years' imprisonment, but spent only two years in jail and were released in 1963.

The arrest of the two Dutch agents happened at the same time as other arrests in the Soviet Union, among them that of the American citizen Marvin W. Makinen. His route was almost the same as the one of Reydon and de Jager – not surprisingly because the official Soviet travel agency Intourist always selected in advance the routes for tourists. Makinen also travelled as a tourist to Kiev and Odessa but planned to continue to Moscow and Minsk and then on to West Berlin via Warsaw. Makinen, who met Reydon and de Jager near Kiev, was arrested and sentenced on 5 September 1961 by a military tribunal to eight years.[36] At almost the same time the German tourists Walter Neuman and Peter Sonntag and also a German married couple named Werner were arrested. When asked over 30 years later whether there was any connection between these arrests and those of Reydon and de Jager, the Cabinet Office of the Dutch Prime Minister explicitly denied the existence of any link.[37]

The British Embassy in Moscow concluded after the trial against Reydon and de Jager that both men 'were of comparatively low intelligence and should never have been used for such a purpose'. The Dutch embassy in Moscow, though fully unaware of the true mission of both Dutchmen, had told the British embassy that both men had been arrested because they had not paid the hotel bill in Odessa. The British embassy commented dryly: 'If this were so, they were very stupid to have drawn attention to themselves unnecessarily in this way'.[38]

Was the CIA involved in this operation? In a review of Reydon's romanticized book *Spy for NATO*[39] the in-house journal of the CIA, *Studies in Intelligence*, commented in 1968 that the IDB operations of Reydon were executed in close cooperation with MI6.[40] However, this is only part of the truth because reliable sources confirm that the CIA as well as MI6 were involved in these kinds of Dutch operations behind the Iron Curtain.[41]

For instance, Reydon confirmed to us that after returning from a maritime trip behind the Iron Curtain he had to deliver his photographs to a MI6 officer in Liverpool or London after the Briton had greeted him with a prearranged password. Apart from this, the Dutch spy was often briefed and debriefed by American officers who always showed identification of, and introduced themselves as belonging to, NATO intelligence.[42]

The doomed operation of Reydon and de Jager had a significant internal fall-out within the IDB. Several senior people had to leave the service, including the Director of the IDB. Criticism of the handling of the operation led to the recruitment of more civilians with university degrees in the political and economical section and to fewer military being employed. Greater priority would be given in future to analysis, and to political and economic intelligence, rather than military data.[43] The targets of the IDB were also broadened, and the Middle East and North Africa were added to the list of key intelligence targets. As a result, the ratio between military and political and economical intelligence shifted from 70:30 per cent to 55:45 per cent.

Nonetheless, the Cabinet Office of the Dutch Prime Minister assured us that this bungled operation had no consequences for the contacts of the IDB with the CIA and other Western intelligence services.[44] The relationship with the CIA had been cemented by Dutch background and logistical support, and probably also Sigint assistance, to the operations of the Agency (and probably also MI6) in Indonesia in 1956–58.[45] The Dutch were engaged in a fierce political battle with the Indonesians over Western New Guinea. There was probably the hope that help to the CIA would pay off on the diplomatic level because the Eisenhower and, later, the Kennedy administrations showed little enthusiasm for the Dutch presence on this island.

However, much of this American-Dutch cooperation is still in the domain of classified documents, although it is clear that the IDB had well informed sources even in the highest ranks of the Indonesian government. Dutch naval intelligence also executed brilliant Sigint operations which gave them an excellent insight into the military operations the Indonesians were planning to execute.[46]

CONTINUED COOPERATION

Despite the Dutch political anger at the continuing lack of United States support in the New Guinea dispute, American-Dutch cooperation in the field of intelligence of course continued. In the 1960s and 1970s the role of the Netherlands as one of the smaller American client-states in the field of intelligence remained unaltered. The exchange of intelligence information between the IDB continued on a strict *quid pro quo* basis but, in the context of the overall American-Dutch intelligence relationship, the IDB remained a junior partner dependent on what the CIA station-chief or the Defense Intelligence Agency (DIA) was willing to deliver to it.

In our interviews many former CIA officials often explicitly stated that they gave high-quality intelligence reports to the staff of the IDB.[47] However, many IDB officers had a different view, and a certain dissatisfaction with the level of CIA reports began to manifest itself in the 1970s. One of the reasons was that within the IDB, an *Analysis* section was established next to *Operations* in which the young academic staff were critical of the quality of the American materials. Partly as a consequence, the relationship with the American intelligence community somewhat cooled.

Another contributing factor was that successive CIA station chiefs in The Hague were kept at arms length by the new director of the IDB, who refused any formal cooperation. Even the exchange of requirements was not greeted with much enthusiasm by the IDB director who also explicitly forbade his employees to have contacts with the CIA. Cooperation with the BVD was much better and many CIA officials regarded this service of much higher quality than the IDB. The overall working relationship improved when the IDB director was sacked in 1978.

In this period the IDB expanded its scope of cooperation with other Western intelligence agencies – notably the Mossad, which became a very important recipient of Dutch intelligence. Particularly in the field of Sigint, the IDB profited enormously from intelligence-sharing, for instance during the war in the Middle East in 1973–74.

However, as stated before, one of the intrinsic risks of liaison is penetration by a foreign service.[48] One of the Israeli services recruited a major in the Royal Netherlands Air Force who worked as a liaison officer in a high ranking position in the Dutch foreign intelligence service. The major had access to intelligence on the Iraqi nuclear programme as well as other highly classified material of interest to the Israelis. The major was exposed and arrested but, unlike the Israeli agent in NSA, Jonathan Pollard, was not tried and was allowed to depart for Israel. It was Israel's then Prime Minister Yitzhak Shamir who – according to a reliable source – personally worked for his release and arranged for his emigration to Israel.[49]

As regards CIA recruitment of members of the Dutch intelligence community and other Dutch officials, not much is known. Retired and still active members of the US intelligence community assured us that this seldom took place because there was a close and intimate relationship with the BVD and other services. The only occasion known to us happened at the beginning of the 1970s when a CIA officer tried to recruit a Dutch politician. The attempt infuriated his own station chief, who had forbidden all such attempts. As one former CIA official candidly told us: 'He was a damn, damn, damn fool to recruit a member of parliament from the Socialist Party.' Another official also described this move as very stupid and said that the CIA official 'probably went on his own'.[50]

At the beginning of the 1980s American-Dutch cooperation intensified again and plans were made for a joint CIA-IDB operation in the former Dutch colony of Surinam.[51] The aim of the operation was to overthrow Surinam's leader Desi Bouterse,[52] whom Washington was afraid would introduce a Cuban-style government. The plan was discussed within the inner circle of the Reagan administration. According to one official involved, the operation in Surinam was eventually 'vetoed by the CIA. The IDB was quite willing to execute the operation but eventually they were overruled'. In Langley, Virginia, it was decided that the operation 'would not bring us anything at all: it would only be counter-productive'.[53]

The CIA had much difficulty persuading the IDB to abort the whole operation. In the end the Dutch Cabinet also decided against the operation because of the potential dangers for the future political relationship with Surinam. The American Congress was unwilling to approve the covert action.[54]

CONCLUSION

From the outset the relationship of the CIA with the Dutch intelligence and security services was generally close. However, liaison with the BVD was always considered to be of a much higher standard than that with the IDB. The ties between the CIA and the Dutch Defence Intelligence Agency were loose because the military attachés at the American embassy in The Hague were usually responsible for this liaison. There was also in some sectors of Dutch naval intelligence a reluctance to cooperate with the CIA. Although some chiefs of station tried to improve this liaison this was most of the time to no avail.[55] The chiefs and other high-ranking officials of Dutch naval intelligence preferred direct contacts and exchange with their American counterparts in the US Office of Naval Intelligence (ONI).

The BVD was and is regarded by the US Intelligence community as one of the best Western European security services, highly respected in Langley, Virginia. Close liaison with this service was therefore always high on the agenda of every CIA station chief posted to The Hague. What of course helped maintain the intimacy between CIA and BVD was that the Dutch and Americans had the same political and military communist enemy at home and abroad. However, although the BVD was willing to accept American material support in this struggle it never tolerated Dutch operations by the CIA without the explicit compliance of the BVD.

American esteem for the IDB was lower than for the BVD. This intelligence service was sometimes viewed by Langley with bewilderment. The level of the personnel and their intelligence reporting were considered to be not of the same quality as those of the BVD. The Dutch government sometimes gave insufficient care in selecting the directors of the IDB. Some directors showed great distrust towards their opposite numbers of the CIA. The IDB also had no explicit requirements to work with, and some of its raw intelligence was of low value. Several CIA officials were even told before they left for The Hague not to expect any fruitful contacts with the IDB.

Despite recurrent American disappointment with Dutch foreign intelligence, it was, interestingly enough, the CIA who apparently vehemently protested against the decision by the Dutch government in 1992 to abolish the IDB, but to no avail. In 1994 the IDB was officially buried, leaving 'eternal vigilance' to others.

NOTES

1. The contribution is partly based on a paper which was presented on the 63rd annual meeting of the Society for Military History, cosponsored by the Central Intelligence Agency (CIA), on 18–21 April 1996 in Washington DC.
2. Bob de Graaff, 'From Security Threat to Protection of Vital Interest: Changing Perceptions in the Dutch Security Service, 1945-91', *Conflict Quarterly* 12/2 (Spring 1992) p.13.
3. F.A.C. Kluiters, *De Nederlandse inlichtingen en veiligheidsdiensten* (The Hague: SDU 1993) pp.253-5.
4. Dick Engelen, *Geschiedenis van de Binnenlandse Veiligheidsdienst* (The Hague: SDU 1995) pp.392–5. The quotation is on p.395.
5. Ibid. p.297.
6. National Archives (henceforth NA), RG 263, CIA-records, Box 1, Folder Allen Welsh Dulles as DCI, Allen Welsh Dulles as Director of Central Intelligence, 26 Feb. 1953–29 Nov. 1961, Vol.IV, Congressional Oversight and Internal Administration by Wayne G. Jackson, pp.47–60.
7. H. Bradford Westerfield, 'America and the World of Intelligence Liaison', unpublished paper for the International Studies Association Annual Meeting, Intelligence Section, Washington DC, 29 March 1994, pp.3–8. Also available in *Intelligence and National Security* 11/3 (July 1996) pp.523–60.

8. Jeffrey T. Richelson and Desmond Ball, *The Ties That Bind* (Sydney/Boston, Allen & Unwin 1990), *passim*. Christopher Andrew, 'The Making of the Anglo-American SIGINT Alliance 1940–1948', in James E. Dillard and Walter T. Hitchcock (eds.) *The Intelligence Revolution and Modern Warfare* (Chicago 1996).

9. Westerfield, 'America and the World of Intelligence Liaison' (note 7) p.14.

10. Interview with former CIA officer.

11. NA, RG 263 CIA records, Box 1, Folder Allen Welsh Dulles as DCI (note 6) p.49.

12. Engelen (note 4) pp.296–305.

13. Ibid. p.306.

14. John Barron, KGB. *The Secret Work of Soviet Agents* (NY: Berkeley Books 1974) p.518.

15. Interviews with former CIA officers.

16. Engelen (note 4) pp.312–13.

17. Ibid. pp.320–36.

18. Interviews with former BVD and CIA officers.

19. Interview with a former American diplomat.

20. NA, RG 263, CIA Papers, Series 'CIA 1949', No. CIA 1-49, 'Review of the World Situation as it relates to the security of the United States, 19 Jan. 1949.

21. For instance: A.R. Kahin and G. McT. Kahin, *Subversion as Foreign Policy: The Secret Eisenhower and Dulles Debacle in Indonesia* (NY: New Press 1995) *passim*.

22. Prior to 1972 it was called *Buitenlandse Inlichtingendienst* (BID).

23. CIA, *The Acme of Skill* (Washington DC, n.d.) pp.6–7.

24. Interviews with former IDB officers.

25. See for instance: James Bamford, *The Puzzle Palace: A Report on NSA, America's Most Secret Agency* (Harmondsworth, Middlesex: Penguin 1985) pp.173-8 and S. De Gramont, *The Secret War. The Story of International Espionage since World War II* (NY: Dell 1963) pp.173–8.

26. NA, RG 457 NSA Records, Box 880, Folder Fried Reports, Memo. by Walter J. Fried on Dutch Hagelin, No.IL 3331-A, 11 March 1944.

27. Ibid. Memo. 'Solution of A Three Deep Hagelin', No.OP-20-GE/MB, 7 June 1944.

28. See also: Bob de Graaff and Cees Wiesbes, 'Codes van vertrouwen', *NRC Handelsblad*, 29 June 1996.

29. Documents concerning the Petersen case can be found in the archives of the Netherlands Ministry of Foreign Affairs (NMFA) in Code 9, Secret Archives, Record Group 921.O B.K.

30. NA, RG 59, Box 3745, 756.5211/10-1154, Memo. by US Secretary of State, J.F. Dulles, 11 Oct. 1954.

31. Ibid. 756.5211/10-2954, Marcy to Dept. of State, 29 Oct. 1954.

32. Public Record Office (PRO, London), FO 371/109482, Chancery The Hague to Foreign Office, CN 10345/3, 3 Nov. 1954.

33. Interview with former Dutch naval intelligence officer.

34. Interviews with former IDB officers.

35. Interview with E. Reydon, 17 June 1992.

36. PRO, FO 371/159596, Trials of Foreign Nationals, NS 1691/3 Chancery Moscow to Foreign Office, 6 Sept. 1961. From this file the documents NS 1691/4 and NS 1691/5 are not yet released. See also: John Ranelagh, *The Agency. The Rise and Decline of the CIA* (NY: Simon & Schuster 1987) pp.252 and 783.

37. Letter to the authors from the Cabinet Office of the Dutch Prime Minister.

38. PRO, FO 371/160708, Chancery, Moscow to Northern Dept., Foreign Office, No.10351/11/10, 11 Oct. 1961.

39. Evert Reydon, *Spion voor de NAVO* (Amsterdam: Van Gennep 1967).

40. CIA Freedom of Information Act Request, FOIA Number C90-0015, *Studies in Intelligence*, 12/1 (Winter 1968) p.75.

41. Interviews with former CIA and IDB officers.

42. Interview with E. Reydon, 17 June 1992. Also: *Parliamentary Proceedings of the Second Chamber 1961–1962*, No.6500, Ch.V, No.17, letter to parliament by Foreign Minister Luns, 18 Dec. 1961.

43. Interviews with former IDB officers.
44. Letter to the authors from the Cabinet Office of the Dutch Prime Minister.
45. See for this: Kahin and McT. Kahin (note 21) pp.143–217.
46. See for instance: R.E. van Horst Pellekaan, I.C. de Regt, J.F. Bastiaans, *Patrouille voor de Papoea's. De Koninklijke Marine in Nederlands Nieuw-Guinea, I* (Amsterdam: Bataafsche Leeuw 1989) *passim.*
47. Interviews with former CIA officers.
48. Westerfield, 'America and the World of Intelligence Liaison' (note 7) p.31.
49. Interviews with former IDB and CIA officers.
50. Interviews with former CIA and IDB officials.
51. Andre Haakmat, *De Revolutie Uitgegleden. Politieke herinneringen* (Amsterdam: Jan Mets 1987) pp.201-11.
52. George Shultz, *Turmoil and Triumph. My Years as Secretary Of State* (NY: Scribners 1993) pp.292-7.
53. Interview.
54. Bob Woodward, *VEIL. The Secret Wars of the CIA 1981-1987* (London: Headline Books 1988), pp.239-41.
55. Interviews with former CIA officers.

4

Science, Scientists, and the CIA: Balancing International Ideals, National Needs, and Professional Opportunities

RONALD E. DOEL and ALLAN A. NEEDELL

The history and immediate prehistory of the American Central Intelligence Agency closely coincide with the emergence of scientific knowledge and scientists as key contributors to American military power and to national security. Intelligence about scientific activities abroad, and the application of the knowledge and the technologies developed and used by scientists to conduct their researches, have been recognized as central to the mission and the operation of the CIA and its predecessor agencies from the very beginning. As a result, the relations between science and the CIA have been intimate, although they have also been marked by strain and by controversy.

There are fundamental differences between the ideals and values of intelligence gathering and the ideals and values that serve to define the international community of scientists. The hallmark of intelligence operations is secrecy and the careful control of information. Knowledge is tantamount to power, usable by an enemy to undermine and to threaten, and as a tool a nation can use to protect itself and its interests. Information is collected from abroad (covertly if necessary); information is withheld from those who would employ it to the nation's detriment. The hallmark of science is openness. There is absolutely no room, in the scientific ideal, for considerations of political ideology or national needs. Indeed, deeply embedded in the traditions and self-image of scientists is the conviction that any attempt by nonscientific interests (religions, states, or political or military alliances) to influence scientific research or to control communications between scientists must be resisted at all costs.[1]

The ways in which these fundamental differences have been negotiated – sometimes reconciled, but mostly not – in the climate of the Cold War have had enormous consequences for the CIA and its ability to recruit and to make effective use of experts of various sorts. They have also profoundly altered the image and practice of science in postwar America.

American scientists faced a profound dilemma with the end of World War II. On the one hand most had dormant professional research careers to tend to, and on the other many had become accustomed to the status and the access to resources associated with war research and organizing activity. The United States' emergence from World War II as the world's leading military and economic power and the major, if not yet precisely defined, role that the US was bound to play in establishing a new global postwar regime, insured that the nation's need to maintain the instruments of military and economic power would not end with the cessation of hostilities. Many scientists were quite willing – even anxious – to continue, at least part-time, working directly for their government. Given the crucial contributions that science-based weapons – the atomic bomb and radar most prominently – had made to the Allied victory, and given the looming threat of new weapons – biological and chemical the most widely anticipated – it is no surprise that the leaders of American intelligence operations recognized the importance that the country's military planners and political leaders should be accurately informed about relevant scientific advances, whereever such advances might occur.[2] Indeed, among the major promoters of this specialized sort of intelligence were scientists, especially the group of influential scientists who had played leading roles organizing weapons research during World War II and those who were intimately familiar with scientific intelligence operations that had been carried out during that conflict.

But those same scientists also knew that scientific intelligence-gathering during World War II had not been well coordinated. The Manhattan Project, under the control of Major General Leslie R. Groves, established its own Foreign Intelligence Branch to spy on related activities abroad, especially on prospecting for uranium ore.[3] The Office of Scientific Research and Development established an office in London and assigned some of the nation's leading scientists to what can be described as intelligence gathering functions. The Army and the Navy, as well as the OSS, did the same. As the war drew to a close a special effort to gather as much information as possible from Germany and Japan was set in motion. And although a special reading panel was set up within the OSRD to review incoming intelligence and attempt to make sure that those who required the information were promptly informed, few were satisfied with the result.[4] How this scientific input was to be arranged was the great unsolved problem.

As the nation began the complex task of demobilization, existing means of gathering scientific intelligence had to be transformed along with so many other war-fashioned or war-expanded organizations. Scientists, who achieved unprecedented status and influence during the war, struggled to define for themselves a permanent postwar role. This study is intended as a sketch of the manner in which that was accomplished, and as a means of raising some of the crucial, if little examined, issues the evolving relations between the intelligence and scientific communities have raised for both.

INTELLIGENCE AND THE POSTWAR ORGANIZATION OF MILITARY R&D

The most important organizational arrangement for continued systematic scientific input into national security planning was the Joint Research and Development Board, established by the Secretaries of War and the Navy in the summer of 1946. Chaired by Vannevar Bush, who had served as both the wartime leader of the civilian Office of Scientific Research and Development (OSRD) and the chairman of the military's own Joint New Weapons Committee (reporting directly to the Joint Chiefs of Staff), the JRDB was charged with the responsibility of reviewing the status of all existing research and development projects and, in the case of overlapping responsibilities or of duplication, to assign primary responsibility to one of the services. As important, the JRDB recruited literally hundreds of civilian scientists from industry and the nation's most prestigious universities to serve on advisory committees and panels. Beginning late in 1946, these panels initiated a systematic inventory of research areas and personnel with the intention of advising the full Board and, through them, the nation's military planners.

To guide its operations the JRDB created a special Policy Council, a high level committee chaired by radio engineer/ionospheric physicist Lloyd V. Berkner (in his capacity as JRDB Executive Secretary).[5] The Policy Council was, in Berkner's own words, 'responsible for critical analysis of the trends of research and development and the vital planning associated with the utilization of new weapons'.[6] Significantly, a representative of the recently established Central Intelligence Group was invited to take part.

Members of the Policy Council quickly recognized that they would require timely analysis of the state of science and scientific research, both within the United States and abroad. To provide itself with high-level scientific input, a formal scientific advisory committee was formed. Appointed were I. I. Rabi and Alfred Loomis, veterans of the World War II radar development effort; William Shockley, the Bell Laboratory electronics expert; Caryl Haskins, the biologist director of the personally-financed Haskins Laboratories in New York and wartime Executive Assistant to the Chairman of the NDRC; and Georges F. Doriot, professor of industrial management at the Harvard Business School and wartime Deputy Director of the War Department's Research and Development Office.[7] This advisory committee was given special top secret briefings about current war plans and strategy.[8]

At preliminary informal meetings with the JRDB leadership in late 1946 the 'technical advisors' discussed an extraordinarily broad range of 'strategic concepts'. They were also given specific tasks, none deemed more essential than responding to a request from General Hoyt Vandenberg, head of the Central Intelligence Group, for assistance in locating qualified technical personnel for national intelligence work.

At their first and second meetings the scientific group discussed a plan for recruiting scientists and for 'evaluating technical intelligence', and agreed to submit that plan to the full JRDB in late December. During the advisors' January 1947 meeting it was noted that their formal paper, which was entitled ' Program for JRDB-CIG Cooperation in the Field of Scientific Intelligence', had been approved by both the CIG and JRDB, and a considerable amount of time was spent going over a list of potential candidates for the job of chief of a planned scientific branch within the CIG.[9]

The qualifications were in certain respects contradictory: the ideal candidate would be a leading researcher well versed in several fields, but also one who grasped the needs of intelligence. As important, the candidate had to be willing to work in anonymity. The technical advisors hoped to provide this scientist a cover position in a Washington-area university, a federal agency, or 'other scientific institutions of note' such as JRDB Chairman Vannevar Bush's Carnegie Institution of Washington. They regarded the physical sciences as critical fields of scientific intelligence, yet recognized individuals of high stature, like themselves and wartime scientific intelligence leader and CIG advisor, Princeton physicist H. P. Robertson, were unwilling to abandon their university chairs and public roles to take on full-time covert assignments of this kind.[10]

PLANNING SCIENTIFIC INTELLIGENCE

The individual that Vannevar Bush and the JRDB eventually recommended to develop this office was Wallace R. Brode. Descended from an old Ohio family with strong science interests (his father and twin brother were also professors), Brode's career typified that of many American scientists who became involved in scientific intelligence in the late 1940s and 1950s. A PhD from Illinois who taught physical chemistry at Ohio State until World War II, Brode had found wartime research much to his liking. The former OSRD liaison office head in Paris, Brode had gained familiarity with European science through a 1926 Guggenheim Fellowship and through a solar eclipse expedition to the Soviet Union. But what particularly drew the Policy Council advisors and Vannevar Bush's attention to Brode was his post-war assignment as director of the Science Department of the Naval

Ordnance Test Station at Inyokern, California, where he had developed plans for scientific intelligence gathering. Bush also appreciated Brode's outspoken disdain for military commandants who regarded scientists as 'merely assigned civilian laborers [directed] to produce such items as a supersonic torpedo, just as he might direct another group to dig a ditch across the road'. Brode's scientific elitism matched Bush's conviction that scientists needed to energetically define their role within the national military establishment.[11]

Installing Brode as the clandestine leader of scientific intelligence required novel accommodations within the American scientific community. Apparently on Bush's urging, Admiral Roscoe Hillenkoetter met with Edward U. Condon, director of the National Bureau of Standards. Condon soon authorized the appointment of Brode as Associate Director with an immediate (and secret) leave of absence, authorizing him to use the position 'as a "blind" ' for his intelligence activities. But Condon also agreed that, after one year, Brode would actually *become* the second-in-command at the NBS. This inducement was intended to buttress Brode's long-term professional standing, since the Ohio chemist was forced to resign his tenured professorship at Ohio State in 1947, having exceeded the number of permitted annual absences.[12]

All these arrangements aside, Brode was not successful. During the year he led the scientific branch within the Office of Research Estimates (ORE), from October 1947 to October 1948, Brode labored to define and have accepted a clear mandate for a scientific intelligence branch within the new agency. He favored an expansive mission. Using the guided missile as an example of a modern weapons system demanding close attention, Brode argued that 'the scientific order of battle' required CIA analysts to examine foreign 'scientific research and development to the point of production'. He championed the idea, earlier advocated by Rabi and Berkner, of building a master biographical database on all foreign scientific and technological personalities; this was later implemented in Intelligence Directive 8 of the National Security Council. (To disguise intelligence interest in the natural sciences alone, Brode recommended persuading a foundation to publish similar studies of drama, education, and music to lend the proposed project a 'cultural' atmosphere.)[13]

Nevertheless, by October 1948 Bush reported to Secretary of Defense James Forrestal that the CIA remained highly inefficient, particularly in the 'scientific and technical area'. Ralph Clark, Bush's director of programs at the now-renamed RDB,[14] more bluntly declared that the 'RDB has received substantially no scientific intelligence of the type wanted from CIA'.[15]

Why Brode failed to develop a viable scientific intelligence organization within the CIA reveals much about the relationship between scientists and the national security establishment during the early Cold War, and the particular difficulties of integrating scientists as a class of experts into the traditional circles of foreign policy-making. The principal problem that Brode confronted was one faced by the intelligence community as a whole: that of coordinating, collecting, and reviewing vast amounts of information from a bewildering range of sources. Brode favored a highly centralized office, modeled after his experience in Army Intelligence and functionally similar to the successful Scientific Intelligence Service created in Great Britain during World War II by the Edinburgh experimental physicist R. V. Jones. But Brode had insufficient resources and standing to deal with existing intelligence sections within the Army, Navy, and Atomic Energy Commission, not to mention information potentially available from the Departments of Justice, Agriculture, Commerce, Treasury and Interior, the Library of Congress, the National Research Council, and the National Advisory Council on Aeronautics. Nor did he have the stature to force these potential sources to share information with him. This gap between information sources and the needs of policy planners presented a daunting management problem that would perplex masters of scientific intelligence for years to come.[16]

Another challenge that Brode faced was creating an organizational structure for the scientific branch. Howland Sargeant, a State Department official tapped to manage scientific matters for ORE before Brode's appointment, had focused on six fields 'of immediate interest': aeronautics, atomic energy, biological warfare, chemical warfare, communications and electronics, and guided missiles. While these categories paralleled standing technical committees within the RDB, and Brode accepted their priority as critical national security concerns, he argued that scientific intelligence would best be served by treating science within such familiar disciplinary frameworks as physics, chemistry, and biology. By recreating the university model within the scientific branch, Brode believed that analysts could best identify potential threats not anticipated by targeted 'fields'. Moreover, by maintaining the professional structure familiar to scientists, Brode hoped to mitigate the problem of recruiting new science PhDs to the CIA. Brode's organizational plan, approved in January 1948, ultimately prevailed as the basis for CIA scientific intelligence. It became his most enduring contribution to this office. Brode's successors maintained the university model into the 1950s, adding new fields, such as medicine and astronomy, as their implications for national security became clear.[17]

A third problem that Brode faced was lack of bureaucratic support within the CIA, particularly from Hillenkoetter, its first director. In contrast to CIG leader Hoyt Vandenberg, who worked closely with Bush in negotiating the interim RDB-CIG agreement on cooperation in scientific intelligence, Hillenkoetter seemed indifferent to the special requirements of scientific intelligence collection, analysis, and production. He allowed competing ORE bureau chiefs to usurp responsibility for gathering scientific information, bypassing Brode's own network of contacts. He similarly left Brode to flounder when a senior official challenged Brode's top-level clearance in nuclear energy. Aware that a Nuclear Energy Branch created in March 1948 in the Office of Special Operations, which ran the CIA's spying activities, violated the Vandenberg-Bush agreement, Hillenkoetter suggested to Bush that the agreement had outlived its usefulness. Angered by Hillenkoetter's nonchalance, Bush reminded him that the RDB was 'probably your principal client in the field of scientific intelligence ... thus far I do not feel that the Board has been supplied with adequate scientific intelligence for its guidance'. His admonition did little however to increase Brode's authority within the CIA.[18]

Ultimately more troubling to Brode than Hillenkoetter's failure to protect him within the CIA was his inability, or unwillingness, to shield him from loyalty review pressures outside the Agency. In the summer of 1948 Edward Condon, planning to attend an international conference on weights and measures in Paris, asked Brode to serve as NBS director in his place. Knowing that Condon was then under investigation by the House Un-American Activities Committee, Hillenkoetter first conferred with HUAC chairman J. Parnell Thomas, who insisted that no CIA official could associate with Condon. Hillenkoetter then refused to grant Brode a temporary leave. Brode argued that the order undermined his covert appointment, and Truman officials, alarmed by Hill's 'peculiar behaviour', asked White House officials John Steelman and Clark Clifford to review the matter. But Hillenkoetter's fecklessness nonetheless was the final straw for Brode. By submitting his resignation, Brode became yet another casualty of the postwar loyalty hearings into US scientific community.[19]

ESTABLISHING AN OFFICE OF SCIENTIFIC INTELLIGENCE

In a September 1948 memo to Hillenkoetter, Brode declared that the organizational problems which had stymied him could be overcome only through the 'drastic' step of creating an Office of Scientific Intelligence on a par with the ORE. At first Hillenkoetter took no action. But by late 1948 the problem of scientific intelligence began to receive attention from several national committees. One was the task force on national security organization, chaired by Ferdinand Eberstadt as part of the Hoover Commission investigation of ways to increase efficiency in the executive branch of government. Alarmed by testimony that medical intelligence was virtually non-existent and that information in the atomic energy and other fields was little better, Eberstadt sternly warned that '[f]ailure properly to appraise the extent of scientific developments in enemy countries may have more immediate and catastrophic consequences than failure in any other field of intelligence'.[20] By securing expert testimony from leading American scientists and RDB officials, Eberstadt ensured that his arguments would reach Hillenkoetter and other intelligence officials. Further pressure came from the internally-run Dulles-Jackson-Correa report on the CIA to the National Security Council (the so-called Dulles Report), which reached similar conclusions about the state of scientific intelligence. In response, Hillenkoetter created a distinct Office of Scientific Intelligence (OSI) on 31 December 1948.[21] Rather than being the origin of scientific intelligence within the CIA, as it is sometimes portrayed, the founding of this office was one climax in the postwar struggle to integrate science within the burgeoning intelligence community.

Hillenkoetter's order to establish a distinct OSI within the Intelligence Directorate affirmed the high standing of the RDB within the national military establishment. His order also reflected a greater willingness by military and intelligence officials as well as scientists to experiment with new ways of gathering and coordinating scientific intelligence. The second Truman administration marked a time of increased attention to science as an instrument of foreign policy and military planning. In his second inaugural address in January 1949, Truman announced the so-called Point IV initiative, which called on Americans to make available their experience and technical know-how to the developing nations of the world. Moreover, through the 1950s science and technology continually gained significance as symbols of national and ideological superiority. Though this evolution of scientific achievements into instruments of foreign policy had only limited influence on the OSI by the time the Korean War began (which in turn highlighted deficiencies in scientific intelligence for military offensive and defensive capabilities), the Korean experience spurred the CIA to expand its involvement in science and deepened its relations with the American scientific community.[22]

The task of defining the function and operation of the new OSI fell to Brode's successor, Willard Machle. Almost certainly Machle's selection as director of new OSI was influenced by Eberstadt's criticism that medical intelligence – particularly involving biological weapons and human physiology – remained unavailable to the CIA. An MD by training and formerly a professor of medicine, Machle had become involved in wartime combat studies within the medical branch of the OSRD and had directed the Armored Force Medical Research Laboratory in Kentucky. In 1946 Machle received the Legion of Honor for his physiological research, just three years before he came director of scientific intelligence, masked by blind appointments at the AEC and the Operations Research Office at Johns Hopkins.[23]

Consolidating the collection and evaluation of 'national' scientific intelligence within the CIA, and establishing this as a priority over the more agency-focused goals of service intelligence units, remained a chief aim of OSI leaders. Through the first half of 1949 this goal seemed as elusive to Machle as it had been to Brode.[24] Earth sciences intelligence remained firmly within the province of Naval Intelligence, for instance, and primarily responsive to Navy requirements. This was so even though such information was critical for evaluating developments in undersea warfare and guided missiles, both highly sensitive intelligence areas of significance to the highest levels of national security planning.[25]

It was detection of the first Soviet atomic bomb test in September 1949, an embarrassing 16 months before the earliest date that the CIA had forecast the previous year, that gave Machle his most powerful opening. In a four-page memo on the 'Inability of OSI to Accomplish its Mission', hurriedly composed as Soviet radioactive debris drifted through the stratosphere, Machle insisted that the non-cooperation of military agencies jeopardized the CIA's ability to provide national scientific intelligence on atomic, biological, and chemical weapons, as well as medical intelligence and basic science fields.[26] Aware of continued RDB frustration with the CIA, Hillenkoetter issued an uncharacteristically bold reorganization plan, DCID 3/3, on 28 October. Bucking powerful military interests, Hillenkoetter's order gave the OSI responsibility not only for basic science but for new weapons systems 'up to the initiation of series production' – that is, technological as well as research developments. Supported by Robertson, Berkner, Bush, and other influential advisors, the move placed CIA scientific intelligence on a parallel course with its British counterpart and temporarily energized relations between the OSI and the RDB.[27]

Machle's task was made easier by the cooperation, and at times direct assistance, of leading members of the US scientific community. After 1948, especially after the Communist takeover of Czechoslovakia, the attitudes of many American scientists darkened along with those of other citizens; they grew particularly distressed as Trofim Lysenko's campaign against Soviet geneticists intensified and published attacks on Western scientists as 'learned lackeys of capitalism' increased. By the time the Korean War broke out in 1950, most American scientists regarded the Soviet Union as a credible threat to American national security, and accepted that Communist Party interference was distorting the Soviet scientific community.[28] As a result, in ways and to a degree long concealed from colleagues and poorly documented in traditional archival materials, scientists began to aid CIA officials in collecting, gathering, and interpreting knowledge about foreign scientific advances.

With manpower shortages common in most fields of science, and restrictions against open publication and clandestine service a bar to future professional employment, few US scientists were willing to work for the CIA full-time.[29] Yet it is increasingly clear that many senior academic researchers contributed to the OSI on a part-time basis. Vannevar Bush, for example, joined the so-called 'Princeton Consultants', which met regularly with Allen Dulles; in 1950, James Killian, George Kistiakowsky, and Jerome Wiesner established the 'Boston Scientific Advisory Panel' to help the Agency address the poverty of US intelligence on Soviet weapons development. All were prominent scientists: Kistiakowsky, a Harvard chemist, was a senior veteran of the Manhattan Project, while Killian was the future president of MIT. All three also went on to serve as Presidential science advisors under Eisenhower and Kennedy. In the final analysis, the goals of scientific intelligence were shaped less by bureaucratic leaders like Brode and Machle than by Bush, Kistiakowsky, and other elite members of the US physical sciences and engineering communities.[30]

The willingness of American scientists to see the goals of national security as commensurate with improving the standing of American science encouraged roles for intelligence in manifestly overt scientific activities. For example, scientists (fully cognizant of their potential intelligence value) were instrumental in the establishment within the State Department of scientific attaché positions within embassies considered strategic for weapons or technological development.[31] Likewise Berkner's so-called Science and Foreign Relations report in 1950 to the State Department (which surveyed its responsibilities in the field of science) was closely coordinated with CIA representatives.[32]

Other American scientists willingly served as brokers of information from their professional communities to the CIA. The extent to which US researchers took part in disciplinary surveys or research projects funded by the CIA cannot be accurately estimated, as official secrecy as well as personal and professional discretion have largely kept such cases from view.[33] But the nature of these interactions is suggested by one instance that has come to light. In 1959 Gerard P. Kuiper, a University of Chicago astronomer and director of its affiliated Yerkes-McDonald observatories, agreed to prepare a lengthy review of Soviet work in planetary and stellar astrophysics, under contract to the CIA. The review was largely written by a visiting Yugoslavian astronomer whose year-long research appointment was made possible by these contract funds. Kuiper, a naturalized US citizen whose wartime service during World War II had included assignments with the Radio Research Laboratory and the *Alsos* mission (a civilian-scientific team deployed behind advancing Allied troops to interview scientists about their progress in weapons research), kept the nature of this contract secret from his colleagues. Concern for national security partly explains Kuiper's willingness to aid the CIA. But he also saw the contract providing professional advantages: by surveying the leading frontiers of Soviet astronomy, Kuiper hoped to improve the competitive edge of his institution and his own research.[34]

Despite inroads of this sort, OSI leaders continued to find it difficult to meet the demand of clients such as the RDB for scientific intelligence. One problem was the State Department's haphazard and ultimately limited use of its science attachés, which always had been intended, in part, to provide a back channel for the collection of sensitive intelligence. Few if any scientific attachés were explicitly instructed about specific collection needs, allowing them to define themselves as ambassadors of American science, a role they clearly preferred.[35] Moreover, career State Department officers, whose training and background shared few common intersections with scientists, often regarded the efforts of scientists to maintain international contacts as synonymous with communist sympathies. Between 1952 and 1957 the number of science attachés fell from 12 to zero (the program was later revived in 1958). Yet it seems unlikely that science attachés could have been expected to fulfil intelligence-gathering roles even with greater State Department backing: French communist intellectuals, including the nuclear physicist Frédéric Joliot-Curie, blasted the attaché program as 'l'activité d'espionage', and West German scientists pointedly ignored Bonn's science attachés until they demonstrated their disinterestedness in sensitive topics. Inadvertent publication of a classified recommendation to shift the backstopping of science attachés directly to the CIA in 1955 prejudiced the situation still further.[36]

A second problem lay in the difficulty that scientific experts, no less than their colleagues in other fields, faced in attempting to decipher the health and vitality of Soviet science. Detailed studies from outside consultants were hardly infallible: Kuiper's first OSI report in 1959 criticized Lunik III's historic images of the lunar farside as possible fakes, a view Kuiper revised the following year after a long private meeting with a chief Lunik project scientist.[37] Although interviews with US scientists returning from the Soviet Union were used to augment these reports (particularly as Soviet participation in international scientific unions ballooned after Stalin's death in 1953), the difficulties of collecting appropriately detailed technical information from such subjects remained formidable.[38]

A final problem for OSI leaders through the early 1950s were their always difficult relations with other chief source of scientific intelligence, the military intelligence agencies. Despite high-level prodding from the first Hoover Commission and the Dulles Survey, Navy and Air Force intelligence services were reluctant to assign additional officers to scientific matters, and even more reluctant to pass on hard-won findings to the CIA.[39] By 1952, leaders of these services, never reconciled to the OSI's heightened authority in scientific and technical assessment following the 1949 Soviet atomic bomb detection, successfully pressured Hillenkoetter's successor General Walter Bedell Smith to restrict OSI analysts to basic science alone. The shift was illuminating, for Smith clearly appreciated scientific intelligence more than his predecessor. H. Marshall Chadwell, a chemist and expert in combat medicine who replaced Machle as head of OSI after Machle had a falling-out over the problem of intelligence access, found this a demoralizing but temporary setback: the line between applied and basic research proved impossible to define, and by the mid-1950s OSI analysts were again involved in weapon studies.[40] A more troubling consequence of OSI's turf battles were continued difficulties in recruiting full-time analysts. As late as 1955 OSI employed just over 200 analysts, a modest number to survey such disparate fields as mathematics, biology and medicine, physics and geophysics, mechanics, thermodynamics, mathematics, and astronomy, as well as foreign scientific institutions and manpower trends.[41]

These limitations were evident in the first reports that OSI analysts struggled to produce. In 1976 the Church Committee probe found that early CIA intelligence estimates were chock with information from 'all manner of subjects' from politics to science – but by 'attempting to do everything, [they] contribut[ed] almost nothing'. Certain early OSI findings seemed irrelevant to the particular needs of policy-makers as well. One late 1949 OSI study offered to President Truman and the National Security Council reported that the number of published abstracts in Soviet chemistry had plummeted below 50 per cent of their 1941 level, indicating the extent of new research now considered classified and linked to weapons development. Quantitative indices of Soviet science were carefully refined by OSI analysts through the 1950s. But this report fell short of predicting the *type* or significance of novel chemical weapons that NSC and RDB staffs needed to plan appropriate responses.[42]

Too much can be made of criticisms of this kind, for several scientific intelligence findings were applicable to specific foreign policy issues. A particular case involved Sweden. In June 1948, Secretary of State George C. Marshall protested to Truman that Sweden's neutrality policy aided the Soviet Union and urged swift adoption of the proposed NATO treaty to tip the Scandinavian system towards the West. The following year OSI analysts produced 'An Estimate of Swedish Capabilities in Science'. This 64-page single-spaced report provided a detailed evaluation of Swedish scientists, universities, research institutions, and technological programs, including highly classified wind tunnel and pulsejet engine research. It tersely concluded that '[t]he USSR would gain distinct, but relatively small, advantage from the point of view of science by overrunning Sweden at the present time'. Following the guidelines for covert action authorized by NSC 10/2 in 1948, OSI analysts also recommended denying certain Swedish scientists and research facilities in case of Soviet invasion. This was precisely the kind of policy paper that the NSC had sought to address Scandinavian neutrality, although its failure to appear in time to join related reports undercut its value.[43]

OSI intelligence estimates gradually established the office within the CIA.[44] But, compared with the Agency's geographic, economic, and political directorates, the mandate and authority of scientific intelligence remained ill-defined and vulnerable. Turf battles with military intelligence (and the creation of the NSA in 1952, with its distinct advisory panels competing for scientific leaders like Robertson) worked against the OSI. Yet continued demand for physical, biological and medical intelligence, and increased recognition by the Eisenhower administration of the prestige value of science in foreign policy towards Latin America, Africa, and India (illustrated by the Atoms for Peace program and more dramatically by the space race), simultaneously placed counter-pressures on the CIA that encouraged catholicism in scientific collection and analysis.[45]

COVERT SCIENCE: CIA MEDICAL RESEARCH

A central task of the OSI during the 1950s remained analysis of scientific intelligence to assist in preparing national intelligence estimates. But CIA officials also sought to justify covert research programs in strategic fields. Given the enormous national infrastructure for nuclear weapons research, intelligence analysts promoted in-house research in other fields, particularly biological toxins and medicine.[46]

In the late 1940s a leading concern for American scientists and military planners remained potential enemy advances in biological, chemical, and radiological warfare (BW, CW, RW). Biochemical weapons were clearly overshadowed by atomic bombs as doomsday weapons during the early Cold War, but absence of international treaties regulating their use – and the modest size of the installations required for their manufacture – made this field a high priority for scientific intelligence. OSI officials were well aware of Japan's use of biological weapons against China during World War II and substantial advances in biochemical weapons research in other belligerent nations, particularly through captured German and Japanese records. A series of reports by former War Research Service director George Merck and other leading specialists suggested a US edge. But they nevertheless underscored that the East-West balance of power could be threatened if the Soviet Union achieved major advances in biochemical weapons (BW), or successfully smuggled BW, CW, or RW agents into the US. The key desiderata was 'much wider information, particularly of an intelligence nature'.[47] Yet, as a frustrated Ferdinand Eberstadt reported to the Hoover Commission in 1948, medical intelligence reaching the CIA was virtually non-existent.[48]

The lack of medical intelligence especially worried leaders of the CIA's clandestine services, who feared foreign advances in mind-controlling techniques of biochemical origin. The widely publicized confessions of Hungary's Cardinal Mindszenty in February 1949 convinced Western observers that mind-altering chemicals had been used to force Mindszenty's testimony, a suspicion bolstered Western impressions of early Cold War trials orchestrated by Joseph Stalin in the Soviet Union.[49] Medical specialists and defectors privately fueled fears of Soviet advances in brainwashing techniques. At a Washington cocktail party, Chadwell was lectured by a medical colleague for paying insufficient attention to 'special interrogations'. Allen Dulles similarly recorded stories from refugees about forced interrogations behind the Iron Curtain.[50]

Analysts worried about two distinct but related matters: the need to extract critical information quickly from captured Soviet agents in the event of hostile acts involving biological or chemical weapons, and ways to better equip US personnel against successful truth-serum or mind-altering agents developed by Soviet researchers. By the late 1940s CIA officials became especially concerned that a combination of hypnosis and drugs could induce unwitting individuals to follow another's will. Anxieties about a hostile government creating a programmed assassination – popularized in the 1959 novel by Richard Condon, *The Manchurian Candidate* – escalated during the Korean War after captured US soldiers publicly 'confessed' to employing biochemical weapons.[51]

CIA scientific analysts, led by Chadwell, responded in two ways. One was to fight for increased domination over the production and dissemination of medical intelligence. Through the first half of 1949, Brode and Machle had no more success in coordinating intelligence in medicine than in other fields of science; despite the recommendations of seven separate committees, the matter had remained unresolved.[52] The broad reorganization of scientific intelligence following the first Soviet atomic bomb enabled Chadwell to consolidate the production of medical intelligence at the CIA. The OSI used its expanded analytical capabilities to identify new medical threats, warning for instance in February 1950 that the Soviets would soon gain the ability to conduct radiological warfare.[53]

The second response – eventually with broad ramifications for the CIA and the biomedical research community – was to set up covert research programs in medical pharmacology, with the goal of influencing and controlling human behavior through psychoactive drugs and other chemical, biological, and psychological means. In April 1950 Hillenkoetter approved a covert plan initially proposed by the CIA's Office of Security, codenamed 'Bluebird', to employ scientific methods and knowledge 'to alter the attitudes, thought processes, and behavior patterns of agent personnel'.[54] Later rechristened 'Artichoke', this program came under the direction of the OSI. A distinct but related project, christened 'MKULTRA', began in 1953 after the CIA's operations branch and its Office of Special Operations (in charge of spying) were merged. MKULTRA was designed to study the use of biological and chemical materials in mind-control, compile information on naturally occurring poisons throughout the world, and carry out covert experiments with LSD and related substances on hundreds of subjects. It is now clear that experiments were carried out on cognizant as well as unwitting subjects, at times with fatal consequences. In at least one case a career army scientist employed in biochemical warfare research, Frank Olson, committed suicide soon after LSD was placed in his drink by CIA colleagues involved with MKULTRA.[55]

That experiments were carried out on humans within five years of the end of World War II, and the Nuremberg trials which had revealed the horrors of Nazi medical experimentation in the concentration camps, demands explanation.[56] Several factors joined to aid CIA efforts to establish an autonomous program in medical research. Deepening Cold War tensions, the detonation of the first Soviet atomic bomb, the outbreak of the Korean War, nuclear testing at the newly authorized Nevada Test Site, and persistent reports from East bloc defectors all made worries about radiological and biochemical warfare seem more credible. But developments within the US national security system were equally significant. The adoption of NSC 68 and 10/2 defined the Soviet Union as an ideological foe bent on world domination and authorized covert activities, while the ascension of Machle and Chadwell as leaders of OSI guaranteed that medical intelligence would become a high Agency priority. Medical curiosity, coupled with the absence of peer review within the CIA's highly secretive OSO, also encouraged researchers to violate contemporary ethical standards. That ethical boundaries had been breached was clearly recognized by the CIA's inspector general in 1957, who labeled Olson's death a result of 'unethical and illicit activities'. This highly embarrassing episode joined covert political assassinations as particularly damaging revelations of the Church Committee hearings on CIA activities in 1975.[57]

It is important to note that biomedical experimentation of this kind, while concentrated at dedicated army facilities like Fort Detrick (which worked closely with the CIA in studying biochemical agents and delivery systems), was not confined to military research installations. Rather, it was diffused within the US scientific community. As with most areas of CIA scientific operations, relatively little is known about extramural Agency support for research in this field. But CIA funds clearly encouraged related studies at American universities and inspired independent scholars to address Agency needs. One example which has come to light involved Georgetown University, the nation's oldest Jesuit university. In 1955 the CIA secretly helped fund a $3 million extension to its hospital complex to make possible MKULTRA Subproject #35, whose goal was 'highly sensitive' research involving biological, chemical, and radiological warfare. A cooperative hospital staff researcher was the Agency's sole point of contact, leaving Georgetown officials in the dark about CIA involvement in the hospital expansion. When Dulles blanched at the price-tag for this effort (which ultimately reached $600 million), Technical Services Staff researchers rushed to its defense, illuminating the value that scientific intelligence agents placed on university-based programs. Their Georgetown 'cutout' would provide cover for three CIA researchers, enhance their scientific status, produce volunteers for medical experiments, and enable Agency personnel to recruit new scientists and contacts.[58] While Subproject #35 was unusually costly, the Georgetown operation appears to resemble covert medical research programs funded at other American universities, including Columbia, the University of Illinois Medical School, and the University of Oklahoma.[59]

CONCLUSION

The successful mobilization of scientific resources during World War II made science a potent national security issue in the Cold War. The advent of the atomic bomb and nuclear diplomacy thrust science into all subsequent deliberations about foreign policy and foreign intelligence. But the most significant contribution of science in World War II was to demonstrate the potential significance of all fields of science – from biomedicine to meteorology – to national defense. 'In the field of science,' as Wallace Brode observed in 1948, 'it is difficult to define that scientific intelligence which may become vital as an economic, social or military factor in the national security and hence it is necessary to maintain broad coverage of scientific advancement and relative status of other countries.'[60] By the end of Hillenkoetter's term as DCI, CIA leaders believed that a sustained flow of information about foreign science was necessary to ensure eternal vigilance for national security.

As the Cold War deepened, US scientists concerned with Soviet advances in atomic and biochemical weapons systems sought to supply government officials with information to strengthen the national defense.

Scientists recognized that questions in these fields could not be addressed by individuals without substantial training in science. But the relationship between scientists and intelligence needs introduced fundamental and largely unresolved tensions. Professional strictures against employing scientific research solely to aid nationalistic aims kept most scientists from participating in intelligence activities on more than an occasional or part-time basis.

In retrospect, the establishment of scientific intelligence within the CIA in the immediate postwar period was at best a mixed success. Early efforts to secure medical intelligence failed, the science attaché system withered, and military intelligence agencies resisted, often successfully, the intrusions of civilian intelligence analysts. The need to install leaders of scientific intelligence in blind official positions led to increased cynicism and distrust within the scientific community, and the ethical lapses of CIA medical specialists in 'Artichoke' and 'MKULTRA' mind-control experiments ranked among the Agency's most troubling violations of national trust. When Brode recommended advising Vice President Richard Nixon in 1959 that 'the majority of all our basic science programs are supported by military agencies as an altruistic gesture but with hidden motives', he unwittingly revealed a fundamental cynicism about the structure of Cold War scientific institutions that the CIA, at least in part, had helped to inspire.[61]

Yet it would be unfair to paint the products of scientific intelligence in a wholly negative light. Western scientists recognized the importance of understanding Soviet achievements as the Cold War deepened, and perceived a Soviet scientific community increasingly oppressed by Communist ideology and statist power. In the early and mid-1950s OSI science analysts produced substantial reports on Soviet scientific capacity and its contributions to economic development, increasing the value of the CIA's National Intelligence Estimates series.[62] Moreover, US scientists found the CIA an ally in their efforts to maintain international contacts in science during the 1950s in the face of State Department hostility to East-West communications from the standpoint of foreign policy. CIA scientific analysts joined civilian counterparts in the mid- and late-1950s in perceiving the prestige value of science for Third World nations. Their reports indirectly helped stimulate scientific and technological assistance programs in Latin America and Sub-Saharan Africa.[63] Finally, the success of CIA science specialists in developing greatly improved remote monitoring means by the late 1950s (including aerial and satellite reconnaissance and electronic eavesdropping) reduced their reliance on military intelligence agencies and helped bring about a further consolidation of scientific resources in the Agency's new Directorate of Science and Technology (created in 1963).[64] While analyses of these developments must await further declassifications, they illuminate the intimate relation between scientific intelligence and the motivations of scientists and the American state in the years following World War II.

NOTES

Both authors acknowledge support from the Smithsonian Institution (Doel for a postdoctoral fellowship in 1994-95), and a grant-in-aid from the Friends of the Center for History of Physics of the American Institute of Physics. In addition, Doel is grateful for travel funds from the National Endowment for the Humanities as well as the Truman and Eisenhower presidential libraries; he especially acknowledges research support from the Pollack Award of the Dudley Observatory and the National Science Foundation (award NSF SBR-9511867). We also thank Rhodri Jeffreys-Jones, Dennis Bilger, and Dwight Strandberg for advice and assistance.

1. On the normative structure and practice of science, see Lorraine Daston, 'The Moral Economy of Science', *Osiris* [2nd ed.] 10 (1995) pp.3–24. Relations between scientists and their patrons are illuminated in Charles Coulston Gillispie, 'Science and Secret Weapons Development in Revolutionary France, 1792-1804: A Documentary History', *Historical Studies in the Physical and Biological Sciences* 23/1 (1992) pp.35-152; for the relationship between scientists and the state in the twentieth century, see for example Monika Renneberg and Mark Walker (eds.) *Science, Technology, and National Socialism* (Cambridge, England: CUP 1994), Loren R. Graham, *Science in Russia and the Soviet Union: A Short History* (NY: Cambridge UP, 1993) and Elisabeth Crawford, Terry Shinn, and Sverker Sörlin (eds.) *Denationalizing Science: The Contexts of International Scientific Practice* (Dordrecht: Kluwer 1992). A helpful overview of recent scholarship is Aaron L. Friedberg, 'Science, the Cold War, and the State [Review Essay]', *Diplomatic History* 20/1 (Winter 1996) pp.107–18.

2. Commission on the Organization of the Executive Branch of the Government (the Hoover Commission), *Task Force Report on National Security Organization* (Washington DC: 13 Jan. 1949), and George S. Jackson and Martin P. Claussen, *Organizational History of the Central Intelligence Agency* [Ch.VI: Problems of Scientific and Technical Intelligence], May 1957, declassified draft in DCI Historical Series, Record Group [hereafter RG] 263, National Archives and Records Administration [hereafter NARA], Washington DC.

3. The intention was, through overt and covert means, effectively to control the world's supply of that essential mineral; see Jonathan E. Helmreich, *Gathering Rare Ores: The Diplomacy of Uranium Acquisition, 1943-1954* (Princeton UP 1985) and Richard Rhodes, *Dark Sun: The Making of the Hydrogen Bomb* (NY: Simon & Schuster 1995) p.109.

4. No single source comprehensively discusses scientific intelligence during World War II; for an introduction see Mark Walker, *German National Socialism and the Quest for Nuclear Power, 1939-1949* (NY: Cambridge UP 1989) pp.153–60 and John Gimbel, *Science, Technology and Reparations: Exploitation and Plunder in Postwar Germany* (Stanford UP 1990).

5. Also included on the Policy Council were the Army and Navy appointees to the JRDB Secretariat, two members appointed by each of the Dept. Secretaries, and the Administrative Secretary of the JRDB. On the establishment of the JRDB and the role of its Policy Council, see Allan A. Needell, 'Rabi Berkner, and the Rehabilitation of Science in Europe: The Cold War Context of American Support for International Science, 1945-1954', in Francis H. Heller and John Gillingham (eds.) *The United States and the Integration of Europe: Legacies of the Post War Era* (NY: St Martin's Press 1994) pp.289–305; and Joint Research and Development Board [hereafter JRDB] 23/1, 30 Sept. 1946, revised 4 Oct. 1946, Research and Development Board [hereafter RDB] records, Box 18, RG 330, NARA.

6. Lloyd V. Berkner to Walker Dyke, 31 Oct. 1946, Folder 'Personal L.V.B. 1946-47', Box 3,

Lloyd V. Berkner [hereafter LVB] Papers, MS Div., Library of Congress [hereafter LC], Washington DC.

7. Biographical information on Doriot is from an obituary published in the *Harvard Business School Bulletin*, Oct. 1987, pp.12–13' and on Haskins from an attachment to a letter from A. N. Richards [President of the National Academy of Sciences] to James E. Webb [Acting Secretary of State] 16 May 1950, Folder NAS/NRC Central File: Int. Relations: Int. Science Policy Study of State Dept.; NRC portion: General, National Academy of Sciences/National Research Council [hereafter NAS/NRC] records, Washington DC.

8. JRDB 57/1 and related documentation in the Folder 'Scientific Advisors to the Policy Council', RDB Subject/Numeric Series, Box 1, Entry 341, RG 330, NARA.

9. J. H. Thach Jr [Navy Secretary, JRDB] to the Navy members of the Board, 'Consultants to the Policy Council, JRDB', 16 Dec. 1946; and agenda for the meeting scheduled on 17, 18, 19 Jan. 1947, both RDB ibid.

10. For Bush's views on scientific intelligence, see Wallace Brode, 'The Responsibilities of the Scientific Branch within the C.I.A.', 4th draft, n.d. [c. Oct. 1948] Box 84 [Box 4 of 11] Wallace R. Brode papers [hereafter WRB] LC; see also untitled notes on possible RDB successors, no date [1948], Box 1651, Official Files series [hereafter OF] Harry S. Truman Presidential Library, Independence, MO [hereafter HST].

11. No comprehensive biography of Brode exists; see 'Personnel actions, WRB' file, undated [1958] and 'Personalities in Your Government', WLW radio program, 9 Feb. 1958, both Box 6 off 11, WRB. Brode's relationship with Bush can be inferred from Wallace S. Brode, '[untitled report on scientific manpower problem]', 18 Nov. 1946 and his cover letter to Bush on this date, both Box 15, Vannevar Bush papers [hereafter VB], LC; see also Steven L. Rearden, *History of the Office of the Secretary of Defense, Volume 1. The Formative Years: 1947-50* (Washington DC: Historical Office, Office of the Sec. of Defense 1984) p.101.

12. Quoted in Brode, 'Responsibilities of the Scientific Branch'; see also cross reference sheet [I.N.P. Stokes], 31 Aug. 1948, Box 61, Confidential File series, HST.

13. National Security Council Intelligence Directive [hereafter NSC ID] 8, 'Biographical Data on Foreign Scientific and Technological Personalities', 25 May 1948 [classified secret], Box 4, RG 263, NARA, as well as Brode to Hillenkoetter, 12 Nov. 1947 and Brode, '[untitled note on CIA scientific intelligence units]' Dec. 1947, both Box 4 of 11, WRB.

14. The 'Joint' designation was dropped following passage of the National Security Act in 1947; see Rearden, *Formative Years* (note 11) pp.23–6, 97–8.

15. V . Bush to Sec. of Defense James V. Forrestal, 13 Oct. 1948, Box 77, John N. Ohly papers [hereafter JNO], HST, R. Clark to Ferdinand Eberstadt, noted in collected abstracts for [Sec. of Defense Robert P.] Paterson, undated [1949], Ferdinand Eberstadt papers [hereafter FE], Seeley G. Mudd MS Library, Princeton U.

16. Rhodri Jeffreys-Jones, *The CIA and American Democracy* (New Haven, CT: Yale UP 1989) p.57. On the founding of British scientific intelligence see Reginald V. Jones, *The Wizard War: British Scientific Intelligence 1939-1945* (NY: Coward, McCann and Geoghegan 1978) and Jones, *Reflections on Intelligence* (London: Heinemann 1989); see also Jackson and Claussen, *Organizational History* (note 2) p.VI-17.

17. Ludwell Lee Montague, *General Walter Bedell Smith as Director of Central Intelligence, October 1950-February 1953* (University Park: Pennsylvania State UP 1992) p.174, and Willard Machle to Prescott Childs, 31 March 1949, File CIA-Miscellaneous, compiled by the Advisory Committee on Human Radiation Experiments, Washington DC 1995 [hereafter ACHRE].

18. Arthur B. Darling, *The Central Intelligence Agency: An Instrument of Government, to 1950* (University Park: Pennsylvania State UP 1990) pp.161–5; Stephen Penrose memo, 'Report on CIA', 2 Jan. 1948, in *Foreign Relations of United States* [hereafter FRUS]: *The Emergence of the Intelligence Establishment, 1945-1950* (Washington DC: US Dept. of State 1996) pp.831–3, Brode to DCI [Hillenkoetter] 11 March 1948, RG CIA-0314495-A, ACHRE; see also Hillenkoetter memo to Bush and Bush memo to Hillenkoetter [quoted], both 24 March 1948, File CIA-Miscellaneous, ACHRE.

19. See Brode memo to files, 20 Sept. 1948, Box 84, 4 of 11, Brode, and cross reference sheet [I.N.P. Stokes], 31 Aug. 1948, Box 61, CF, HST. The Condon loyalty hearings (particularly

ironic in light of his willing, covert accommodation to the CIA) are explored in Jessica Wang, 'Science, Security, and the Cold War: The Case of E. U. Condon', *Isis* 83/2 (1992) pp.238–69. While John Prados [*Presidents' Secret Wars: CIA and Pentagon Covert Operations from World War II through Iranscam* (NY: Morrow 1988) pp.80–1] notes that Hillenkoetter, laboring with a limited network of contacts, has received undue criticism, his indecision towards scientific intelligence better supports Christopher Andrew's assessment that Hillenkoetter was 'probably the weakest' Director of Central Intelligence; see *For the President's Eyes Only: Secret Intelligence and the American Presidency from Washington to Bush* (NY: HarperCollins 1995) p.170.

20. Quoted in Jackson and Claussen, *Organizational History* (note 2) p.VI, 1, and F. Eberstadt to V. Bush, 12 Aug. 1948, Box 28, FE.

21. Jackson and Claussen, *Organizational History* (note 2) pp.VI, pp.1–4.

22. Needell, 'Rabi Berkner' (note 5) pp.289–93; on the evolving relationship between scientists and the state in the early Cold War, see especially Stuart W. Leslie, *The Cold War and American Science: The Military-Industrial-Academic Complex at MIT and Stanford* (NY: Columbia UP 1993) pp.1–13 and Allan A. Needell, 'From Military Research to Big Science: Lloyd Berkner and Science-Statesmanship in the Postwar Era', in Peter Galison and Bruce Hevly (eds.) *Big Science: The Growth of Large-Scale Research* (Stanford UP 1992) pp.290–311.

23. Montague, *Smith* (note 17) pp.174–5; Howard A. Rusk and Richard L. Meiling, MDs, to F. Eberstadt 28 Sept. 1948, Box 73, FE; and 'Machle Receives Legion of Merit', *New York Times*, 22 Feb. 1946, p.16, col.7.

24. Even in the field of medical intelligence, arguments voiced in favor of retaining intelligence functions within service agencies dominated intelligence circles through early 1949; see [name deleted] to Machle, 18 Feb. 1949, File CIA-030695-A, ACHRE.

25. Beno Gutenberg to E. C. Watson, 29 Sept. 1946, Box 18.3, Beno Gutenberg papers [hereafter BG], California Inst. of Technology archives, Pasadena, California [hereafter CIT], 'Organization and Direction of Committee on Geophysical Sciences', 27 May 1947, Box 227, RG 330, NARA, and 'Scientific Intelligence: excerpts from file tabbed Progress Reports', 11 July 1952, Box 2, RG 263, NARA. Popular accounts occasionally blame Vannevar Bush for failing to recognize the strategic value of guided missiles, enabling the Soviet Union to beat Americans in launching the first artificial satellite (see e.g. William B. Breuer, *Race to the Moon: America's Duel with the Soviets* [Westport, CT/London: Praeger 1993] pp.100, 116–17. Yet recently declassified records (for instance, Bush to James Forrestal, 13 Oct. 1948, Box 77, JHO-HST) reveal that Bush stressed the importance of these weapons to military and intelligence officials; for historical discussions of guided missile policy in the early Cold War, see Michael A. Dennis, 'Our First Line of Defense: Two University Laboratories in the Postwar American State', *Isis* 85/3 (1994) pp.427–55 and David H. DeVorkin, *Science with a Vengeance: How the Military Created the U.S. Space Sciences after World War II* (NY: Springer-Verlag 1992).

26. Machle to Prescott Childs, 31 March 1949, CIA-miscellaneous file, ACHRE, and Machle to Hillenkoetter, 29 Sept. 1949, Box 4, Entry HRP 82-2 00286, RG 263, NARA; see also Rhodes, *Dark Sun* (note 3) p.363.

27. Montague, *Smith* (note 17) p.174, Jackson and Claussen, *Organizational History* (note 2) p.VI-47-9, and memo for SIC working committees, 13 Oct. 1950, Box 2, RG 263, NARA. This order, known as DCID 3/3, also established a new Science Advisory Committee, composed of OSI representatives as well as representatives from service intelligence agencies, a move that consolidated OSI leadership in providing scientific intelligence for the RDB.

28. See Daniel J. Kevles, 'K1S2: Korea, Science, and the State', in Peter Galison and Bruce Hevly (eds.) *Big Science: The Growth of Large-Scale Research* (Stanford UP 1992) pp.312–33 and Ronald E. Doel and Robert A. McCutcheon, 'Introduction [to Astronomy under the Soviets]', *Jnl for the History of Astronomy* 26/3 (1995) pp.279–96, esp. pp.285–6.

29. 'Tenth Meeting of the Committee on Geophysical Sciences', RDB, Box 226, RG 330, NARA. Hillenkoetter himself testified before Eberstadt's Task Force that money was not a problem in recruiting scientists, but rather the inability to publish; see testimony recorded by

Ferdinand Eberstadt for the Hoover Commission task force, compiled for [Sec. of Defense Robert] Patterson, n.d. [1949], Box 73, FE.

30. Montague, *Smith* (note 17) pp.175–6 and Jeffreys-Jones, *CIA* (note 16) pp.79, 108.

31. 'Verbatim Minutes of a Meeting of the Intelligence Advisory Committee', 3 Dec. and 17 Dec. 1948, in FRUS, *Emergence* (note 18) pp.881–95.

32. Needell, 'Rabi, Berkner' (note 5) pp.297–8; see also Allan A. Needell, 'Truth is our Weapon': Project TROY, Political Warfare, and Government-Academic Relationships in the National Security State', *Diplomatic History* 17/3 (Summer 1993) pp.399–420.

33. On this issue see particularly Ronald E. Doel, 'Scientists as Policymakers, Advisors, and Intelligence Agents: Linking Contemporary Diplomatic History with the History of Contemporary Science', in Thomas Soderqvist (ed.) *The Historiography of Contemporary Science and Technology* (London: Harwood Academic Publishers, forthcoming 1997) pp.33–62 and 'ACHRE Information Collections', *ACHRE Final Report*, Supplemental Volume 2: Sources and Documentation (Washington DC: US Government Printing Office 1995) pp.91–113.

34. Ronald E. Doel, 'Evaluating Soviet Lunar Science in Cold War America', *Osiris* [second series] 7 (1992) pp.238-64. Answering a list of questions supplied by his CIA handlers [which has not survived], Kuiper made clear that he would not deliberately deceive his Soviet colleague, as he was apparently asked to do (see p.257). Professional allegiances allowed scientists to contribute to national defense needs but not at the cost of compromising personal relations with foreign colleagues or their research communities.

35. Joseph Koepfli Oral History Interview [hereafter OHI] (Ronald E. Doel, interviewer, 3 Aug. 1995, transcript at Niels Bohr Library of the American Institute of Physics [hereafter AIP], and Richard T. Arnold OHI (Doel, 10 Aug. 1994, AIP).

36. Frances G. Knight to Scott McLeod, 6 April 1953, Box 2.4, Joseph B. Koepfli papers [hereafter JBK], CIT; Arnold OHI, AIP; and 'What's Happened to Science in State?' *Chemical & Engineering News* 34/2 (9 Jan. 1956) pp.112–15. For foreign reactions, see *Un Plan U.S.A. de Mainmise sur la Science* (Paris: La Nouvelle Critique 1953) quoted on p.71 and J.B. Koepfli, 'Summary of Translation of Brochure, A U.S. Plan for Dominating Science', Box 2.3, JBK. On the Hoover Commission's admission of the CIA backstopping plan, see Koepfli to Earl A. Evans Jr, 9 Feb. 1956, Box 1.3, JBK.

37. Doel, 'Soviet Lunar Astronomy', pp.257–8.

38. See particularly Robert G. Leonard, 'Communication to the Editors [re. 'Covert Scientific Collection'], *Studies in Intelligence* 3 (1959) pp.129–32, Box 12, RG 263, NARA. That no criticism of the practice appeared in the flagship journal *Science* before 1962 suggests that the community of American scientists accepted the practice as legitimately helpful to US national security; this first instance was Patrick D. Wall, 'Scientists and the CIA', *Science* 136 (13 April 1962) p.173.

39. Only in atomic energy, handled by the Joint Atomic Energy Intelligence Committee, was there a satisfactory resolution of these tensions; see Montague, *Smith* (note 17) pp.175–7.

40. Final Report of the Select Committee to Study Governmental Operations with Respect to Intelligence Activities (Church Report), *Senate Report*, 94 Cong., 2 sess., no.94-755 (1976) [hereafter Church Committee]: Book 4: Supplementary Detailed Staff Reports on Foreign and Military Intelligence, p.60 and Ray S. Cline, *Secrets, Spies and Scholars: Blueprint of the Essential CIA* (Washington DC: Acropolis Books 1976) p.147.

41. This figure is noted in Annex B to DCI Directive 3/4, Box 2, RG 263, NARA, although the total number of support personnel in this office was much higher; see Church Committee, Book IV: Supplementary Detailed Staff Reports on Foreign and Military Intelligence, p.57. By the mid-1960s, as scientific intelligence functions expanded to include spy satellites and related fields, the number of core employees swelled to 1,300; see Church Committee, Book VI: Supplementary Reports on Intelligence Activities, pp.262–3.

42. Church Committee, Book 1: Foreign and Military Intelligence, p.20, and 'Abstracting Services as an Intelligence Tool for Assessing Soviet Chemical Research', CIA/OSI report 4/49, 19 Dec. 1949, Box 257, Psychological Strategy Board files [hereafter PSB], HST. This technique is discussed in J.J. Bagnall, 'The Exploitation of Russian Scientific Literature for Intelligence Purposes', *Studies in Intelligence* 2 (1958) pp.45–9, Box 12, RG 263, NARA.

43. 'An Estimate of Swedish Capabilities in Science', CIA/OSI report 1/49, 9 Aug. 1949, Marshall to Truman, 3 June 1948, Box 257, PSB, and 'Report of NSC on Position of US with Respect to Scandinavia', 16 Dec. 1948, NSC record series, both HST. US diplomatic reactions to Sweden's neutrality policy are discussed in Melvyn P. Leffler, *A Preponderance of Power: National Security, The Truman Administration, and the Cold War* (Stanford UP 1992) pp.217-18 and Rearden, *Formative Years* (note 11) pp.470-3. OSI conclusions about the state and direction of Swedish science are generally in accord with those of recent histories of Swedish science; see Doel, 'Scientists as Policymakers' (note 33) p.39.

44. One such example is 'Soviet Scientific and Technical Manpower', June 1953, Box 3, White House NSC Staff, NSC Registry Series, Dwight D. Eisenhower Presidential Library, Abilene, Kansas [hereafter DDE], originally classified secret.

45. See Memo to Special Staff, NSC, 5 June 1953, Series White House-NSC Registry, Box 3, DDE. On the role of the NSA, see Jeffreys-Jones, *CIA* p.68 and Rear Adm. J.N. Wenger to H.P. Robertson, 14 Jan. 1953, Box 12.11, Howard Percy Robertson papers [hereafter HPR], CIT.

46. Jackson and Claussen, *Organizational History* (note 2) pp.VI-11-34; Montague, *Smith* (note 17) pp.177-8.

47. Quoted from the Ad Hoc Committee on Biological Warfare [Caryl P. Haskins, chair, 1949] in Susan Wright, 'Evolution of Biological Warfare Policy: 1945-1990', in Wright (ed.), *Preventing a Biological Arms Race* (Cambridge, MA: MIT Press 1990) pp.26–68, on p.30. By 1946 this issue also was a growing concern for chemist and Harvard president James B. Conant; see Conant to Roger Adams, 9 Sept. 1946, Roger Adams papers [hereafter RA], University of Illinois archives. US efforts to assess foreign scientific advances immediately after World War II are noted in David Cassidy, 'Controlling German Science, I: U.S. and Allied Forces in Germany, 1945-1947', *Historical Studies in the Physical and Biological Sciences* 24/2 (1994) pp.198–235 and R.W. Home and Morris F. Low, 'Postwar Scientific Intelligence Missions to Japan', *Isis*, 84/3 (1993) pp.527–37.

48. Eberstadt to Bush, Box 28, FE, and Machle to Hillenkoetter, 29 Sept. 1949, Box 4, Entry HRP 82-2 00286, RG 263, NARA.

49. The most comprehensive discussion of this issue is John Marks, *The Search for the "Manchurian Candidate"* (NY: Norton 1991); see also Church Committee, Book II: 'Intelligence Activities and the Rights of Americans' [hereafter Book 2], pp.57-9. On the larger issue of US perceptions of Soviet research, see Susan Gross Solomon, 'Reflections on Western Studies of Soviet Science', in Linda Lubrano and idem (eds.) *The Social Context of Soviet Science* (Boulder, CO: Westview Press 1980) pp.1-30.

50. Chadwell to Deputy Director, Administration, 25 April 1951, and memo on ARTICHOKE conference, 4 Dec. 1952, File CIA-0314495-A, ACHRE.

51. Marks, *Search* (note 49) p.9, and Church Committee, Book 2, pp.57-8.

52. Prescott Childs to DCI [Hillenkoeter], 20 May 1949, Box 2, RG 263, NARA.

53. CIA/OSI, 'Soviet Potentialities to Conduct Radiological Warfare' [WP-40-50, classified top secret], 23 Feb. 1950, CIA-miscellaneous file, ACHRE.

54. John Ranelagh, *The Agency: The Rise and Decline of the CIA: From Wild Bill Donovan to William Casey* (NY: Simon & Schuster 1986) p.204.

55. Marks, *Search* (note 49) pp.73–86, Church Committee, Book 2, p.58, and *ACHRE Final Report* (Washington DC: US GPO 1995) pp.184–7. The merger of the Office of Policy Coordination and the Office of Special Operations is examined in Jeffreys-Jones, *CIA* (note 16) p.70.

56. For an introduction to relevant literature, see Alan Beyerchen, 'What We Now Know about Nazism and Science', in Margaret C. Jacob (ed.) *The Politics of Western Science, 1640-1990* (Atlantic Highlands, NJ: Humanities Press 1994) pp.129–56.

57. Quoted in Church Committee, Book 2, pp.57–8; on the Church Committee, see Andrew, *President's Eyes* (note 19) pp.414–22.

58. Deputy Director (Plans) to DCI re MKULTRA, Subproject 35, 15 Nov. 1954; Memorandum for the record, [information deleted], re. Subproject 35, 5 May 1955, File CIA-0314495-A; and memorandum, 'SUBPROJECT 35 of PROJECT MKULTRA', 10 May 1955, all File CIA-0314495-A, ACHRE; and Marks, *Search* (note 49) p.202.

59. Marks, *Search* (note 49) p.59.
60. Brode, 'Responsibilities of the Scientific Branch' (note 10).
61. Wallace R. Brode to John A. Armitage, country desk officer, USSR, State Dept. n.d. [July 1959], Box 6 of 11, WRB.
62. Ranelagh, *The Agency* (note 54) pp.196–7. By the 1960s, as opposition to scientists' participation in Vietnam War effort increased and recruitment for the CIA became more difficult, scientific intelligence in less central fields became marginal; a revealing example is provided in Bruce Murray, *Journey into Space: The First Thirty Years of Space Exploration* (NY: Norton 1989) pp.99–100.
63. E.B. Skolnikoff to James R. Killan Jr, 23 Oct. 1958, Executive Office of the President, Office of Science and Technology, RG 359, Box 111, NARA; see also Doel, 'Scientists as Policymakers' (note 33) p.40.
64. See John Lewis Gaddis, *The Long Peace: Inquiries into the History of the Cold War* (NY: OUP 1987) pp.195–214, Ranelagh, *The Agency* (note 54) pp.24, 490-1, Church Committee, Book IV, pp.77–8, Scott D. Breckinridge, *The CIA and the U.S. Intelligence System* (Boulder, CO: Westview Press 1986) p.33 and Jeffrey Richelson, *The U.S. Intelligence Community*, 2nd ed. (Cambridge, MA: Ballinger 1989) pp.17–18 and *passim*. It is interesting to note that the corresponding elevation of science within the State Dept., through the creation of its Bureau of Oceans and International Environmental and Scientific Affairs, did not come about until 1973/74; see *Science and Technology in the Department of State*, Science Policy Research Division, Congressional Research Service, Committee Print (Washington DC: US GPO 1975) and *Science and Technology in U.S. International Affairs: A Report of the Carnegie Commission on Science, Technology, and Government* (NY: Carnegie Commission 1992) p.50.

5

The Wizards of Langley:
The CIA's Directorate of Science and Technology

JEFFREY T. RICHELSON

To most of the public, reference to the Central Intelligence Agency elicits visions of espionage and covert operations. To the more knowledgeable it also signifies an agency responsible for the production of finished intelligence. Far fewer think of it in terms of its efforts to exploit science and technology for intelligence purposes. Even an 800-page history of the CIA, published in 1986, included only a few references to the Directorate of Science and Technology. Yet the history of the directorate is a key element in the history of both the CIA and the entire intelligence community.[1]

The directorate has had an enormous impact on the collection and analysis of intelligence. It has designed and operated key intelligence satellite systems, been heavily involved in signals intelligence (Sigint) collection operations, and established the CIA's role in the technical analysis of foreign missile and space programs. It is also responsible for a number of scientific advances which have been made available for medical and other purposes.

It has also been the focus of bureaucratic battles. Its control or attempts to control key components of the CIA resulted in intense disputes within the agency. Its involvement in overhead reconnaissance and technical intelligence analysis also brought protests from the Air Force. The resolution of those battles helped shape the nature of the US intelligence effort throughout the Cold War.

ORIGINS

The earliest suggestion that the CIA needed to make a concerted effort to harness science and technology for intelligence purposes came from the Technological Capabilities Panel (TCP), which had been established in July 1954 by President Dwight D. Eisenhower, in response to concerns about US vulnerability to surprise attack.[2]

Key members of the TCP were James R. Killian Jr, President of the Massachusetts Institute of Technology, and Edwin H. Land, President of the Polaroid Corporation. Killian chaired the TCP, while Land headed its Project Three, charged with examining ways of enhancing the nation's intelligence capabilities through technology.[3]

Its formal report, *Meeting the Threat of Surprise Attack*, was issued on 14 February 1955. Even before that day Land, in writing Director of Central Intelligence (DCI) Allen Dulles concerning the proposal to build a reconnaissance aircraft to overfly the Soviet Union, offered the opinion that 'we feel you must assert your right to pioneer in scientific techniques for collecting intelligence ...'[4]

The report would echo those sentiments at greater length. It noted that 'We obtain little significant information from classical covert operations inside Russia ... We cannot hope to circumvent ... [Soviet security] measures in an easy way. But we can use the ultimate in science and technology to improve our intelligence take'. Specific recommendations included 'adoption of a vigorous program for the extensive use, in many intelligence procedures, of the most advanced knowledge in science and technology'.[5]

In response, the CIA established a Scientific Advisory Board. Chaired by Land for almost a decade, it would come to be better known as the Land Panel. Within the CIA's organizational structure, the panel was attached to the office of the DCI's Special Assistant for Planning and Coordination, Richard Bissell.[6]

Bissell, as head of the U-2 effort and the Development Projects Staff, served as the key agency figure in the CIA's exploitation of technology for intelligence collection purposes. In early 1958 he was appointed as co-director of the 'Corona' photographic reconnaissance satellite project, and also served as the CIA official responsible for the program to develop a successor to the U-2, which resulted in the CIA's A-12/'Oxcart', and in modified form the Air Force's SR-71.[7]

In late January 1959 Bissell became the Deputy Director for Plans, responsible for the CIA's espionage and covert action operations. However, he also took the Development Projects organization with him – which upset Land, who believed it should be separated from the type of activities conducted by Plans. Land became particularly distressed in 1961 after learning that Bissell had 'involved' the U-2 program in the Bay of Pigs fiasco, employing the aircraft to photograph the airfields that had been attacked by the CIA's Cuban pilots.[8]

That fiasco led to the resignation of DCI Allen Dulles and his replacement by John McCone on 29 November 1961. At one of his first meetings with the President's Foreign Intelligence Advisory Board (PFIAB), which was chaired by Killian and included Land, he discovered the PFIAB's concern that the CIA's exploitation of science and technology might be constrained by continued connections with Plans. Killian and Land told McCone of their strong belief that a separate component of the agency should be established for its scientific and technical endeavors.[9]

After the session, McCone ordered a review of the organization and structure of the CIA by a three-man panel. All deputy directors were asked to comment on the Killian-Land proposal. Bissell registered his strong objections in a 10 January 1962 memorandum to McCone, entitled 'Technical Intelligence Collection'.[10]

Those arguments did not persuade McCone, who told Killian on 22 January that he intended to establish a deputy director for technical collection. The new directorate would include Bissell's Development Projects unit, now a Division. Bissell, as a result of the Bay of Pigs misadventure, was on his way out as Deputy Director for Plans, but not necessarily on his way out of the agency. In the fall of 1961 McCone and Bissell agreed that he would resign at the end of December. However, McCone's wife died and he requested Bissell delay his resignation until he determined whether he would continue as DCI. When McCone returned in January he decided that he wanted Bissell to become head of a Directorate of Research. After receiving approval from Attorney General Robert Kennedy, and then President John Kennedy, McCone extended the offer to Bissell.[11]

But in a 7 February letter to McCone, Bissell rejected the offer and again questioned the whole concept. He objected to moving the Office of Scientific Intelligence (OSI) and the National Photographic Interpretation Center (NPIC) from the Directorate of Intelligence to the new directorate. In addition, while he understood that the DCI might need a policy adviser on reconnaissance matters, he noted his personal distaste for the role – in contrast to being involved in an operational or managerial position.[12]

Third, he expressed his belief that there were 'grave disadvantages' to the proposal to split the Technical Services Division of the Directorate of Plans, which produced disguises, miniature camera and recording devices, secret writing kits, and other devices to support clandestine operations. Research and development activities were to be placed under the new directorate while operational support functions would continue to reside in Plans. He argued that 'progress in the exploitation of advanced techniques can be accelerated only by forcing a closer integration of developmental and operational activities which will be far easier to accomplish if they remain under common command'.[13]

The responsibilities he did feel would be appropriate to place outside of the Plans and Intelligence Directorates, apparently concerned aerial and space reconnaissance matters. Such a job, he explained, would more appropriately be assigned to a special assistant than a deputy director. As such, for him to accept it, 'would mean a long step backward'. He resigned, effective 17 February 1962.[14]

THE DIRECTORATE OF RESEARCH

Bissell's letter of 7 February 1962 signaled his imminent departure from the agency, and left McCone with the need to find a new manager for the CIA's reconnaissance programs. Killian and Land were concerned that he act quickly, so that none of the programs would suffer from a lack of direction. They again urged McCone to establish a science and technology directorate with no connection to covert activities.[15]

On 14 February McCone approved Headquarters Notice (HN) 1-8, which announced that a deputy director for research and development would be established at some later date. On 16 February HN 1-9 established, effective 19 February, the position of Deputy Director for Research. The notice also informed its readers that certain activities of the Development Projects Division (DPD) would be transferred to Research, along with other research and development activities. Two months later, HN 1-15, effective on 15 April, transferred the Special Projects Branch and supporting elements of the DPD to the Research directorate.[16]

Appointed to head the new branch was Dr Herbert (Pete) Scoville Jr, promoted from his position as Assistant Director for Scientific Intelligence. In accepting the new position Scoville placed himself at the center of a bureaucratic war. The mission statement of the Deputy Director (Research) was spelled out in HN 1-23 of 30 July 1962, assigning the deputy director responsibility for conducting 'in depth, research and development in the scientific and technical fields to support intelligence collection by advanced technical means'. It assigned the directorate 'primary responsibility for Agency Elint activities', to be conducted by an Office of Elint (OEL), and established an Office of Special Activities (OSA) – which absorbed most personnel and functions of Development Projects. OSA was involved in four ongoing collection programs – the 'Corona' and 'Argon' reconnaissance satellite programs, the 'Oxcart' (A-12) and 'Idealist' (U-2) aircraft programs – as well being responsible for development of further aerospace intelligence systems. Also established was an Office of Research and Development.[17]

However, HN 1-23 did not specify cognizance over the Office of Scientific Intelligence or the Technical Services Division. The Deputy Director for Intelligence, Ray Cline, refused to give up OSI, viewing such a move as 'weakening CIA's analytical voice' and incompatible with the principle that one unit should not both collect intelligence and evaluate the results. Richard Helms, Deputy Director for Plans, was adamant about the importance of his directorate retaining control of TSD.[18]

Even with a less extensive mandate than expected, Scoville found himself in charge of an undermanned directorate. Virtually all of the scientific expertise in the agency remained in the Office of Scientific Intelligence. As a result, the Directorate of Research 'never had a fighting chance', according to a CIA historian.[19]

Two additional sets of problems made it difficult for Scoville to build the kind of directorate that Land and Killian had in mind. Several intelligence problems occupied center stage at CIA in 1962, which drained time and energy that might have been devoted to establishing a true science and technology directorate. One was to determine if a newly-discovered Soviet missile installation in Estonia was an anti-aircraft or anti-missile installation. The second, and most time consuming, stemmed from the discovery of Soviet intermediate-range ballistic missiles in Cuba. Scoville's background, as technical director of the Air Force Special Weapons Project, made him a key source for policy-makers with regard to the specific nature of the nuclear threat.[20]

Towards the very end of his tenure Scoville found himself in a bureaucratic battle with Brockway McMillan, who became Director of the National Reconnaissance Office (NRO) on 1 March 1963, but may have been involved in NRO matters before that time as a result of his position as Assistant Secretary of the Air Force for Research and Development.

The NRO had been established on 6 September 1961 to provide a framework under which the Air Force, CIA, and Navy would develop and operate space (and selected aerial) reconaissance systems. Whereas Bissell and the first NRO director, Joseph Charyk, had enjoyed an amicable partnership, Scoville and McMillan did not.[21]

Part of the problem was that McCone had undercut Scoville's position. Secretary of Defense Robert S. McNamara, who had sought to consolidate space programs under the Air Force, told McCone that the CIA should limit itself to defining requirements, possibly doing some advanced research, and interpreting the photographs brought back by the Air Force satellites. McMillan followed up on McNamara's wishes and on McCone's agreement by attempting to implement the policy. He informed the CIA that he was transferring its responsibilities for 'Corona' to the Air Force Office of Special Projects. McCone could not decide whether he should accept McMillan's decision or insist on continued CIA participation.[22]

By late 1962, Scoville was frustrated with his internal and external battles and the lack of McCone's support. That frustration came to the attention of Killian, still chairman of the PFIAB, in early 1963, and served as catalyst for Killian and Land, who had not been satisfied with the

Directorate of Research concept, to provide McCone with additional (and more specific) guidance concerning the CIA exploitation of new developments in science and technology. Thus, in March 1963, the PFIAB approved 'Recommendations to Intelligence Community by PFIAB', and sent it on to the DCI.[23]

Three of the key points were recommendations for:

(a) The creation of an organization for research and development which will couple research (basic science) done outside the intelligence community, both overt and covert, with development and engineering conducted within intelligence agencies, particularly the CIA.

(b) The installation of an administrative arrangement in the CIA whereby the whole spectrum of modern science and technology could be brought into contact with major programs and projects of the Agency. The existing fragmentation and compartmentation of research and development in CIA severely inhibited this function.

(c) The clear vesting of these broadened responsibilities in the top technical official of the CIA, operating at the level of Deputy Director. Recasting and extending the CIA's present [Directorate for] Research might accomplish this.[24]

THE DIRECTORATE OF SCIENCE AND TECHNOLOGY

Despite the PFIAB's push for change, McCone did not take immediate action. In a 15 April 1963 response he made only generalized claims of progress. The only specific information was not of the sort Land or Killian would be pleased with – McCone acknowledged that he had considered including OSI and TSD in the directorate but had suspended his plans. He did promise to 'move ahead with additional changes' that would give the Research directorate expanded responsibilities.[25]

But before McCone moved to fulfill this promise, Scoville decided he had enough of the bureaucratic wars, packed up, and headed for his New England summer home. On 25 April he submitted his resignation, to take effect on 1 June, noting that he had been frustrated in his attempts to consolidate the Agency's scientific and technical functions. McCone sent Dr Albert (Bud) Wheelon, who had replaced Scoville as Director of the Office of Scientific Intelligence, to try to change his predecessor's mind. Scoville, however, was adamant.[26]

Once McCone was convinced Scoville would not return, he offered the

34-year old Wheelon the job. The OSI chief had received a doctorate in physics from MIT at the age of 23 and worked on space reconnaissance design at TRW. In 1956 he was selected to assess the results of a 'major breakthrough of heretofore denied intelligence on the Soviet missile program' for the US Intelligence Board – U-2 photography of Soviet facilities, sometimes facilities whose existence and purpose had been unknown. Wheelon was one of those brought in to assess the puzzling images.[27]

Wheelon wanted no part of the job because, as he told McCone, it was a no-win situation unless the directorate controlled all of the Agency's scientific and technical efforts. McCone was only able to budge his subordinate by agreeing to turn over the Office of Scientific Intelligence and the Directorate of Support's Automated Data Processing Staff. Wheelon then decided to accept the position, but insisted that the directorate be renamed the Directorate of Science and Technology and that the PFIAB's March 1963 recommendations become the directorate's charter. On 5 August 1963 HN 1-36 announced the immediate renaming of the Directorate of Research, the transfer of the Automatic Data Processing Staff, renamed the Office of Computer Services, to Science and Technology, as well as the transfer of the Office of Scientific Intelligence.[28]

Predictably, Wheelon's absorption of the Office of Scientific Intelligence left Ray Cline furious. In his memoirs, he would characterize McCone's transfer of analytical functions to Wheelon's organization as 'a major change in the CIA's structure [which] I disapproved of'. He characterized the result as being that 'CIA advocacy of its own scientific collection techniques became mixed up with its objective analysis of all scientific and technical developments. The appearance of objectivity was hard to maintain when analysis and collection were supervised by the same staff'.[29]

Wheelon was also willing to take on those outside the Agency who stood in the way of the directorate playing the role he envisioned for it. Included in this set of external (to the agency) foes were two powerful Air Force generals, Bernard Schriever and Curtis LeMay, and NRO Director McMillan.

On 7 November 1963 Wheelon established a Foreign Missile and Space Analysis Center (FMSAC) in the directorate, employing personnel from OSI. Carl Duckett, who had been the Army's missile intelligence chief, was named FMSAC director. The center, which would consist of approximately 270 personnel, would evaluate collection activities, and perform detection and trajectory analysis, signal analysis and optical data analysis. Thus the CIA now had an in-house capability in the field.[30]

Predictably the Air Force, whose Foreign Technology Division had a similar mission to FMSAC, was not happy. In September 1963 Air Force Chief of Staff Curtis LeMay had learned of Wheelon's intentions. In December, after the center's creation, General Bernard Schriever, head of the Air Force Systems Command, wrote to LeMay to urge that 'immediate action should be taken to slow down or block CIA action to duplicate DOD missile and space intelligence'. He recommended that General Joseph Carroll, head of the Defense Intelligence Agency, and thus the senior military official on the US Intelligence Board, be encouraged to protest CIA activities in the area 'at least until an agreement on respective responsibilities and mutual support can be reached'.[31]

But Schriever believed that since 'the problem could not be solved through intelligence channels alone ... I recommend that you and the Secretary act to protest this expensive and unnecessary duplication of DOD space and missile intelligence analysis by CIA'. Schriever characterized the Air Force capability in the area as representing 'a significant investment in manpower and resources and ... an extremely vital function which must not be lost or permitted to be eroded by another government agency'.[32]

LeMay apparently responded that he shared Schriever's concern about the FMSAC and proposed that he submit a memorandum to the Joint Chiefs of Staff (JCS) which would hopefully provide the foundation for a JCS memo to the Secretary of Defense expressing their concern. As LeMay saw it, the memo would request the Secretary to consult with McCone 'in an effort to prevent a major CIA effort competing with and largely duplicating activities well underway in Department of Defense agencies'.[33]

It is not clear whether a JCS memo was produced, or if it was, whether McNamara took up the subject with McCone. If he did McCone would have known he had the backing of Land and Killian in fending off Defense. It is clear that such protestations, irrespective of how far up they went, did not affect the operations of the center.

Wheelon's other major external problem was the situation that he inherited from Scoville with regard to the CIA-NRO relationship. After reviewing the situation Wheelon concluded that the era of cooperation between the CIA and Air Force on reconnaissance matters was over, telling McCone that 'there is no point in screwing another light bulb into a socket that is shorted out'. The director asked him to further analyze the situation and make a recommendation.[34]

After talking to Scoville and others, Wheelon concluded that CIA participation was in the national interest, and if cooperation was not possible, then competition was mandatory. McCone accepted Wheelon's judgement and told him that the CIA should once again play a strong role in the overhead programs. According to Wheelon 'I immediately assumed responsibility for for all overflight activities with the U-2 and development of ... 'Oxcart'. I also became responsible for the CIA role in 'Corona' '. The partnership between the CIA and Air Force resumed on 'Corona', after 'a period of readjustment in the expectations of the Air Force'.[35]

ORGANIZATIONAL EVOLUTION

The Directorate of Science and Technology of 1964 consisted of six offices – the Office of Computer Services, Office of Elint (renamed the Office of Sigint Operations in 1978), the Office of Research and Development, the Office of Special Activities (which would be renamed the Office of Development and Engineering in May 1973), the Office of Scientific Intelligence, and the Foreign Missile and Space Analysis Center. The two scientific and technical organizations that remained outside were the Technical Services Division and NPIC – although it is not clear that Wheelon wanted either. Even without those organizations the new directorate represented an impressive concentration of systems development, collection, and analytical responsibilities.[36]

Wheelon, as Ray Cline would note in his memoirs, 'stayed only a short time before going back to industry'.[37] In 1966 Wheelon did depart, for Hughes Aircraft, although not before having established a science and technology directorate similar to that envisioned by Killian and Land. He was succeeded by Carl Duckett, first as Acting DDS&T (until 20 April 1967) and then as DDS&T (till 1 June 1976).

Six years after Wheelon's departure the directorate's organization chart showed virtually no change. However, there were significant changes, beginning in 1973, that reshaped the directorate over the next decade – and for a few years made it an even more extensive empire than it was under Wheelon. In 1973 DCI William Colby transferred the Technical Services Division from Operations (as Plans had been renamed) to Science and Technology, 'as a start in breaking down the walls of compartmentation between the Operations Directorate and the Agency's other directorates'.[38]

More importantly, 1973 also saw the transfer of the National Photographic Interpretation Center from the intelligence directorate to Science and Technology. The NPIC is the successor to the CIA photographic interpretation unit first established in 1953 as the Photographic Intelligence Division (PID). Under the provision of National Security Council Intelligence Directive (NSCID) 8 of 1961 and its successors, the NPIC is run by the CIA as a 'service of common concern' serving the entire intelligence community.[39]

NPIC's transfer had been in the works for several years. It was clear to key individuals in the center that to extract the most intelligence from the images that would be produced from the KH-9 camera system, first orbited in 1971, upgraded equipment would be required. NPIC director Arthur Lundahl explained to DCI Richard Helms that with good quality equipment NPIC could minimize the probability of any successful Soviet deception. Another problem that needed to be addressed was the requirement for new equipment, such as adjustable chairs, that would take the physical strain out of photographic interpretation.[40]

But money was difficult to get while NPIC was in the intelligence directorate. Furthermore, according to Dino Brugioni, a former senior manager at NPIC, contractors were not interested in working with NPIC because it had relatively little money to spend. A million dollar contract was not worth the trouble, and the DI had no leverage with such contractors. However, the Directorate of Science and Technology, which did hundreds of millions of dollars of business with them, had considerable leverage. Accepting work from NPIC, even if it was for relatively little money, would be a smart business move if it was part of the S&T directorate.[41]

With the acquisition of TSD, and particularly NPIC, Duckett's directorate had an even greater role in the intelligence collection and analysis work of the CIA than Wheelon's. But it was an influence that Duckett's successor Leslie Dirks would not completely retain after assuming the deputy director's position on 1 June 1976.[42]

In 1976, at the initiative of Deputy Director of Intelligence Sayre Stevens, OSI and the Office of Weapons Intelligence (OWI), which had been created in 1975 by merging FMSAC with some elements of OSI, were transferred to the Directorate of Intelligence. Stevens felt that the separation of the two offices from the rest of the intelligence production effort was artificial. Further, he was concerned about the lack of interdisciplinary analysis on foreign military forces – particularly for nuclear proliferation. Bringing the technical people from OSI and OWI into his directorate, he felt at the time, was a solution. He succeeded in selling DCI George Bush on the idea and the two offices were transferred.[43]

The DS&T did receive something in return – the Foreign Broadcast Information Service, whose open source collection activities provided a significant portion of the information used by agency analysts. It was felt that FBIS was more of a collection activity than an analytical unit, and thus belonged in the DS&T.[44]

One further organizational change was set in motion by the late 1980s creation of a new Office of Special Projects within the directorate, whose function was the design of emplaced sensors for the collection of measurement and signature intelligence (Masint) and signals intelligence. In 1993, in order to eliminate redundancy, Special Projects and the Office of Sigint Operations were merged to form the Office of Technical Collection (OTC).[45]

While one aspect of the history of the Directorate of Science and

Technology involves its creation and evolution as an institution, another is its role in systems development, collection operations, analysis, and research and development.

COLLECTION SYSTEMS DEVELOPMENT

The CIA's role in the 'Corona' program and Wheelon's unwillingness to surrender the CIA's role in strategic reconnaissance set the stage for agency involvement in the development of new overhead reconnaissance systems.

The groundwork for one program had been laid in 1963. While 'Corona' represented a substantial improvement in US intelligence capability, photo-interpreters were having a hard time finding strategic and military facilities in the vast amount of film. Wheelon asked an advisory group chaired by Stanford physicist Sidney Drell to look at two questions: what resolution photo-interpreters needed to confidently find and identify strategic installations in broad area coverage, and whether 'Corona' could be improved to provide the required resolution.[46]

The Drell group would inform Wheelon that a substantial improvement in resolution was needed and that it was unlikely that incremental improvements in 'Corona' would achieve it. Those conclusions led to a CIA effort to develop a new system, and a fierce battle with the Air Force over which organization's proposed new area-surveillance system should be funded. The CIA, and Wheelon, emerged victorious. They produced the KH-9 camera system, capable of producing images encompassing thousands of square miles with a resolution of 1–2 feet. The first KH-9 would be launched in 1971, and a total of 19 successful launches would take place through 1984.[47]

A second system under development at the CIA by 1965 had a quite different purpose from 'Corona' or 'Hexagon': the interception of telemetry from Soviet and Chinese missile tests. The analysis of telemetry signals was crucial to producing high-quality intelligence on the capabilities of Soviet and Chinese strategic weapons systems. The Office of Special Activities sought to determine whether such signals could be intercepted from geostationary orbit, in which a satellite at 22,300 miles above a point on the equator revolves around the earth at the same speed at which the earth turns. A space-based system had the potential to provide data irrespective of the launch site, flight path, or presence of intercept facilities in a particular nation.[48]

The result was the award of a contract to TRW, to build a series of satellites, which would be first codenamed 'Rhyolite'(and subsequently 'Aquacade'). The first of the satellites would be launched in June 1970, and be followed by single launches in 1973, 1977, and 1978. With the 1973 launch a two station pattern – one satellite over the Horn of Africa, the other over Borneo – was established. The program would continue well into the

1980s, with the satellites exhibiting extraordinary lifetimes.[49]

Another key space intelligence program of the directorate was codenamed 'Kennan' (and subsequently 'Crystal'). Its success satisfied a requirement for 'real-time' intelligence that had existed since the beginning of the space reconnaissance program, but had been technically unattainable. The Air Force attempt to produce such a system ended in failure in 1962. As a result, the CIA and the Air Force had developed several systems that returned film in capsules, which introduced a delay, sometimes of weeks, between a target being photographed and an interpreter seeing the photograph.[50]

By the late 1960s technological advances had made such a program theoretically feasible. In 1972, the CIA, after another battle with the Air Force, was given the go-ahead to develop its proposed system. The first of the new satellites produced under the 'Kennan' program, with an optical system designated KH-11, would be launched in December 1976. Another seven would be built before production would be terminated in favor of a more advanced model.[51]

The KH-11 life span would continue to grow from approximately two years for the first models to over five years for later versions. While the first models would be able to operate for only a few hours each day, owing to power limitations, later models could be employed whenever needed. The result was a revolution in intelligence and warning capabilities. Imagery of an event could be on a photo interpreter's desk shortly after the event occurred, and a finished analysis could be in the hands of a decision maker within an hour. In addition, the digital form of the imagery allowed for extensive computer manipulation in pursuit of extracting as much intelligence as possible from the images.[52]

In addition, the directorate's 'Indigo/Larcrosse' program produced radar imagery satellites which relied on transmitting radio signals at a target below and constructing an image from the returned reflections. Since radio waves penetrate cloud cover, the satellites could provide imagery, in contrast to the KH-11s, even when the target below was covered by clouds, albeit with lower resolution. The first of the satellites was orbited in December 1988.[53]

COLLECTION OPERATIONS

One element of Science and Technology collection operations has been the role of the Office of Special Activites and its successors in operating the ground stations for systems such as 'Rhyolite' and the KH-11 at Pine Gap, Australia and Fort Belvoir, Virginia respectively.

All of the chiefs of the 'Rhyolite/Aquacade' ground station at Pine Gap were senior officers of the Science and Technology directorate, and the facility has been staffed largely by CIA analysts. Meanwhile, the main KH-11/Advanced KH-11 ground station at Fort Belvoir, Virginia, also known as Area 58, hosts the Primary Exploitation Group (PEG), whose personnel examine imagery from the satellites as it arrives.[54]

Aside from running and manning stations such as Pine Gap and Fort Belvoir, the directorate has been involved in air, land-based and sea-based collection programs. CIA A-12s began flying over Vietnam in May 1967 in order to determine if surface-to-surface missiles had been introduced into the country. Twenty-two missions would be flown by the end of 1967.[55]

The CIA constructed Sigint collection sites in several countries. Among the most important sites established by OEL/OSO were those in Norway, Iran and China. The Norwegian stations have been operated by personnel from Norwegian military intelligence. Originally personnel from the CIA and NSA were regularly on assignment at those stations, a practice which subsequently ceased. Included among the Norwegian stations is (or possibly was) the one located at Vardo. Its targets have included signals from the Soviet space and missile test center at Plesetsk and the telemetry from SS-N-18 and SS-N-20 SLBM tests from the White Sea and Barents Sea.[56]

By the mid-1960s OEL had established sites in Iran that were even more advantageous than the sites in Turkey (operated by NSA and the Air Force) for monitoring the progress of the Soviet ICBM program, owing to their ability to intercept telemetry from earlier stages of the missile's flight. Two of the most important Iranian sites were the ones known as Tacksman I and Tacksman II – located at Kabkan, 650 miles south of the Tyuratam space center and ICBM test facility, and at Behshahr, on the southeastern corner of the Caspian Sea.[57]

When the Shah fell from power in 1979, the United States lost the outposts. Kabkan was besieged by militiamen, and 22 US technicians were captured and subsequently returned to the United States. On 31 January 1979 the US technicians abandoned the post at Beshahr.[58]

The US initially suggested setting up intercept stations in China in 1978, prior to the establishment of diplomatic relations. At first, the Chinese were reluctant. However, during a January 1979 visit to Washington, Deng Xiao Ping offered to cooperate with the US in collecting and sharing intelligence on the Soviet Union. Discussions between Deng and National Security adviser Zbigniew Brzezinski produced an agreement in principle to pursue a joint effort to establish new collection facilities in western China.[59]

The negotiations were completed in late December 1980 and early 1981 by DCI Stansfield Turner during a secret visit to Beijing. Collection operations from the resulting sites, at Qitai and Korla in Xinjiang province, began in the fall of 1980. The stations were constructed by the Office of

Sigint Operations, and operated by the Technical Department of the People's Liberation Army's General Staff. OSO trained the Chinese technicians and still periodically sends advisers and service technicians as required. The initial equipment allowed for the interception of telemetry from Soviet missile and space shots conducted from two major Soviet launch sites, Tyuratam and the Sary Shagan ABM test site.[60]

A second aspect of land-based OEL/OSO operations has been its joint operation with the National Security Agency of eavesdropping equipment deployed to US embassies and consulates. The Special Collection Service and its Special Collection Elements can 'deliver verbatim transcripts from high-level foreign-government meetings in Europe, the Middle East and Asia, and phone conversations between key politicians'.[61]

One of OSO's lesser known collection operations involved the operation of a signals intelligence ship, disguised as a fishing trawler, near the Kola Peninsula. The ship would often sail close to Soviet naval maneuvers, intercepting whatever communications or other electronic signals were available.[62]

Emplaced sensors developed by the directorate, most recently by its Office of Special Projects, have also been instrumental in the collection of intelligence. In 1965 the CIA planted a nuclear monitoring device on the summit of Nanda Devi in Garhwal, India. The device was intended to monitor Chinese nuclear tests being conducted at China's Lop Nor nuclear test site, approximately 900 miles away. After it was swept away in an avalanche, a second device was placed, in 1967, on the summit of the neighboring 22,400 foot Nanda Kot. That device remained in place for a year before being removed.[63]

Some of the most exotic emplaced sensors developed were those used in an attempt to monitor various Soviet weapons programs. One was a round device that could be hidden in a tree stump, and sent data to a satellite. Another appeared to be a tree branch. It could be fitted around the stump of a tree and contained a sensor at one end to detect signals from a nearby Soviet laser test facility.[64]

The directorate's Foreign Broadcast Information Service (FBIS) is a major open source collector. It monitors the public radio and television broadcasts of foreign nations, foreign print media, as well as the broadcasts of 'black' or clandestine radio stations and prepares summaries and analyses of publications and broadcasts of interest for use by intelligence analysts and officials. To do this FBIS employs high-frequency receivers, satellite channels, subscriptions, news agencies, wire services, and foreign databases.[65]

During May 1989, US monitoring of Chinese radio broadcasts provided important data on the support for the student protesters in Beijing. The reports indicated that 40,000 students, teachers, and writers in Chengdu marched in support of democracy in mid-May. Altogether, radio reports indicated that there had been demonstrations of more than 10,000 people in at least nine other provinces.[66]

In a December 1992 address the Deputy DCI, Admiral William O. Studeman, noted that, 'Each week FBIS monitors 790 hours of television from over 50 countries in 29 languages. Foreign television programs, such as news programs and documentaries, give analysts a multi-dimensional feel for a country or material that other open source media cannot provide. TV allows us to broaden our knowledge of more restrictive societies'.[67]

ANALYSIS AND PROCESSING

As elements of the science and technology directorate from 1963 to 1976, OSI and FMSAC/OWI played a key role in CIA and intelligence community production of scientific and technical intelligence.

OSI's production focused on issues such as foreign developments in computers, lasers, nuclear energy, and communications technology. Its 1964 report on the 'Japanese Nuclear Energy Program' discussed the number and type of research reactors in Japan, her exploration for and production of uranium and research into the production of heavy water, a variety of applications – from the study of the use of plutonium for advanced reactors to the application of nuclear energy in research, medicine, and industry.[68]

Its 1965–67 production effort employed approximately 215 analysts. Twenty-five of those analysts spent about a quarter of their time on China, specifically on scientific resources; research, development, and prototype testing of air defense systems, cruise missiles, aircraft, and naval vessels; scientific space activities; nuclear energy; unconventional warfare; and the physical, engineering, and life sciences.[69]

FMSAC focused on the technical details of foreign missile and space systems. Its primary concern was not with production numbers, deployment locations, or employment strategies but rather the accuracy of a missile and its warheads, the size and yield of the warheads, the maximum operational range of the missile, reentry angles, burn time, propellant flow rate, and some other technical details.

As would be expected during the 1963–76 period, China and the Soviet Union were the main focus of its work. In the 1965–67 period, and beyond, it studied the full range of Chinese systems – tactical short-range missiles, MRBMs, IRBMs, and ICBMs. Subsequently, it added Chinese space launch activities to the list.[70]

With respect to the Soviet Union the 1963-1976 period saw the testing of a variety of offensive and defensive missile systems, as well as frequent space launches. In addition to the testing of air defense and anti-ballistic missiles the Soviets tested the SS-9, SS-11, SS-13, SS-17, SS-18, and SS-19 ICBMs as well as the SS-N-6 and SS-N-8 SLBMs. From Tyuratam and Plesetsk the Soviets orbited many photographic reconnaissance, Elint, navigation, and communications satellites.[71]

FMSAC's analysis would play a role in the highly publicized 1969 debate over the capabilities of the SS-9. Near the end of the Johnson administration, a National Intelligence Estimate concluded, without any dissents, that the SS-9 was not MIRVed. The estimate did note that the SS-9 might be able to dispense its three warheads in a manner that could allow them to damage or destroy several Minuteman sites. In 1969 the Nixon administration, and most particularly Defense Secretary Melvin Laird, argued that the triangular footprint of the SS-9 made it 'functionally equivalent to a MIRVed missile', and that the Soviets might be attempting to develop a capability to destroy a sizeable portion of the US ICBM force in a first-strike. Laird's position, supported by the Defense Intelligence Agency and Air Force, was fundamental to the administration's case for the Sentinel Anti-Ballistic Missile system, designed to protect ICBM forces.[72]

The battle between the CIA and the Nixon administration over the SS-9 dragged on for several months. FMSAC provided the technical analysis which, along with the work done by the Office of Strategic Research in the Directorate of Intelligence, was used in producing the agency's conclusion that the SS-9 was not a credible threat to US ICBMs. One key factor in reaching that conclusion was FMSAC's analysis of SS-9 multiple warhead accuracy. The test data showed that the warheads often missed their targets by more than a nautical mile. Even the warhead's projected five megaton yield would not compensate for that degree of inaccuracy. Thus, FMSAC's David Brandwein was 'convinced that the SS-9 was not MIRVed, was not a first-strike weapon . . . '.[73]

With the departure of OSI and OWI, which would be merged to form the DI's Office of Scientific and Weapons Research, from Science and Technology, and the acquisition of FBIS, the directorate's remaining analytical components became FBIS and NPIC. In addition to collecting open source material, FBIS also produces a variety of finished intelligence products. Such FBIS reports include *Soviet Public Statements on SALT, September – December 1980: Commitment to Negotiations, Flexibility on SALT II* (1980), and *China's Evolving Arms Control Policy* (1988).

RESEARCH AND DEVELOPMENT

While every office in the Directorate of Science and Technology conducts some research and development in support of its activities, the Office of Research and Development has a charter to 'push beyond the state of the art, developing and applying technologies and equipment more advanced than anything commercially available'. Specific areas of research have included imagery (which comprises a third of the office's resources), communications, sensors, semiconductors, artificial intelligence, image recognition, process modeling, database management, and high-speed computing.[74]

The winner of the CIA's 1996 award for the agency's top scientist, John Craven, received the award for his work on three projects. One involved the application of microwave technology to produce a hundredfold increase in the speed of computer operations. (The speed of current computers is limited by the power they consume and heat they generate. Microwave technology can operate at low power levels, thereby conserving energy and reducing heat generation.) A second involved reducing the problems associated with using laser beams for communication over long distances, such as the susceptibility to interrupted communications due to minor misalignment.[75]

The work presently done by ORD falls in three main areas. One area is imagery-related work performed for the National Imagery and Mapping Agency and the Office of Development and Engineering. A second is the work that benefits primarily OTS. The remaining research generally has a dual-use potential, and is now frequently provided to other elements of the government or the medical and scientific communities. This transfer of knowledge goes back to the 1970s, when CIA research into lithium iodine batteries, conducted to insure the prolonged operation of reconnaissance satellites, was made available to the medical community. It subsequently became the dominant technology used in heart pacemakers.[76]

Among the present dual use areas relevant to law enforcement, the environment, and medicine are:

Natural Language Processing – developed to permit computer sorting of cables arriving at the CIA's Counter-Terrorism Center to weed out irrelevant ones. It reduced the time required from 1–3 hours for humans to 90 seconds for computer sorting. NLP can be used to locate documents containing the type of information the user desires or locate specified information within a text. NLP can be used to automate the construction of data bases.

Facial Recognition – identification of an unknown person against a set of known people. (It has been used by the INS to identify a convicted rapist who crossed from Mexico to Texas.)

Chemical Pollution Detection – detection and measurement of pollutant gases through remote spectroscopy. It can be used to monitor and measure the levels of pollutant gas above manufacturing and waste management facilities.

Hyperspectral Imaging – detects spectral signatures not obtainable through other sensors and can be used to make measurements relevant to geology, forestry, agriculture and environmental management.

Pattern Recognition – technology developed to pick out changes from succeeding satellite images of a given target area are being tested to determine if it can significantly improve the accuracy of mammograms.[77]

Other dual use areas in the physical and computer sciences include advanced optical and magnetic recording systems, optical character recognition, hypertext systems, image perspective transformation modeling and visualization, and multilingual text processing. The image perspective and transformation modeling system developed by ORD 'takes overhead photography and through use of image modeling and and rendering tools, warps the images to appear as if the perspective is on the ground'. Its applications range from familiarizing an intelligence officer with an area in which he or she will be operating to allowing an urban planner to examine the impact of new structures on the local community.[78]

Research and development work is also conducted in the social sciences. Substantially prior to the collapse of the Soviet Union, ORD funded research into the use of social choice theory to analyze high-level Soviet decision making. It has also developed a methodology called FACTIONS, which attempts to help analysts determine the relative influence of leaders and groups, the likely degree of US influence in foreign political debates, the potential for change of leadership or regime, and patterns of conflict and cooperation.[79]

PAST IMPACT AND FUTURE ROLES

The Directorate of Science and Technology was established because key presidential advisors felt it was imperative that the CIA properly harness the powers of science and technology for the acquisition of intelligence. It flourished initially and for a long period because of the influence and abilities of its first head, Albert (Bud) Wheelon, and his successor, Carl Duckett.

It was during their tenure that three key satellite systems vital to both worldwide intelligence collection and the monitoring of arms control treaties – 'Rhyolite', the KH-9, and the KH-11, were developed. The directorate also established the CIA's role in the technical analysis of data on foreign missile and space programs, thus providing for alternatives to estimates produced by the Defense Intelligence Agency and military services. And as noted, its scientific activities have had significant spin-off benefits – both for other parts of the government as well as for the scientific and medical fields.

For much of its existence, because of its concentration of collection systems development, collection operations, and analysis functions, it arguably represented the single most influential element of the US intelligence community. However, it is unlikely to wield as much influence as it did in the past, in quite the same way.

While it acquired the Office of Technical Services, Foreign Broadcast Information Service, and NPIC subsequent to Wheelon's departure it lost key analytical components at the time of Duckett's retirement – the Office of Scientific Intelligence and Office of Weapons Intelligence.

Further, its control over NPIC was weakened in 1991, and then eliminated in the late 1996. In 1991 the Senate Select Committee on Intelligence directed that the Director and Deputy Director of NPIC positions be rotated between CIA and Defense Department officials every three years. The rationale was that the change would be 'a first step toward making the Center more responsive to military requirements'. Even more threatening was the plan of DCI John Deutch to establish a National Imagery and Mapping Agency (NIMA) within the Department of Defense, which succeeded in October 1996.[80]

Third, the 1992 restructuring of the National Reconnaissance Office changes the place of the Director of the Office of Development and Engineering in the reconnaissance program. Prior to the restructuring the CIA maintained its own element of the NRO, known as Program B (Program A was the Air Force Office of Special Projects, Program C was the Navy element; in the second half of 1989 or early 1990 the Director of ODE was designated head of Program B). With the restructuring, Programs A, B and C were terminated while imagery and Sigint directorates were established under the Director, NRO. While the CIA still details employees to work at NRO, it no longer owns programs in the way it once did.

It would also appear that with the collapse of the Soviet Union and the shifting of targets, the role of the directorate in Sigint collection has diminished in importance, as the merger of OSO and OSP into OTC would indicate. The Iranian sites are long gone. The other key sites that it operated for many years, in Norway and China, are no longer of the significance they once were.

Thus, DS&T's impact may increasingly not be the result of its control of an entire development-collection-analysis process, but lie in producing scientific breakthroughs that can be applied to intelligence collection and analysis performed by other organizations within and outside of the CIA – the Directorates of Intelligence and Operations, NRO, NSA, NIMA as well as governmental elements outside the intelligence community.[81]

NOTES

1. John Ranelagh, *The Agency: The Rise and Decline of the CIA* (NY: Simon & Schuster 1986).
2. Donald E. Welzenbach, 'Science and Technology: Origins of a Directorate', *Studies in Intelligence* 30 (Summer 1986) pp.13–26 at p.13.
3. Ibid. p.15.
4. Edwin H. Land to Allen W. Dulles, 5 Nov. 1954, cover letter to Memorandum for: Director of Central Intelligence, Subject: A Unique Opportunity for Comprehensive Intelligence, 5 Nov. 1954.
5. Welzenbach, 'Science and Technology: Origins of a Directorate' (note 2) p.16.
6. Ibid.
7. Richard M. Bissell, *Reflections of a Cold Warrior: From Yalta to the Bays of Pigs* (New Haven, CT: Yale UP 1996) p.135.
8. Welzenbach (note 2) p.22; Peter Wyden, *Bay of Pigs: The Untold Story* (NY: Simon & Schuster 1979) pp.193–4.
9. Welzenbach (note 2) p.22.
10. Ibid.
11. Ibid.; Bissell, *Reflections of a Cold Warrior* (note 7) p.203.
12. Letter Richard M. Bissell to John McCone, 7 Feb. 1962.
13. Ibid.
14. Ibid. Central Intelligence Agency (hereafter CIA), HN 1-8, 14 Feb. 1962, National Archives and Records Administration (NARA), CIA Historical Review Program (CIA HRP) 89-2 RG 263, NN3- 263-94-010, Box 1, HS/HC 706, Folder 7.
15. Welzenbach (note 2) p.23.
16. CIA, HN 1-8, 14 Feb. 1962; CIA, HN 1-9, 16 Feb. 1962 and HN 1-15, 'Transfer of Special Projects Branch', 16 April 1962 – both NARA, CIA HRP 89-2, NN3-263-94-010, Box 5, HS/HC 706, Box 7.
17. CIA, HN 1-23, Deputy Director (Research), 30 July 1962, NARA, CIA HRP 89-2, RG 263, NN3-263-94-010, Box 5, HS/HC 706, Box 7.
18. Ibid. Welzenbach (note 2) p.23; Ray S. Cline, *Secret Spies and Scholars, Blueprint of the Essential CIA* (Washington DC: Acropolis Books 1976) p.200.
19. Welzenbach (note 2) p.24.
20. Ibid. pp.23–4.
21. William E. Burrows, 'Imaging Space Reconnaissance Operations during the Cold War: Cause, Effect, and Legacy', in Svein Lundestad (ed.), *U-2 Flights and the Cold War in the High North* (Bodo, Norway: Bodo College 1996) p.84, n.13; Interview with Herbert Scoville, 1984.
22. Albert D. Wheelon, 'Lifting the veil on CORONA', *Space Policy*, Nov. 1995, pp.252–3.
23. Welzenbach (note 2) p.24.
24. Ibid. p.25.
25. Ibid. p.26.
26. Ibid.
27. Wheelon, 'Lifting the veil on CORONA (note 22) p.252; CIA, Biographic Profile of Albert Dewell Wheelon, 10 May 1966.
28. Welzenbach (note 2) p.26; CIA, HN 1-36, 5 Aug. 1963, NARA, CIA HRP 89-2, RG 263, NN3-263-94-010, Box 5, HS/HC 706, Folder 7.
29. Ranelagh, *The Agency* (note 1) p.491; Cline, *Secrets, Spies, and Scholars* (note 18) pp.199–200.
30. John Prados, *The Soviet Estimate: U.S. Intelligence Analysis and Russian Military Strength* (NY: Dial Press 1982) p.201; Letter Gen. B.A. Schriever, Commander, Air Force Systems Command to Gen. Curtis E. Le May, Chief of Staff, USAF, 26 Dec. 1963.
31. Letter, Schriever to Le May.
32. Ibid.
33. Draft of Letter, Curtis E. LeMay to Gen. B. A. Schriever, Commander AFSC, 7 Jan. 1964.
34. Wheelon (note 22) p.253.
35. Ibid.

36. US Congress, Senate Select Committee to Study Governmental Operations with Respect to Intelligence Activities, *Final Report, Book IV: Supplementary Detailed Staff Reports on Foreign and Military Intelligence* (Washington DC: US GPO 1976) pp.100, 102; Desmond Ball, *Pine Gap: Australia and the US Geostationary Signals Intelligence Program* (Sydney: Allen & Unwin 1988) pp.5–6.

37. Cline, *Secrets, Spies, and Scholars* (note 18) pp.199–200.

38. US Congress, Senate Select Committee to Study Governmental Operations with Respect to Intelligence Activities, *Final Report, Book IV* (note 36) p.101; William Colby with Peter Forbath, *Honorable Men: My Life in the CIA* (NY: Simon & Schuster 1978) p.336.

39. Prados, *Soviet Estimate* (note 30) p.156; NSCID No.8, Photographic Interpretation, 17 Feb. 1972; George Wilson, 'N-PIC Technicians Ferret Out Secrets Behind Closed Windows,' *Los Angeles Times*, 12 Jan. 1975, p.25; Curtis Peebles, 'Satellite Photographic Interpretation', *Spaceflight*, Oct. 1982, pp.161–3.

40. Telephone interview with Dino Brugioni, 21 May 1996.

41. Ibid.

42. Ball, *Pine Gap* (note 42) pp.5–6; US Congress, Senate Select Committee to Study Govenmental Operations with Respect to Intelligence Activities, *Final Report, Book IV* (note 36) p.102.

43. Telephone interview with Sayre Stevens, 29 May 1996. Stevens now characterizes his action as a 'foolish move on my part'. He recalls that he was warned that 'you'll leave or get thrown out and they'll put some political scientist in there' who would ruin everything and 'to some extent that happened'.

44. Interview with CIA official.

45. Ronald Kessler, *Inside the CIA: Revealing the Secrets of the World's Most Powerful Spy Agency* (NY: Pocket Books 1992) pp.77–8; CIA document fragment, 22 July 1988.

46. Wheelon, 'Lifting the veil on CORONA', p.259.

47. Ibid.

48. Ball, *Pine Gap* (note 42) pp.5–6.

49. Jonathan McDowell, 'U.S. Reconnaissance Satellite Programs, Part 2: Beyond Imaging', *Quest* 4/4 (1995) pp.40–5.

50. Jeffrey T. Richelson, *America's Secret Eyes in Space: The US Keyhole Spy Satellite Program* (NY: Harper & Row 1990) pp.23–132.

51. Ibid. pp.123–56.

52. Ibid. pp.136–7.

53. Ibid. pp.217–27.

54. Ball, *Pine Gap* (note 42) pp.58, 80.

55. Thomas P. McInnich, 'The Oxcart Story', *Studies in Intelligence* 26/2 (Summer 1982).

56. Owen Wilkes and Nils Petter Gleditsch, *Intelligence Installations in Norway: Their Number, Location, Function, and Legality* (Oslo, Norway: PRIO 1979) p.35; Seymour Hersh, '*The Target is Destroyed': What Really Happened to Flight 007 and What America Knew About It* (NY: Random House 1986) p.4.

57. Hedrick Smith, 'U.S. Aides Say Loss of Post in Iran Impairs Missile-Monitoring Ability', *New York Times*, 2 March 1979, pp.A1, A8.

58. Dial Torgeson, 'U.S. Spy Devices Still Running at Iran Post', *International Herald Tribune*, 7 March 1979, pp.A1,A8.

59. Robert Gates, *From the Shadows: The Ultimate Insider's Account of Five Presidents and How they Won the Cold War* (NY: Simon & Schuster 1996) pp.122–3.

60. Ibid. p.123; Robert C. Toth, 'U.S., China Joint Track Firings of Soviet Missiles', *Los Angeles Times*, 18 June 1981, pp.1, 9; Philip Taubman, 'U.S. and Peking Jointly Monitor Russian Missiles', *New York Times*, 18 June 1981, pp.1, 14; Murrey Marder, 'Monitoring Not-So-Secret-Secret', *Washington Post*, 19 June 1981, p.10; George Lardner Jr and R. Jeffrey Smith, 'Intelligence Ties Endure Despite U.S.–China Strain', *Washington Post*, 25 June 1989, pp.A1, A24.

61. Bob Woodward, *Veil: The Secret Wars of the CIA, 1981-1987* (NY: Simon & Schuster 1987) pp.30–1.

62. Private information; Central Intelligence Agency, *Cost Reduction Program FY 1966, FY*

1967, 1 Sept. 1965, NARA, CIA HRP 89-2, RG 263, NN3-263-94-010, Box 7, File HS/HC 713, Folder 3.

63. 'The Indian Connection', *India Today*, 31 Dec. 1983, p.10; '$ Diplomacy', *India Today*, 1–15 May 1979, p.107.

64. NBC, *Inside the KGB: Narration and Shooting Script*, May 1993, p.39.

65. Kessler, *Inside the CIA* (note 45) p.78; *Fact Book on Intelligence*, 1993, p.9; CIA, 'Foreign Broadcast Information Service', brochure, n.d.

66. Robert Pear, 'Radio Broadcasts Report Protests Erupting All Over China', *New York Times*, 23 May 1989, p.A14.

67. Remarks by Adm. William O. Studeman, Deputy Director of Central Intelligence to the First International Symposium on National Security and National Competitiveness: Open Source Solutions, 1 Dec. 1992, McLean, VA, pp.12, 20.

68. Office of Scientific Intelligence, Central Intelligence Agency, 'Japanese Nuclear Energy Program', OSI-SR/65-55, Nov. 1964.

69. China Task Force, 'The Production Effort', July 1965 – June 1967, p.20–2, NARA, RG 263, CIA HRP 89-2, NN3-263-94-010, Box 9, File HS/HC 735, Folder 2.

70. Ibid. p.20.

71. Robert P. Berman and John C. Baker, *Soviet Strategic Forces: Requirements and Responses* (Washington DC: US GPO 1982) pp.104–5.

72. Ranelagh, *The Agency* (note 1) pp.493–4; Russell Jack Smith, *The Unknown CIA: My Three Decades with the Agency* (NY: Berkeley 1989) p.241; Prados, *Soviet Estimate* (note 30) p.209.

73. Kirsten Lundberg, *The SS-9 Controversy: Intelligence as Political Football* (Boston, MA: John F. Kennedy School of Govt 1989) pp.5, 18.

74. *Office of Research and Development, Directorate of Science and Technology, Central Intelligence Agency*, n.d., n.p.; Interview with senior DS&T officer, 1996.

75. Peter Maass, 'From His Bed, CIA's Best Makes His Breakthrough', *Washington Post*, 21 April 1996, pp.A1, A20.

76. Interview with senior DS&T official, 1996.

77. CIA, Office of Public Affairs, 'Dual Use Technology Projects: Law Enforcement and the Environment', 1996; Office of Research and Development, *TIPSTER Text Program Overview*, Fall 1995; Ulysses Torassa, 'CIA Technology Might Improve Mammography', *Cleveland Plain-Dealer*, 12 March 1996, p.7-E.

78. CIA, Office of Public Affairs, 'Image Perspective Transformation Modeling and Visualization', 1996.

79. CIA, Office of Public Affairs, 'FACTIONS', 1996.

80. US Congress, Senate Select Committee on Intelligence, *Report 102-117: Authorizing Appropriations for Fiscal Year 1992 for the Intelligence Activities of the U.S. Government, the Intelligence Community Staff, the Central Intelligence Agency Retirement and Disability System, and for Other Purposes* (Washington DC: US GPO 1991) p.7.

81. The directorate is in the process of reorganizing and has added three new offices that reflect such a focus. The Clandestine Information Technology Office will address collection capabilities within emerging information technologies. The Office of Advanced Analytical Tools will address the problem of information overload. The Office of Advanced Projects will focus on the 'insertion of technology into the intelligence process'. (CIA, Office of Public Affairs, 'Restructuring in the DS&T', 27 June 1996).

6

The Committee of Correspondence: CIA Funding of Women's Groups 1952–1967

HELEN LAVILLE

In January 1967, the left-wing periodical *Ramparts* published an exposé of the CIA funding of the National Student Association. The allegations were quickly taken up by the mainstream press, and provoked a widespread outcry about the covert activities of the Agency. Ramparts proclaimed its expose was a 'case study in CIA corruption'.[1] The *New York Times* concurred that the revelations of covert CIA funding had not only been hugely damaging to America's reputation abroad, but threatened the very essence of American democracy; 'Faith in American institutions has been besmirched in a way that would have evaded the reach of any foreign enemy.'[2]

In the general rush to both expose and condemn the level of CIA covert and sinister behaviour however, one group escaped the intense media scrutiny. In February 1967 the *New York Times* announced, 'A fourth fund with apparent CIA connections, the J. Frederick Brown Foundation of Boston, Mass. has been making contributions to a New York based women's group called the Committee of Correspondence'.[3] Indicative of the lack of real concern produced by the *Times* article was a letter written by the Metropolitan Editor of the *Times* to the Committee of Correspondence. Requesting the home telephone numbers of the members of the Committee, the letter, addressed 'dear Gentlemen', met with no response.[4]

Contemporary ignorance regarding the nature or function of the Committee of Correspondence has not been corrected by subsequent historical research. This oversight is regrettable, since the history of the Committee and its relationship with the CIA reveals important insights into the relationship between the private/voluntary sphere and the public/governmental sphere in Cold War America. First, the rhetoric and activities of the Committee illustrate the vitality and importance of the voluntary principle in American ideology and its potential in the propaganda effort. Second, the CIA funding of an organization which was supposedly 'private' demonstrates that the government felt the need to support, direct and manipulate the private sphere for its own propaganda ends. Finally, contrary to contemporary journalistic characterizations of the CIA as an organization bent on the corruption of all that was good in American life, the relationship between the CIA and the Committee of Correspondence reveals the extent to which the private sphere was complicit in its own 'corruption'.

The role of American private organizations in the Cold War propaganda effort was an important one. Eisenhower's championship of the efforts of private organizations was based on two premises. First, the scale of propaganda necessary to secure the defeat of the Soviet Union was so immense as to be beyond the limits of government resources. As Rhodri Jeffreys-Jones has pointed out, Eisenhower's 'New Look' defence policy depended not only on an increase in nuclear capabilities in an effort to limit military expenditure, but also upon an increased remit for the covert arm of the CIA.[5] I would argue that a third, often overlooked part of the 'New Look' was an attempt to devolve a large part of the responsibility for overseas propaganda on to the private sector. The message about the American way could thereby be spread further at a lower cost. As Eisenhower wrote to Anna Lord Strauss of the League of Women Voters:

> There will never be enough diplomatic information officers at work in the world to get the job done without help from the rest of us. Indeed, if our American ideology is eventually to win out in the great struggle being waged between the two opposing ways of life, it must have the active support of thousands of independent private groups and institutions and of millions of individuals.[6]

The input of private organizations was important not only for financial reasons. The importance of the private sector in maintaining the 'free way of life' so vital to America had been noted and lauded by observers from de Tocqueville to Arthur Schlesinger Sr.[7] During the Cold War, the celebration of voluntary associations became even more vociferous. Oscar and Mary Handlin, for example, claimed in their work *The Dimensions of Liberty* (1961) that 'the emergence of a distinctive pattern of voluntary associations was inextricably bound with the history of liberty in America'.[8] By 1969 Grant McConnell's study of voluntary associations recognized the consensus which had sprung up regarding their importance to maintaining the democratic way of life:

> For a rather long time now, at least since the end of World War II, we have seen the rise and consolidation in a position of dominance of a

body of doctrine which exhaults the private association as an essential feature of American democracy, perhaps of any genuine democracy.[9]

The significance of the private sector in the Cold War lay in its representation of the voluntary and therefore genuine nature of American people's allegiance to their system of government. As such, the overseas discourses of private organizations in the Cold War operated on a different level to these of the overt agencies of government. Information which came from 'private' sources was perceived as genuine and sincere. Information from a government source was more likely to be seen as propaganda, and therefore received with a greater degree of scepticism or hostility. By covertly funding private organizations, the US government could disseminate information which had a far greater chance of being believed, rather than being simply dismissed out of hand as propaganda.

To a certain extent CIA funding of the Committee was in no way different from its involvement in voluntary associations in other constituencies, such as the National Student Association, or labor organizations. However, in funding a voluntary organization which was run by and aimed at women exclusively, the CIA sought to address certain gender specific problems. The growth in international women's organizations as a consequence of World War II created an important Cold War battlefield. To many women, the activities of this 'private' arena were of greater importance than the arguments and pronouncements of governments. Few women had a tradition of direct participation in 'traditional', public political life, therefore the language of women's organizations seemed of greater relevance to women than governmental pronouncements. Information was directed to attributes which were assumed to be shared by women of all nations in an attempt to claim the 'natural' allegiances of this specific identity group. This information, furthermore, came not from alien and distant officials, but from other women.

The idea that women were more responsive to appeals from women of other nations than they were to appeals from their own or other governments posed a significant problem for the merchants of American propaganda programs. As a constituency with no 'natural' loyalty to their nation state, women of all nations were particularly vulnerable to a well-targeted propaganda campaign sponsored by another nation. A particular worry was that women would be easily swayed by emotive appeals in the name of 'peace'. Concern ran particularly high in Germany. The Women's Affairs Branch's Semi-Annual Report 1 July 1949 – 31 December 1949 noted, 'There is evidence of systematic efforts from the Eastern Zone to undermine the Western German state by appealing to certain women's organizations through the slogans of peace and unity'.[10]

This concern was not limited to government agencies. In 1952, the American women's organizations became increasingly concerned that Soviet-sponsored women's organizations were embarking upon an orchestrated campaign to subvert the worldwide network of women's organizations into an anti-American stance. Soviet-sponsored groups such as the Women's International Democratic Federation (WIDF) by-passed governments and spoke directly to women, claiming a shared gender identity of peace-loving, nurturing motherhood. These activities were typified in a letter sent to the 'Women of America' from the Women's International Democratic Federation (WIDF), accusing the American government of using germ warfare in Korea, and begging American women, in the name of the 'women of the world' to protest this action.[11]

The letter confirmed the worst fears of the leaders of American women's organizations. On 16 April 1952, Rose Parsons, head of the Women's Liaison Committee of the UN, called a meeting in her New York apartment of leaders of prominent women's voluntary associations. Parsons, acting at the request of the Liaison Committee, presented a report, 'What steps should be taken to Rally the women of the Free World to counter-act Communist Propaganda'. Parsons described the 'intensive propaganda campaign which is being waged by Communists', pointing out 'that women of the free world are for the most part unaware of these tactics'. She identified the new Cold-War battlefield that the women's international voluntary association represented upon which communist organizations were waging an assault by:

> holding large conferences, organizing letter-writing campaigns, and using other mass communications media which in many cases appeared above reproach on the surface, yet were really only clever disguises for their communist aims.[12]

The Committee, which took the temporary title 'The Anonymous Committee', agreed that it was vital that women around the world be alerted both to the techniques of the Communist women and to the true nature of American women, and retired to consider its response to the letter.

By the time of the second meeting of the Committee, on 20 May, all connections with the Liaison Committee of the UN, and with the various organizations of which the members of the Anonymous Committee belonged, had been severed. The Committee members were acting as individuals in order, in Parsons' words, to 'get along faster'.[13] Mrs Hester, a member of the Committee, drafted a response to the letter, and a report on its implications.

Hester claimed that the picture the rest of the world was receiving of the United States through Soviet propaganda was one of 'a depraved, immoral country, where the few rich imperialistic warmongers are preparing a new war to exterminate women and little children and that they are deliberately corrupting the poor, hungry masses of Americans by means of brutal comic books, gangster films and pornographic literature to soften them up for cannon fodder. Our God is the dollar.'[14] Hester suggested that the purpose of the group should be to 'assume the role of a catalytic agent. We should be a kind of planning Committee where ideas originate and be put into effect through many different channels.' Suggestions for action included requesting information about the WIDF through the CIA, persuading the *Saturday Evening Post* to publish an article on Soviet propaganda, and supporting a more extensive information service by the US government.

Mrs d'Estournelles, member of the Committee and an executive director of the Woodrow Wilson Foundation, drafted a response to the WIDF's letter. The letter vehemently denied the use of germ warfare by the US troops. It was impossible that this could be happening without the knowledge of American women since 'in our country every citizen can express his views through newspapers, organization and government, and thereby, assert his influence in public affairs. Therefore, no official act such as germ warfare could take place without its becoming known'.[15] The women of America, the letter asserted, 'want peace and are working for peace in every possible way. We resent this spreading of false accusations because it creates hate and does not help towards a peaceful solution'. Following the advice of the State Department the letter was signed by Eleanor Roosevelt, Anna Lord Strauss of the League of Women Voters, and Edith Sampson, the first American black woman delegate to the UN. The letter was well publicized, with reports in the *New York Times*, *New York Herald Tribune* and *Washington Post*. Two hundred copies of the letter were distributed to US information services abroad through the State Department. The letter was broadcast to South-East Asia on Radio Free Asia and in Eastern Europe on Radio Free Europe. Parsons sent a further 75 copies of the letter to the heads of various women's organizations.[16]

Whilst women's organizations were prepared to launch their own 'private' campaigns to counter Soviet propaganda (and many individual women's organizations did maintain their own programs), the Anonymous Committee was to become a small but effective agent of the American government. Rose Parsons had complained in a letter to Eleanor Roosevelt of the drawbacks of self-financing women's organizations:

> This whole problem of finances is very bothersome to me because we, in the voluntary agencies in this country, especially the women's organizations spend at least half our time trying to raise money, whereas the communist women have only to put out their hand and

money is poured in from the government. This, of course is why they can so easily do such a terrific propaganda job.[17]

In the case of the Committee, Parsons side-stepped this problem by simply not bothering to attempt to secure private funds and instead relying on government money. At the first meeting of the Committee it had been suggested that 'maybe the Government could subsidize the enterprise (though this would have to be done secretly to achieve the desired results)'.[18]

All mention of government funding was quickly dropped, however, as an anonymous grant of $15,000 was made to enable to Committee to set up. This anonymous funding allowed the aptly titled 'Anonymous Committee' to operate as a private, non-governmental organization. The gift of money, however, coincided with an interest in the organization by individuals connected with the government. Dorothy Bauman, following a tour of Europe sponsored by the State Department, had drafted a plan for the CIA to counter communist propaganda aimed at women. In Bauman's words the plan envisaged 'a group of very competent women who would form a nucleus and then start doing some constructive work with women'.[19] Bauman then met with her friend, Rose Parsons, who told her about the Anonymous Committee: 'She thought it was a fine idea so I went back to the government and said that she was willing to get this small group of women together and start this thing with me.' Bauman first attended a meeting of the Committee in August 1952. By then the Committee of Correspondence, named after the Committees established by individuals such as Thomas Jefferson and Samuel Adams in the early American colonies,[20] was running.   Within six months the committee was corresponding with 1,200 women in 73 different countries.[21]

The original focus of the committee fell on countering Communist propaganda through personal letters and a newsletter to individual contacts of the members of the Committee. This list quickly grew and split into two sections – personal friends (A category) and 'friends of friends' (B Category). Initially the tone of the letters was anti-Communist in the extreme. A circular letter from Parsons, Bauman, and a Mrs Mahon, dated 24 November 1954, focused upon 'the present Hate campaign of the Soviet Union against the Free World and the US in particular'.[22]   In December 1952, the plan for the Committee presented to the members outlined the need for a campaign to strengthen the position of women in the 'free world' as 'protagonists of the principles of the free world and against the onslaught of communism'.[23] This campaign was necessary since,

> Communist proselytising and infiltration of women's organizations is not new, but their expansion of activities and their use of every

available means to press their attack on the United States is an emphasis which was not so obvious a few years ago. Therefore it seems reasonable that the answers to these attacks, as well as constructive information about women's efforts, should be provided by American women leaders.[24]

The newsletters produced by the Committee were subsequently vehemently anti-Communist in tone. The Bulletin for 15 April 1953, for example, criticized the Soviet government for paying lip-service to the ideals of family life, whilst at the same time putting into practice a 'clever device...to disrupt family life', namely 'forcing the mother to work outside the home'.[9] This, argued the Committee, resulted in the removal of the mother's influence over her children, a deliberate tactic to 'give the Communists absolute control over the child with the opportunity to mould him into the pattern of well-disciplined little robots'. This approach was contrasted with the findings of the International Study Conference on Child Welfare, held in Bombay in December 1952. The Conference had concluded by calling upon all countries 'to do everything you can to preserve and strengthen family life, since a happy home life is essential to the greatest growth and development of every child'.

However the tone of these communications was a little too strident for the non-American market to swallow. Bauman complained that 'Europeans think we are ... too hysterical on the subject of Communism'.[26] Rose Parsons' visit to Belgium and Holland resulted in similar conclusions: 'I felt at once a certain distrust and resentment of our communications. The criticisms were too much US Propaganda, too obvious a campaign against the USSR.'[27] Therefore, in August 1953 Anne Hester, the Executive Director of the Committee, recommended a new approach. Hester argued that the Committee had begun its work with the assumption that 'misunderstanding of the US hostility towards us, was primarily caused by Communist propaganda. The Committee itself felt that combating Communist propaganda would help correct the situation'. After six months' operation, however, the time had come to reappraise the situation 'in the light of cold realism and realize that every great foreign power, especially when it has only recently achieved such power, is bound to arouse envy, hatred, resentment and misunderstanding. Hester's analysis of the situation concentrated on the 'rising tide of Neutralism and anti-Americanism throughout the world':

> Europe is afraid the US is going to push her into a war against the USSR. She resents us. There are many other causes for resentment, including the natural psychological reaction against the donor of financial help on the part of the recipient. Resentment in Asia, South

America and the Middle East likewise result from US foreign policy – economic, social or political.[28]

Hester concluded 'the Committee has a great deal more to do than counteract Communist propaganda. It must try to contribute to the restoration of confidence in the US, the leader of the free world.' The Bulletin began to concentrate on putting forward a positive image of the United States, rather than relying on attacks on the Soviet Union. Issues were published on topics such as 'The Negro in the US' and 'Atomic Power for Peaceful Purposes'. Bulletin 18 was devoted to showing 'Typical days in the Lives of Five American Women' in order to 'counteract Hollywood publicity and anti-American propaganda which depicts American women as selfish idlers'.[29]

The Committee did not limit itself to correspondence.[30] Eight conferences were organized in the years 1956 – 1963, starting with 'The Responsibility of Freedom' for 13 correspondents from South and South-East Asia. The Committee also produced a great deal of educational material such as the 'Community Action Series' designed to help voluntary organizations. Fieldworkers were sent to Africa and South America to encourage women's participation in public life.

These praiseworthy efforts were almost entirely bankrolled by the CIA. From the first Anonymous Grant of $25,000 in 1953 to the revelations about funding in 1967, the Committee was financed almost totally though the CIA. The first grant of money to the Committee in January 1953 was made through Dorothy Bauman on behalf of a 'donor, representing a group of people, [who] prefers to remain anonymous'.[31] Jean Picker claimed that the source of the money was through Parsons' friend, CIA director Allen Dulles.[32] The next year funding had become a more complicated affair. From 1954 to 1958 the Committee was supported almost entirely through grants from the Dearborn Foundation. Unusually for a charitable foundation, Dearborn wrote to the Committee of Correspondence on 23 February 1954, soliciting an application from them for funds. Subsequently the foundation made a grant for 1954 of $25,000. In 1955 this grant increased to $34,000, as the foundation wrote to the Committee asking them to consider making a bigger application next year for the purpose of 'non-administrative activities'. A grant of $17,750 was made in 1956 to cover the expenses of the Conference for South-East Asia. In all the Dearborn Foundation contributed $587,500 between 1954 and 1966.

Though not named in the 1967 allegations, the Dearborn Foundation was undoubtedly a CIA front. Oral histories confirm that the CIA supported the Committee from the start and Dearborn was the only contributor to the Committee from 1954 to 1957, remaining their chief contributor until

1965.[33] The foundation is not listed in the Foundation Directory and has no tax records.

As the activities, and therefore the budget of the Committee of Correspondence grew the CIA developed an increasingly complicated method of channelling funds. The Agency established fronts which would make grants to foundations which would then make grants to the Committee of Correspondence. The McGregor Educational Institutions Endowment Fund, for example, described its purpose in the third edition of the Foundation Directory as 'endowment grants for higher educational institutions, including technical schools, located exclusively in Vigo County (Indiana)'. In 1964 it made grants of $8,051. Of this sum, $8,000 was a grant to the Committee of Correspondence, which had never expressed a particular interest in Vigo County, Indiana. The Florence Foundation served a similar purpose, receiving exactly $15,000 in gifts in 1964, and making a grant of exactly $15,000 that year to the Committee of Correspondence. The Hobby Foundation also channelled money into the Committee ($20,000 in total). On being named as a recipient of CIA money, trustee William Hobby admitted to channelling 'substantial amounts' and declared, 'I'm glad to have co-operated with the CIA.[34]

This complicated system of funding made it impossible, when news of the funding scandal broke, to assess the extent of the subsidy. A February 1967 memo from the then Executive Director of the Committee, Anne Crolius, considered the allegations made in the press regarding CIA funding. Crolius pointed out that the Brown Foundation, which had been accused of being a CIA front and which had given the Committee of Correspondence a total of $25,000, had also made grants to organizations such as 'Notre Dame Law School, Urban League and the New York Zoological Society'.[35] The implication is that a Foundation which gave money to the harmless New York Zoological Society could not be a CIA front, but a legitimate organization. In fact, it was probably both.

The confusion over the source of funding, however, allowed the 'witting' members of the Committee (those who were aware of the CIA's involvement) to hide their complicity in CIA support from the other members of the Committee. Crolius insisted, 'Regardless of whether the foundations mentioned did receive CIA funds and pass these same funds on to us, the Committee of Correspondence was not aware of any connection of these foundations with the CIA'. The Press Statement released by the Committee was able to argue, with some plausibility, 'We, with other educational organizations , have evidently been caught up in a situation of which we were not aware. Our policy has always been to seek funds for our program from private sources. The Committee of Correspondence have never sought or received direct support from the CIA, nor has it knowingly received CIA support indirectly'.[36]

However, as the Committee faced increasing disarray, witting members were forced to acknowledge their complicity in the funding to unwitting colleagues. A meeting of the witting members of the group on 3 April 1967 acknowledged that the lack of funding was likely to lead to difficult questions from the unwitting participants in the Committee. Since legitimate foundations would know of the CIA funding, they would not believe denials of the Committee's staff, and would be unlikely to make grants to a group that was dishonest with them. The minutes of the meeting summed up the dilemma of the witting members: 'If the knowing members acknowledge to a foundation our past connections, we run the risk of this information reaching our unknowing members as well as others in the US and abroad; if we do not acknowledge, we will get no money.'[37]

In an emotionally charged special meeting on 24 July 1967, Spencer Arnold, 'a representative of our past donors', came from Washington to speak to the Committee.[38] Arnold was at pains to assure the women that they had not been the front of a propaganda campaign, like that of the Soviets, but rather a policy of 'orderly development, avoiding the Soviet approach ... and at the same time building to insure that in the future these countries would not be susceptible to propaganda'. The work of the Committee was genuinely important and constructive and 'the propaganda was icing on the cake if and when it came'. Arnold emphasized the idea that the CIA and the Committee had had common interests:

> In working with groups like the C of C, it came down to the fact that we had the same goals, methods, techniques, and experience to do the same thing that the government wanted to see done for long-range United States policy.

Arnold attempted to soothe the feelings of the unwitting members of the Committee, explaining, 'You keep the circle of knowledgability as small as you can as long as you can.'

Members of the Committee argued over whether the Committee would be able to carry on and if it would be ethical to do so. In fact, without CIA support, funds quickly dried up. An emergency donation of $5,000 was made in 1967 by Committee member Jean Picker. The purpose of this donation was more to avoid the embarrassment of folding immediately after the revelations, rather than to ensure the long term future of the Committee. In February 1969 the Committee sent its last correspondence to its readers. Since many of the readers were still unaware of the CIA funding, the letter made no reference to the Agency and instead attributed its retirement to the huge growth in the number of concerned women and the variety and range of their interests. This, the letter argued, made it impossible for the Committee to continue in its pattern of person-to-person relationships.[39]

The last months of the Committee were fraught with tension and recriminations. The minutes of the July special meeting recorded, 'Someone said that some of the members of the Committee let the rest of them stick their neck out.' Rosemary Harris complained, 'we have set ourselves up as an example of what an organization that is private can do. We couldn't have done it without government help.' A statement in the files of the Committee went further in its expression of disapproval of the way in which the unwitting members of the Committee had been used. Its signatories, Eleanor Coit, Elizabeth Jackson and Alice Clark, wrote:

> It is not in keeping with our philosophy to have CIA funds used for an organization with a goal such as that of the Committee of Correspondence which was to strengthen the free world by encouraging citizen responsibility and democracy.[40]

The differences in outlook between the witting and unwitting members of the Committee mirror the important contradictions in the relationship between private groups and the public sector in Cold War America. While many of the unwitting members of the Committee felt that, if they were to retain any significance, the distinctions between private and public must be maintained, the witting members did not recognize any boundaries between the sectors. Amidst the confusion of the funding revelations in 1967, many commentators argued from the moral high ground, that the blurring of distinctions between the private, voluntary sphere and the realm of government was unacceptable and had caused irreparable damage to the American ideal of voluntarism. Covert CIA funding destroyed the strength of American voluntary organizations, which lay according to the *New York Times* in 'their freedom from government domination'.[41] Such distinctions were not always as clear-cut to members of the Committee since it was impossible to separate their public and private roles. The Committee worked through a combination of their own private contacts and liaison on various levels with the government. The first Annual Report of the Committee established that members of the Committee travelled extensively overseas on behalf of their own organizations. However, the report continued, 'On these trips, they have created new contacts and had the opportunity to sound out "correspondents" on their reaction to the work of the Committee'.[42] For example, Mrs Parsons had travelled to France, Germany and Italy in her role as the Chairwoman of the American branch of the International Council of Women, as well as touring in Japan, South-East Asia and the Middle East. On both occasions, Parsons provided the

Committee of Correspondence with detailed reports on the conditions in the country, the strength of communism and opportunities for the Committee. Other members of the Committee travelled, not as direct representatives of their organizations, but at the expense of the government as a result of that affiliation. For example, Anna Lord Strauss, head of the League of Women Voters, visited Japan, Burma, Indonesia and the Philippines under the auspices of the State Department's Leader Exchange program.

Liaison with various government agencies was common. All material produced by the Committee was made available to the US Information Agency, who awarded the Committee a Certificate of Merit in 1954 in recognition of its help in developing 'world understanding of American concepts and purposes'.[43] USIA Public Affairs Officers co-operated closely with the Committee, 26 of them sending in 'carefully selected' lists of women in their communities who the Committee should add to its mailing lists.[44] Minutes of a Committee meeting on 9 December 1958 recorded a discussion 'concerning sharing confidential information received from our correspondents with the US Department of State. There was a general agreement that this would be done'.[45]

To the witting members of the Committee, attempts to make distinction between their roles as private citizens and public servants were meaningless. Experience of voluntary work during World War II, together with the crisis atmosphere of the Cold War, made redundant the distinction between the individual as private citizen and as government employee. Working for America was the important thing, not squabbles over funding. The CIA's Donald Jameson explained in a television interview:

> It's hard, I think, for people, particularly of a younger generation, to understand the degree to which the Government and its activities had the confidence of its people. There was almost nobody that I couldn't go to in those days and say I'm from the CIA and I'd like to ask you about so-and-so and at the very least get a respectful reception and a discussion.[46]

Amid the bitter debates that ended the Committee, Rose Parsons felt the need to rescue this motivation from the more squalid arguments and recriminations. Somewhat pathetically, she reminded the Committee, 'It was important to remember that when this started it was a real emergency and there was a great need for this kind of program. We knew it would be impossible to raise money. We tend to forget now that it was a patriotic thing.'[47]

As experts in the field of women, the leaders of women's organizations were frequently called upon to lend their expertise to the government through co-operation in various projects. From the US government's point of view, the 'private' contacts of these women through their work in international women's organizations were invaluable. Few in the Government had any knowledge of international women's organizations. Arguably, few cared. Dorothy Bauman complained, 'It was amazing to me how little interest and how little knowledge our government had about women's effectiveness and certainly not abroad'.[48] It was probably something of a relief to be able to hand much of the responsibility for propaganda aimed at women to a competent, enthusiastic outside group. Thus the relationship between the government and the Committee was based on shared goals and an understanding by government that the members of the Committee were the experts in the field. A letter from the Dearborn Foundation stated:

> We believe the Committee has the stature and competence to propose and develop means by which American women can make a responsible, co-ordinated contribution to non-communist Women's organizations . . . We want to assist you in your program but feel you have the specialized and detailed knowledge not available to us, to provide the necessary leadership.[49]

It is clear that the members of the Committee who were aware of the source of their funding thought it unimportant. Connie Anderson, for example, argued there was little pressure from the CIA, 'Just a little bit, not very much . . . they told us some people to see and some people not to see in other lands. But that really amounted to very little. It was mostly our own selves'.[50] The witting members of the Committee did not subscribe to the doctrine that he who pays the piper calls the tune, rejecting the argument that inevitably direction and control came hand in hand with financial assistance. Evidence of the CIA's intervention in the running of the Committee is rare, although this may be because of the destruction of such evidence or of the failure to commit directions to paper. Connie Anderson asserted that control over the work of the Committee was exercised through personal meetings between her and two men who would visit her apartment once a month and 'talk about things, and what we should do and so on'. She insisted, however, that the control was of a limited nature, 'It was a simple thing, there was never any direction, there was just hearing about what we were doing rather than any direction on their part.'[51] Anne Crolius concurred, 'It was a good program and as far as I know there was no hanky-panky, no underhanded action, no influence on the Committee to do anything other than what it intended to do'.[52]

Some allowance must obviously be made for the willing suspension of reality on the part of these Committee members; no-one likes to think they are being used as a puppet. It is important to recognize, however, that the issue of funding is important in and of itself regardless of the level of control the CIA actually exercised. The fact that the CIA chose to fund the dissemination of information through the efforts of a 'private' group, rather than operating on their own, demonstrated the importance they placed upon the attachment of the 'private' tag on information.

By masquerading as a private organization, the Committee was able to present itself as living proof of the vitality of the voluntary organization in American life. As Louise Backus pointed out, the Committee wound up exploiting this ideal:

> We say we are an example and this is a democracy. You can have enough voluntary interests to carry the load. In other countries it is truly impossible for organizations to exist without government help. Now we discover that individual organizations just don't seem to be able to exist without government help.[53]

If it was, as Bauman, Anderson, Picker and others argued, unimportant that the money came from the CIA, why go to the trouble to hide it? Bauman claimed in her article 'Right or Wrong?' that

> From my observation, it would have made little difference to most participants had it been said that government funds were involved, for they were accustomed to having their own governments control most delegates to international meetings and provide transportation.[54]

In an oral history, however, Bauman was more realistic about the importance of being private. Jacqueline Van Voris, who wrote the official history of the Committee, asked her, 'Why did you not want to be identified with the government? Were you more effective?'. Bauman readily admitted, 'Oh much, yes...The moment you put the government's label on it that would have caused suspicion and resentment..I think it was the only way they could do things and it was so obvious that the communists controlled organizations, they were all underwritten by their government'.[55]

By presenting itself as a 'private' group the Committee was able to influence people who would have been hostile to governmental, 'public' propaganda. The Committee had quickly found how hostile many of its correspondents were to any suggestion of government propaganda. Rose Parsons, in her report to the Committee on Japan in 1954, had written of the Japanese people's fear of propaganda, describing how the Committee for Free Asia had offered Japanese women a free room for their meetings, 'which they had enjoyed very much and were most grateful for until they found that CFA propaganda was so exaggerated in favor of the US and against the USSR that they refused to meet there any more'.[56] Information from a 'private' group was 'purer' than that which was disseminated by a government.

Committee Bulletins were at pains to point out that the Communist women's organisations were funded by their government and therefore were mere mouthpieces of the Soviet government. A letter to correspondents from Rose Parsons (6 May 1953), about WIDF, detailed the position of its leaders and the Soviet bankrolling of the WIDF's propaganda campaign. Referring to the WIDF's call for a Congress of Women in Copenhagen, in June 1953, Parsons declared, 'The Committee of Correspondence feels very strongly that when a Congress is called in the name of all women in the world, women should be able to obtain accurate information as to the sponsorship, aims and purposes of that Congress'. Since, according to a WIDF bulletin, 'expenses for the delegates visits to Copenhagen are being provided', Parsons worried that 'many women, unaware of the Communist sponsorship of the "World Congress of Women" and of the tactics used to attract them there will no doubt be tempted to avail themselves of this opportunity to travel'.[57] The difference between this situation and the Committee's convening of a Conference of Women's Non-governmental Organizations in 1962, where delegates were paid travel and living expenses, lay entirely in the Committee's assumption of a double standard.

But if the Committee symbolized the infiltration of the public world into the private sphere, it was also an important example of the willingness of private groups to co-operate with the government. By the time the revelations of CIA funding were made in 1969, public hostility and suspicion towards government involvement in private groups were rife. CIA involvement could only be a bad thing, a threat to the 'free society'. Thus the editorial in *Ramparts* proclaimed moralistically:

> The spectre of CIA infiltration of domestic institutions – and the covert creation of co-ordinated leadership among them – must horrify those who regard unfettered debate as vital to representative democracy.[58]

However, in their attempt to vilify the shady agents of the CIA as instruments of corruption, such accounts fail to take into account the willingness of the private sector to be 'corrupted'. In her account of the activities of the Committee, 'Right or Wrong?', Bauman clearly implies that the acceptance of CIA funding was 'Right':

> With today's questioning of all of CIA's activities, it seems to me only fair to tell of one operation that was highly constructive and successful and where no overt pressure from the CIA was ever used on a group of competent, individualistic women.[59]

Bauman's argument is that, rather than being a corrupting influence in their private organization, the CIA merely facilitated what the group would have done anyway, given sufficient funds. Mrs Papanek, who had worked harder than any other member to secure private funding, concurred, telling the Committee that 'she couldn't understand why the exposure of the fact in *Ramparts* has made the CIA evil. We were asked to do a job we were considered fit for'.[60]

One-dimensional interpretations of the covert funding of private organizations which cast the CIA as the Machiavellian puppet-masters of simple-minded, if well-intentioned citizens overlook the willingness of these 'private citizens' to accept funding. The frustration of people such as Rose Parsons at the difficulties in opposing Soviet state-funded organizations with the meagre resources of the private sector was genuine. However, protestations of an 'uneven playing field' in terms of funding were disingenuous. Elizabeth Wadsworth, an unwitting member of the Committee, commented:

> You cannot do everything to give the impression that you don't take government money and take it. If it's important that you not take government money then you don't take it. If it's not important that you not take government money then take it. That's the point. It's not a question of whether you take government money or not. *It's whether you make an issue of it.* We did make an issue of it and then we took it. Dumb.[61]

Members of the Committee were not the unthinking lackies of the US government. The original motivation behind the Committee was a response by concerned, informed citizens to a perceived problem rather than an initiative by scheming Government officials. Many of the members of the Committee, far from working at the direction of the CIA, contributed their voluntary effort completely unaware of the source of their funding. In the end, however, covert government funding of the organization was a direct contradiction of the Committee's message of what voluntary, concerned women's organizations could achieve. The notion of an independent private sector in the US campaign against the Soviet Union was an illusion.

The lack of attention which the Committee received, both in 1967 and by subsequent historians, is a serious error. The funding of a women's organization by the CIA reveals the importance they attached to the growing network of international non-governmental organizations amongst women and their fear that such organizations would not be effectively reached by official channels of propaganda. Conversely, the willing participation of American women in such a programme, irrespective of their knowledge of the CIA's involvement, is an important example of the role of the private sector in America's Cold War.

NOTES

1. *Ramparts*, March 1967, p.38.
2. *New York Times*, 20 Feb. 1967, p.36.
3. Ibid. 16 Feb. 1967, p.26.
4. Metropolitan Editor, *New York Times*, to Committee of Correspondence, 17 Feb. 1967, Committee of Correspondence Papers, Sophia Smith Collection, Smith College, Northampton, Massachusetts (hereafter referred to as CoC Papers), Financial File, Unnumbered Box.
5. Rhodri Jeffreys-Jones, *The CIA and American Democracy* (New Haven, CT: Yale UP 1989) p.83.
6. Eisenhowever to Strauss, 24 May 1956, Anna Lord Strauss Papers, Schlesinger Library, Radcliffe College, Cambridge, Massachusetts, Box 9, File 182.
7. De Tocqueville asserted that the importance of voluntary associations to democratic life was such that 'if men living in democratic countries had no right and no inclination to associate for political purposes, their independence would be in great jeopardy' (Alexis de Tocqueville, *Democracy in America*, Vol.II, London 1862, p.130. Schlesinger argued that Americans, 'in mastering the associative way of life, have mastered the democratic way', and argued that the repression of voluntary associations by the axis powers was evidence of their importance in the maintenance of democracy (Arthur Schlesinger Sr, 'Biography of a Nation of Joiners', *American Historical Review* 50/1 (1944).
8. Oscar and Mary Handlin, *Dimensions of Liberty* (Cambridge, 1961) p.89.
9. Grant McConnell, 'The Public Values of the Private Association', in J. Roland Pennock and John W. Chapman (eds.) *Voluntary Associations* (NY: Atherton Press 1969) p.147.
10. Women's Affairs Branch Semi-Annual Report, 1 July 1949 – 31 Dec. 1949, Ruth Woodsmall Papers, Sophia Smith Library, Smith College, Northampton, MA, Box 51, File 7.
11. Women's International Democratic Federation open letter, 1952, Lena M. Phillips Papers, Schlesinger Library, Radcliffe College, Cambridge, MA (hereafter referred to as Phillips Papers), Carton 7.
12. Report of 1st meeting of Anonymous Committee, 16 April 1952, Phillips Papers, Carton 7.
13. Parsons to Phillips, 8 May 1952, Phillips Papers, Carton 7.
14. Comments and suggestions by Anne Hester, Phillips Papers, Carton 7.
15. Draft reply to WIDF, read at 2nd Meeting of Anonymous Committee, 20 May 1952, Phillips Papers, Carton 7.
16. Parsons reports at meeting of the Anonymous Committee, 22 Aug. 1952, Phillips Papers, Carton 7.
17. Parsons to Roosevelt, 19 June 1958, Records of the National Council of Women, Library of Congress, Washington DC, Microfiche 707.
18. Report of 1st meeting of the Anonymous Committee, 16 April 1952, Phillips Papers, Carton 7.
19. Oral history of Dorothy Bauman, CoC Papers, Box 54, File 888.
20. Other names that the Committee of Correspondence considered in its first year included Committee on Constructive Action, Blank Committee, and, referring to its work in countering Communist propaganda, the Wreckers Committee.
21. Personal views and recommendations of the Executive Director for the program and activities of the Committee of Correspondence, Phillips Papers, Carton 7.
22. Letter from Parsons, Mahon, and Bauman, 24 Nov. 1952, Phillips Papers, Carton 7.
23. Minutes of the Committee of Correspondence, Dec. 1952, Phillips Papers, Carton 7.
24. Ibid.
25. Committee of Correspondence Bulletin, 14 April 1953, Phillips Papers, Carton 7.
26. Hester to Phillips, undated, Phillips Papers, Carton 7.
27. Report of the Committee of Correspondence, 13 Aug. 1953, Phillips Papers, Carton 7.
28. Personal views and recommendations of the Executive Director for the program and activities of the Committee of Correspondence, 27 Aug. 1953, Phillips Papers, Carton 7.
29. Committee of Correspondence Bulletin, Feb. 1955, CoC Papers, Box 2, File 20.
30. It is not the intention of this essay to provide a comprehensive survey of the activities of the

Committee of Correspondence. For greater detail, see Jacqueline Van Voris, *The Committee of Correspondence – Women with a World Vision* (Northampton, MA: Interchange 1989).

31. Quoted in Van Voris, *The Committee of Correspondence.*
32. Oral history of Jean Picker and Harvey Picker, CoC Papers, Box 54, File 901.
33. 'Foundations which have supported the Committee of Correspondence', 1 March 1967, CoC Papers, Financial File.
34. *New York Times*, 21 Feb. 1967.
35. Crolius to Picker, 27 Feb. 1967, CoC Papers, Box 4, File 32.
36. Statement drawn up by Jean Picker, CoC Papers, Box 1, File 3.
37. Memorandum of meeting, 3 April 1967, CoC Papers, Financial File.
38. Notes on Special Board Meeting, 24 July 1967, CoC Papers, Financial File.
39. Letter to be sent to correspondents, Feb. 1969, CoC Papers, Box 1, File 3.
40. Statement by Coit, Jackson, and Clark, Dec. 1970, CoC Papers, Box 19, File 9.
41. Ibid.
42. Committee of Correspondence Annual Report, 1 March 1953 – 1 April 1954, Phillips Papers, Carton 4.
43. Streibert to Parsons, 16 April 1954, Phillips Papers, Carton 4.
44. Hester to Members of the Committee, 12 Aug. 1954, Phillips Papers, Carton 4.
45. Minutes of Meeting, 9 Dec. 1958, CoC Papers, Box 2, File 2.
46. Donald Jameson interview in Channel 4 Television, 'Hidden Hands: A Different History of Modernism' 1995.
47. Notes on Special Board Meeting, 24 July 1967, CoC Papers, Financial File.
48. Oral history of Dorothy Bauman, CoC Papers, Box 54, File 888.
49. Dearborn Foundation to Parsons, 7 March 1955, Phillips Papers, Carton 7.
50. Oral history of Connie Anderson, CoC Papers, Box 54, File 887.
51. Ibid.
52. Oral history of Anne Crolius, CoC Papers, Box 54, File 892.
53. Notes on Special Board Meeting, 24 July 1967, CoC Papers, Financial File.
54. Dorothy S. Bauman, 'Right or Wrong', CoC Papers, Box 54, File 890.
55. Oral history of Dorothy Bauman, CoC Papers, Box 54, File 888.
56. Rose Parsons, Report of a Trip, 28 Aug. – 6 Nov. 1953, Phillips Papers, Carton 7.
57. Parsons letter, 6 May 1953, Phillips Papers, Carton 4.
58. *Ramparts*, March 1967.
59. Dorothy Bauman, 'Right or Wrong?', Oct. 1974, CoC Papers, Box 54, File 890.
60. Notes on Special Board Meeting, 24 July 1967, CoC Papers, Financial File.
61. Oral history of Elizabeth Wadsworth, CoC Papers, Box 54, File 902 (author's italics added).

7

The CIA and the Soviet Threat:
The Politicization of Estimates, 1966–1977

LAWRENCE FREEDMAN

I

In January 1976, during the last weeks of the administration of President Gerald Ford, reports appeared in the press of an extraordinary exercise conducted by the US Intelligence community. In addition to the normal National Intelligence Estimate (NIE) covering Soviet offensive strategic nuclear forces, a second estimate had been commissioned from outside experts, known to have a hawkish disposition. The first, known as Team A, took a moderate view of Soviet capabilities and the second, Team B, took a much more alarmist view. The two teams were obliged to argue their case before the President's Foreign Intelligence Advisory Board, a body which had itself been set up to provide a distinctive view to that of the intelligence establishment. Senior figures in the outgoing administration made it clear that their sympathies were with Team B. The Director of Central Intelligence barely defended his own analysts.

For the intelligence professionals, and in particular the CIA, this dismal situation represented the culmination of institutional developments which had been set in motion right at the start of the Nixon administration, almost eight years earlier. Up to that point the civilian leadership of the Department of Defense had found CIA estimates congenial, not least because they contradicted what were seen to be the inherent tendency of military intelligence to exaggerate Soviet strategic capabilities. Since then the civilian leadership in the Pentagon had taken the view that the CIA was too biased in the other direction. In this they were supported by at least one leading defence analyst.[1] The debate focused on estimates of Soviet ICBM capabilities, and their implications for American policy on ballistic missile defence (BMD) and the Strategic Arms Limitation Talks (SALT).

Because of these policy connections, this article covers the period from the decision taken in November 1966 by the administration of President Lyndon B. Johnson to propose arms control negotiations to the Soviet Union and the end of the Ford administration in January 1977, by which time SALT had become a source of immense controversy within the United States. The debate on this estimating record was sustained after the Team B episode,[2] and then rumbled on until after the end of the Cold War.[3] The declassification of the relevant NIEs allows for a new evaluation of the performance of both the CIA and its critics.[4] This essay considers this particular issue, but only briefly. The main concern is with the relationship between the estimating process, strategic policy and the politicization of the intelligence community.

This study opens with a description of the position of the CIA within the estimating process by late 1966 and what can now be seen as a developing crisis over its highest priority estimates – those covering the strategic forces of the Soviet Union. The next section demonstrates the importance of this estimate in the context of the developing debate over strategic arms control which gathered pace as the negotiations proceeded and the first agreements were signed with the Soviet Union in May 1972 and then implemented. I then demonstrate the various ways in which opponents of SALT sought to discredit and marginalize the CIA. The final section assesses the performance of the CIA in the light of the charges then made against it and the pressures to which it was subjected.

II

The start of our period finds the CIA in a strong position. At this time the estimating process was following well established lines. In addition to the CIA, it involved the Defense Intelligence Agency (DIA), the agencies of three armed services, the State Department's Bureau of Intelligence and Research (INR) and the National Security Agency (NSA). The responsibility for producing estimates rested with the Board of the Office of National Estimates (ONE), a relatively small and coherent group of intelligence professionals, supplemented by retired military officers, diplomats and academics, backed by about 50 professional staff, and accountable to the Director of Central Intelligence (DCI). In late 1966 the chairman of the Board was Sherman Kent, in the last year of his 16 year tenure.[5] He served a new DCI, Richard Helms, who had just taken over from the unfortunate Vice Admiral William F. Raborn Jr. The final approval to an estimate would be given by the US Intelligence Board (USIB) on which all the agencies were represented.

Around 50 National Intelligence Estimates (NIEs) were produced each year. Some were urgent responses to developing crises: others, including those in Soviet strategic forces, were routine and followed an annual cycle. Those dealing with the Soviet Union were the NIE-11 series, with the estimate of Soviet strategic defence and offensive forces NIE-11-3 and NIE-11-8 respectively. The estimating process involved a request for studies from all parts of the intelligence community, a collating process undertaken by ONE which would produce a draft estimate ready to be submitted to the various agencies for review. This draft would not be a loosely organized composite but would be tightly argued and take a clear position. This would then be subject to an inter-agency review, chaired by a member of the Board of National Estimates, which would go through the draft in great detail to produce an agreed document. The skill of the drafters would be in using style and structure to manage areas of difference. Where no agreement could be reached, a dissenting agency could footnote a page of the estimate explaining why it disagreed with a particular passage. After being approved by the USIB it would be sent to the National Security Council.[6]

For our purposes the important feature of this estimating process was that it favoured the CIA.[7] Although ONE was notionally separate from the CIA it shared the same offices in Langley, Virginia and often recruited from the CIA. There was mutual respect between the staffs and they tended to reinforce each others' views. In the estimates on Soviet strategic forces, ONE had a long-standing distrust of military estimators. They were fortified in this belief by the fact that it was shared by the most substantial figure in the defence establishment – Secretary of Defense Robert S. McNamara.[8] Although McNamara had set up the DIA to reduce the influence of the individual military agencies, he had become disillusioned with the continuous promotion of what he considered to be exaggerated claims about Soviet potential. The DIA faced problems in establishing itself in the career aspirations of military officers, while the individual service agencies were left depleted, and even reduced in status to non-voting members of the USIB.

McNamara had been through a searing experience with Vietnam and, belatedly, had come to rely on the CIA which had been consistently more sceptical on the state of the war.[9] This recent experience combined with the earlier experience of the 'missile gap' saga of the late 1950s when Air Force intelligence in particular had argued vigorously but erroneously that the Soviet missile programme was ahead of that of the United States.[10] John F. Kennedy had campaigned for President denouncing the dire state of the nation's defences only to discover in office that the strategic balance was moving positively in America's direction. One reason for confidence in the optimistic presentations of the strategic balance was that from 1961 the United States began to receive high-quality imagery from reconnaissance satellites. These removed critical uncertainties as to what was going on within the Soviet Union. Given the size and secrecy of the Soviet Union there had been no other source of reliable information, especially since the downing of a U-2 reconnaissance aircraft in May 1960.

For the first half of the 1960s there seemed to be every reason to adopt a sanguine perspective on Soviet strategic strength. NIE-11-8-64, for example, took the view that Moscow was concentrating on its overall deterrence position rather attempting a 'rapid numerical buildup'. The Soviet Union was not believed to be attempting to match 'the US in numbers of intercontinental delivery vehicles', for reasons both of cost and the anticipated American response, and nor was it attempting to develop a first-strike capability.[11]

In April 1965 McNamara reflected the optimistic perspective on Soviet intentions in an interview when he claimed, with regard to strategic nuclear forces, that 'the Soviets have decided that they have lost the quantitative race, and they are not seeking to engage us in that contest.'[12] However, a few weeks later the intelligence community began to reconsider the pace of ICBM deployment. The estimate for mid-1966 had been raised from 285–320 ICBMs to 350–400. Moreover some of the silos spotted under construction appeared to be for a new missile, yet to be test-fired. The speed with which this was being brought into service 'could stem from a desire to reach a planned ICBM force level more quickly than would otherwise be possible'.[13]

By now the estimators were prepared to admit the possibility of an attempt at parity, albeit at the top end of the range for 1975 of between 500 and 1,000 ICBMs. The issue was one of priorities. The lower end of the range meant a concentration on high-quality, large 25-megaton SS-9, which was just becoming operational; the higher end would involve the much smaller and less capable one-megaton SS-11, which was still being tested. For this reason DIA took the unusual step of dissenting from the NIE by claiming that it was exaggerating the likely number of Soviet ICBMs in 1970 and 1975. This was because the main issue now was the composition of the Soviet missile force, and the DIA was expecting a much greater emphasis to be given to the SS-9.[14]

By the summer of 1966 this had become the basis of the Pentagon appreciation of what was clearly a Soviet build-up in all areas of military capability. By the end of that year, and the start of our period, it was evident that deployment of both the SS-11 and the SS-9 was proceeding apace. That summer the Soviets had been seen to have 250 ICBMs; by the end of the year it had risen to 340, and construction work indicated to the Americans that these numbers were set to double to 670–765 ICBMs by mid-1968. It was now apparent that SS-11s were being introduced at a faster pace than SS-9s. It appeared that Moscow was determined, at the least, to achieve numerical parity with the United States, which was then reaching its plateau of 1054 ICBMs.[15] The NIE considered the possibility of a combined offensive and defensive force sufficient to achieve a first strike capability but concluded that it would not be feasible for it to achieve by the mid-1970s 'strategic capabilities that would make rational the deliberate initiation of general war'. A force of 800–1,100 operational launchers was now estimate for mid-1971. This would rise only to 800–1,200 by mid-1976, except by this time it was assumed that the second-generation SS-7 and SS-8 missiles, numbering around 210, would have been dismantled.[16]

The major divisions at this time, however, were not over the future of the Soviet ICBM force but over its defensive aspirations. It had been known for some time that the Soviet Union took strategic defences, against both air and missile attack, far more seriously than did the United States. From early 1965 construction work at what appeared to be an anti-ballistic missile (ABM) system to protect the Moscow area picked up after a period of modest and occasional activity. The NIE at the end of that year confirmed that the Russians were starting to deploy an ABM system in earnest. Construction accelerated again during the second half of 1966, so that full operational capability appeared likely by 1970.[17]

For reasons discussed below this development was troublesome to McNamara. Nonetheless he could be comforted by the general assessment that the system being deployed, codenamed 'Galosh' in Washington, was relatively mediocre and would not be difficult for American missiles to penetrate. Against this had to be weighed the possibility that another system with apparently nationwide coverage was being deployed. This was known as the 'Tallinn Line' after the Estonian capital where the system was first observed. In 1963 the consensus had been that this was an ABM system but then the CIA began to have doubts. By the 1964 NIE it was being suggested that the primary mission might be either air or missile defence. By 1966 the CIA was convinced that it was the former rather than the latter and this was reflected in the NIE. This was by no means a unanimous view. DIA, along with Army and Air Force intelligence, argued that 'on balance ... they believe it is more likely that the systems being deployed are for defense against ballistic missiles with an additional capability to defend against high flying supersonic aerodynamic vehicles.'[18] The argument continued for some time thereafter.

McNamara went public on the Soviet ABM activity at a news conference in November 1966.[19] The timing was critical because at this time he was engaged in a fierce debate with the Joint Chiefs of Staff over his unwillingness to sanction an American ABM system, despite the fact that one had been under development for some time and was now considered by its advocates to be ripe for deployment.[20]

IV

The argument over ABM deployment went to the heart of a developing strategic debate which dominated American policy-making for the subsequent two decades. It was a debate from which the intelligence community could not escape because it turned on the question of whether the two superpowers were driven by the same logic in their search for a stable nuclear deterrent, as McNamara believed, or whether the two were influenced by quite distinct strategic concepts which were likely to be reflected not only in their emerging force structures but also in their behaviour at times of crisis, which was the view of his opponents. The intensity of the debate was in part due to the fact that, in important respects, both views were correct. McNamara may have been correct in broad terms about the logic of mutual deterrence, and this may have therefore served as a satisfactory basis for American policy, but the Soviet strategic view of the time was undoubtedly different and it took many years before they were persuaded of the McNamara line – by which time, of course, American views had changed substantially.

The rigorous, systematic nature of McNamara's view of deterrence, captured by the concept of 'mutual assured destruction',[21] provided a template against which all other positions came to be judged. It had not been his initial position at the Pentagon. For a while he had been convinced that mass destruction might be avoided in the event of war through a concentration on military targets, but he soon realised that neither side was able to prevent the destruction of the other in war. He set about making a virtue out of a cruel necessity. To assure destruction of the enemy meant being able to destroy a sizeable portion of its population and industry even after absorbing a surprise first strike. It was best that this was made absolutely clear to Moscow because then it would be reluctant to attempt a first strike. Equally he was ready to acknowledge that the United States was also obliged to be cautious because of the Soviet ability to assure its destruction.

This did not mean that a nuclear war would have been fought in this way, although the attempts to devise alternative and less cataclysmic types of nuclear attacks did not meet with great success. The value of the concept was that it reduced the risks that either side might take chances with deterrence but also, and for McNamara this was very important, it provided a criterion against which to evaluate the sufficiency of strategic forces. So long as American forces could assure destruction in the face of all conceivable improvements in Soviet strategic forces then there was no need to purchase excess capacity. This was the origin of concepts such as the 'greater-than-expected-threat'. This was not, as has been supposed, a device to exaggerate Soviet strength to trigger an equally exaggerated American response, but more a means of demonstrating that the United States could cope with the maximum conceivable Soviet threat.[22]

The logic of assured destruction was that an offensive missile attack would always get through. In principle this logic could be undermined by two types of development. The first would be the design of an attack that would destroy the other side's retaliatory capability, with urban areas left at the mercy of forces still held in reserve. Since the introduction of ballistic-missile carrying submarines (SSBNs) in the early 1960s a first-strike of this nature had seemed extremely unlikely. Nonetheless, there were concerns that air and missile bases could become vulnerable as accuracies improved, and this was the danger which was believed to be raised by the large Soviet SS-9 ICBM.

An attack on bombers and ICBMs would only make sense if the retaliatory threat posed by any escaping weapons, and the relatively invulnerable submarine-launched ballistic missiles (SLBMs), could be handled by a defensive system. Hence the importance of ABMs. A serious breakthrough in this area could undermine the other side's confidence in its assured destruction capacity. The problem with an ABM system, as well as with civil defence, was that it could readily be overwhelmed. The cost of adding extra offensive capability seemed to be far less than that of adding extra defensive capability. The defence could be blinded by dedicated attacks on its radars or spoofed by decoys and chaff released by incoming missiles. McNamara had particular reason to be confident in the ascendancy of the offense in 1966 because of the development of techniques for greatly increasing the number of actual warheads a defence would face by means of multiple independently-targetable re-entry vehicles (MIRVs).

To McNamara therefore ABMs were a waste of money. They would reduce security rather than enhance it as any deployment would probably trigger offensive counter-deployments by the other side. His problem was that the Soviet Union did not seem to be as satisfied as he was with the level of capability attained by the United States by the mid-1960s. He blamed himself in part for this, wondering whether if he had not encouraged the build-up of American ICBMs during the first half of the 1960s the Soviet Union would not have been so determined to catch up during the second half. However, he also had to accept that Moscow did not share his distaste for ABMs but seemed to be investing in them – mightily according to those who believed that the Tallinn Line was also an ABM system – to the point where continued American restraint appeared to be conceding a strategic advantage to the Russians.

This debate gathered steam through 1966. To the Joint Chiefs of Staff this became symbolic of all their frustrations with McNamara and his 'whizz-kid' systems analysts and his cavalier disregard for military judgements. In the summer of 1966 the Chiefs agreed to maintain a united front in pressing their demands on McNamara, a concordat which was reflected immediately in debates in the intelligence community, and they put a nationwide ABM system at the top of their list.

The issue came to a head in November 1966 as President Johnson hosted the Chiefs and McNamara at his Texas ranch to sort out the next year's budget. One part of McNamara's response was not controversial. He gained approval for the development of a MIRVed ICBM (Minuteman III) and SLBM (Poseidon) to defeat the Soviet ABM.[23] On the question of ABMs he won from Johnson a reprieve before he was obliged to deploy. Johnson would offer the Soviet Union talks to see if they could agree on mutual restraint. This he duly did in his State of the Union message in February 1967. To McNamara's frustration the Soviet Union (still possibly in ignorance of MIRVs) did not respond. In June 1967 he harangued a bemused Alexei Kosygin on the futility of ABMs when the Soviet premier met Johnson at Glassboro'. Kosygin, who had seen himself as something of a dove because of his preference for defensive weapons as against offensive, was appalled by McNamara's grim logic.[24] It was only the next year that Moscow began to appreciate his analysis, slowed down ABM construction,[25] and agreed to SALT. By then McNamara had left government, his valedictory speech on strategic arms taken up with a painful combination of a warning about how arms races can develop their own 'mad momentum' with an announcement that approval had been given for a 'thin' ABM system designed, somewhat unconvincingly, to defend the United States against a Chinese attack. The two sides moved towards talks, only for the exercise to be aborted at the last minute by the August 1968 Soviet invasion of Czechoslovakia.[26] It took over a year before the talks could get going in earnest with the new administration of Richard M. Nixon.

V

In the short-term this debate strengthened the CIA's position in the estimating process. With McNamara's encouragement it developed an Office of Strategic Research (OSR) in 1967 to strengthen its technical competence when debating strategic forces with the Pentagon agencies. This did not last long. With the arrival of the Nixon administration the CIA along with ONE soon found themselves exposed and beleaguered. One can surmise that its position would have eventually come under some pressure even if Hubert Humphrey had won the 1968 Presidential election instead of Richard Nixon. It has been argued that its position had been steadily weakening since its failure to anticipate the secret delivery of Soviet missiles to Cuba in 1962, and later estimates on Vietnam. The evidence for this is scant, but it was in something of an institutional rut.[27]

Even with the protection of a more sympathetic administration, the increasingly polarized debate would have led to the CIA's positions being subjected to increasing scrutiny. In this it would not have been helped by the fact that Moscow appeared to have embarked upon an expansion of its strategic capability that belied the presumption of mutual restraint. At the end of 1968, for example, the best guess was that the Soviet ICBM force would tail off at around 1,200 launchers, although it could reach as high as 1,500. This still assumed that the second-generation missiles would be removed, though this had yet to happen.[28] A year later a force of around 1,400 missiles was already under construction and ONE had abandoned all attempts to 'estimate the maximum size it might reach'.[29] This required some explaining.

What made the past error particularly awkward in 1969 was that the debate on ABMs had suddenly intensified, with Congress now actively involved, and it appeared to turn on the credibility of alternative estimates on Soviet strategic forces. The Johnson administration never really made a serious effort to justify its ABM programme by reference either to the Soviet or Chinese threats and an attempt to do so could well have caused dissension within the intelligence ranks. In the light of apparent Soviet second thoughts about its own system and presuming an earlier start to SALT (Johnson had even been tempted to get a quick agreement during the last months of his Presidency) the programme, known as 'Sentinel', might well have been abandoned. As it was the Nixon administration found itself with an awkward inheritance, as citizen groups sprang up to protest against the imminent deployment of major ABM installations in their vicinity, and indicated that they at least were more worried that the ABMs would draw fire than confident that incoming attack would be successfully deflected. The Nixon administration could not bring itself to abandon a programme that Republicans had argued for so vehemently, but it did reorient it. In doing so it took care not to challenge directly the doctrine of assured destruction, for though its programme, now known as 'Safeguard', was designed to defend against a Soviet attack, only Minuteman sites were to be protected and not American cities.[30]

This may have made domestic political sense, was more wasteful than provocative in strategic terms, and could be justified diplomatically as strengthening the American position in the imminent SALT negotiations. However, it was still difficult to rationalize on its own terms. The argument was that without 'Safeguard', Minuteman would become vulnerable to a surprise first strike. Initially the new Secretary of Defense Melvin Laird even tried to claim that a strike against American ICBMs might be combined with one against SLBMs based on a breakthrough in anti-submarine warfare techniques, but this line had to be abandoned as the US Navy insisted that this was pure fantasy.[31]

This left the question of why it would matter if one or even two arms of the US strategic triad (of bombers, ICBMs and SLBMs) were eliminated so long as one remained intact, capable of launching a devastating retaliation. A simple answer – to the effect that it had long been American policy to maintain a degree of survivability in each separate arm of the triad might have sufficed. McNamara had authorized a study (STRAT X) in 1966 which was published in June the next year precisely to consider the question of how to cope with ICBM vulnerability in the future and a case had been made that it was better to have a survivable ICBM force than not, even though the enemy's destruction could still be assured without one.[32]

Eventually the administration latched onto a specious, though widely supported, scenario according to which after being disarmed of ICBMs an American president would be left with no other option but to launch a counter-city attack using SLBMs in the full knowledge that this would result in retaliation in kind against the United States. The problem with this scenario was that it understated the carnage that would result from an attack solely targeted against missiles and bombers, which would not be experienced as confined to military targets, the range of options that would still be available in terms of retaliation, and the difficulty that would be faced in eventually designing a truly invulnerable ICBM force.

Many of these problems were for later. For example, the intractability of the problem of ICBM vulnerability was illustrated by the tortured history of the search for a basing mode for the M-X missile during the Carter and Reagan administrations. In the first instance the critics did not ask why it mattered if one arm of the triad should become vulnerable but contented themselves with demonstrating that either it was not going to become vulnerable or else, if it did, then the 'Safeguard' programme would be unable to cope. The charge was that the threat was being tailored to fit the weapon system: if it had been too little then no ABM would be needed but if it was too large then the projected ABM would not be able to cope.

This debate ensured that a sharp light was cast on the intelligence community's view of what the Soviet Union was up to. The most important questions concerned the SS-9. It could carry three warheads, and the questions were whether they could manage the correct footprint to destroy three Minuteman ICBM silos, and then whether sufficient numbers of these were likely to be built to warrant substantial American expenditure on ballistic missile defences. During 1969 the differing perspectives on this issue were ventilated before the Senate Foreign Relations Committee[33] and were the subject of a special working group in the National Security Council staff, which in retrospect can be seen as the beginning of the end for the established estimates process.[34]

Behind this particular issue was a more general problem of Soviet objectives. As the ABM debate gathered pace the United States was also preparing to open discussions on strategic arms limitations. These talks had been inspired in the first place by presumptions that both sides could recognize an equivalent stake in the stability resulting from the condition of mutual assured destruction (MAD). What if the Soviet Union did not understand MAD in the same way as did the United States but was convinced that there were still meaningful forms of nuclear superiority to be had and it was determined to have them? The readiness to build up offensive weapons so rapidly (now also including submarine-launched ballistic missiles) indicated that, at the very least, Moscow had a quite distinctive strategic perspective.

For these reasons the 1969 NIE was unusually controversial and difficult. The previous year's estimate had reported test-firings of the SS-9 triplet in the late summer of 1968. Although these were compatible with an attempt to obtain a MIRV capability, early deployment would mean degradation in overall accuracy and reliability. A MIRV system capable of attacking hard targets would not be available until 1972.[35] This view was repeated in the text in the 1969 NIE, with the initial operational capability for a hard-target MIRV now seen as between 1972 and the mid-1970s. The SS-9 tests had not shown independent guidance, and the system seemed best explained as a copy of the US Polaris A-3 warhead and a response to possible American ABM developments. Although deletions do not make this wholly clear the case for a more capable MIRV rested largely on the Soviet Union being able to vary the pattern of impact of the SS-9 to match the standard footprint of Minuteman deployment. The sceptics argued a hard-target capability could not be readily projected from what had been seen so far. All the Pentagon agencies claimed that an intention to develop this capability was evident, given the yield of the individual re-entry vehicles and the attempts to reduce the degradation of accuracy consequent on the move to this new system.[36]

The controversy was now extending into the overall objectives of the Soviet programme. In a discussion of Soviet military policy a year earlier several uncertainties in estimating Soviet strength had been noted. Moscow attached great importance to attaining parity with the United States but it was by no means clear how they defined parity. The possibility that it might seek 'strategic superiority of such an order that it could be translated into significant political gain' was dismissed, as it had been before, on the grounds of the economic burden involved and the likelihood of an American response.[37]

In drafting the NIE 11-8-69, the Board of National Estimates had inserted a paragraph consistent with this previous judgement, arguing that 'the Soviets recognize the enormous difficulties of any attempt to achieve strategic superiority of such an order as to significantly alter the strategic balance' and that it was therefore 'unlikely that they will attempt ... to achieve a first strike capability'. Because this contradicted the public position of Melvin Laird, the Pentagon demanded that this paragraph be removed despite being cleared by the inter-agency review. Richard Helms, the DCI, complied. In the event, the State Department reintroduced the text as a dissent, while the Air Force (unusually in combination with the NSA) noted that it was 'more likely than not that the Soviets are seeking some measure of superiority'.[38]

V

In the event the administration's threat assessment did not sustain the 'Safeguard' system. Nixon and Kissinger effectively determined that McNamara's initial call had been correct and that arms control was a more effective way of dealing with the problem. The strategic arms agreement signed by Presidents Richard Nixon and Leonid Brezhnev in May 1972 contained a Treaty which severely limited ABM systems and a five-year interim agreement on offensive arms which capped the number of ICBMs that the Soviet Union could deploy to 1,400. This limit, it was hoped, would also reduce Washington's concerns about the vulnerability of the American Minuteman force. This was also now frozen at its established level of 1,000 systems but with no restraints on MIRVing.

Much to the irritation of Congressional hawks, the administration justified the SALT accords by using exaggerated assessments of the level of Soviet capability that might have emerged had no cap been imposed. This led to the Jackson Amendment (after Senator Henry Jackson) which insisted that future treaties must be based on equality in systems between the two superpowers.[39] The main problem for the administration, however, was that having raised the bogey of ICBM vulnerability it could not bury it. This was especially true given its failure even to pursue limits on MIRVs in SALT. The agreements removed the option of anything more than a marginal ABM defence of ICBMs, yet had not cut off the Soviet threat because of the options that opened up for the Soviet Union once it put multiple warheads on its ICBM force, which was much more substantial in terms of both overall numbers and individual capacity.

While the accuracy of the SS-9 triplet came to be played down, in early 1974 the Pentagon warned that a whole series of new generation Soviet ICBMs were about to be deployed and at least some of these would be

MIRVed. The awkward issue this posed for the administration was aggravated as a result of the evidence that the Soviet Union had exploited the drafting of the agreement on offensive arms to maximize the size of its new force. Soon these particular issues of strategic arms became intermingled with a more general debate on Soviet foreign policy, and what appeared to be an attempt to assert its position in sensitive areas of the Third World despite the claims made by both sides on the virtues of detente. All this encouraged those who believed that the Soviet Union had never taken detente seriously but was using the high-level summits and the wide range of negotiations to encourage the United States to lower its guard while it continued to strengthen its own position. The coincidence of a more confident Soviet foreign policy with an apparent ascendancy in the arms race was used to suggest that Moscow did indeed believe that a lead in the strategic arms race translated into a favourable 'correlation of forces' that could in turn be used for great political effect in those parts of the world where the two superpowers still competed for influence.

Those inside and outside government who believed that detente still had value, and that arms control was worth pursuing, argued that whatever Moscow might want to achieve by way of strategic superiority and global power there were still inherent limits on what it could achieve in practice. In retrospect this view seems correct. However at the time it relied on analysts in Washington having a more realistic appreciation of the Soviet Union's strategic prospects than those in Moscow, and it could still not eliminate the troubling thought that a Soviet Union straining against the limits could be almost as dangerous for international security as one able to transcend these limits with ease.[40]

This argument was felt in the debates over Soviet strategic capabilities. By and large the CIA and the State Department stressed the sources of caution in Soviet strategic doctrine and foreign policy while the Pentagon-based agencies insisted that the evidence pointed to much greater risk-taking propensities.

VI

This issue was at the heart of a fierce debate over what had been the centrepiece of American foreign policy during the two Republican administrations. By the end of his term in office President Ford dare not utter the word 'detente' and had to ask his Secretary of State, Dr Henry Kissinger, not to attempt to complete a new strategic arms limitation treaty. After his successes with SALT in 1972, Kissinger had found himself fighting a rearguard battle in his efforts to sustain a more moderate view of the threat.

Part of his problem was the weakness of those parts of the intelligence community that might have been able to support him in this struggle. For this he had himself to blame. As he set about securing his own supreme position in the foreign policy establishment during Nixon's first term he sought to marginalize and fragment potential bureaucratic opponents. The Board of National Estimates (BNE) was a natural target. An agreed NIE, emanating from an elite Ivy League group beyond his control, was inimical to his wider purposes. He critiqued the estimates for their convoluted judgements and for seeking to gloss over rather than expose divergent views. He was not alone among policy makers in feeling that he was being told what the intelligence professional could agree upon rather than what he wanted to know.[41] He pressed for the estimates to be stronger on raw data and more transparent on areas of disagreement. The inevitable result of this was that the considered judgements of the intelligence professionals counted for less and the policy-making clients were able to assess the material according to their own prejudices and predilections. This dispute took place against the backdrop of Congressional disquiet at revelations which cast doubt on the overall management of the CIA, especially its covert operations.[42]

Nor was there any shortage of willing challengers to the BNE from within the intelligence community. By the end of 1969 the Pentagon had already decided to use its own estimates of Soviet strategic forces rather than the NIEs. The classified version of Melvin Laird's posture statement of 1970 contained DIA figures. The NIEs themselves had been subjected to critical, largely conservative, scrutiny by the President's Foreign Intelligence Advisory Board (PFIAB)[43] set up during the great controversy of 1969. By the start of Nixon's second term the BNE had few friends. The new DCI was James Schlesinger, who while still at the RAND Corporation in 1971 had conducted a scathing review of the estimating process. He set in motion reforms which were picked up by his successor, William Colby, when Schlesinger was moved to the Pentagon after a few months in office. Colby accepted that BNE did not have much of a future given Kissinger's dislike of its agreed, compromise estimates.[44] With the resignation of its Chairman, John Huizenga, in October 1973, it was dissolved. Under the new National Intelligence Officer (NIO) system, individual, senior analysts prepared the estimates which were reviewed by the USIB. The NIOs themselves tended still to rely on the CIA for their analytical support, but found their time taken up with managing an estimating process that was becoming much more haphazard. The influence of the NIEs declined further as a result.[45]

Because of the continuity in mainstream CIA perspectives in the NIE drafts, the new system still did not satisfy the critics. When the Rockefeller

Commission reviewed PFIAB in 1975 it urged that it played an even greater role in assessing the quality of foreign intelligence and estimates.[46] In 1975 the Chairman of PFIAB, George Anderson Jr wrote to Ford advising a 'competitive analysis of the intelligence on Soviet intentions and capabilities.' Colby argued the wisdom of waiting to see how the 1975 NIE looked. This was agreed but the critics were still not satisfied and the call for a competitive estimate was renewed.

When Colby was replaced as DCI in November 1975 by George Bush the estimators were left even more exposed. Bush saw his job in a largely political light and was more inclined to accept the demands for a competitive estimate. Also the Pentagon was now pushing hard for such a move, led by Robert Ellsworth, a new assistant secretary for intelligence.[47] So it was that a 'Team B' was established to provide an alternative view to the NIE-11-76, which was produced by Howard Stoertz, a senior analyst with long experience on the Soviet estimates. The composition of Team B was agreed following discussions between Bush and William Hyland, Deputy Assistant for National Security Affairs.[48] Its members were chosen from the right and could boast formidable academic, military and intelligence experience. Several investigations of technical issues were sponsored, including the accuracy of Soviet missiles, and the team offered a general overview. The results of their deliberations were as predictable as they were opinionated.

This was not a straightforward competition as the two teams were playing different games. Team A's estimate covered future Soviet capabilities, but, as was normal in NIEs, it was heavily footnoted and contained contrary opinions not dissimilar to those developed in the Team B Report.[49] By contrast there was no dissent or refutation allowed for in the Team B Report. Moreover this was not so much an alternative estimate as a critique of the performance of the intelligence community over the previous decade. Its concern was less with the detail of Soviet capabilities, though it certainly had points to make here, and more with the assessment of the Soviet attitudes to overall nuclear strategy. The two estimates did not engage.

The central charge made by Team B, that the estimates had underestimated the Soviet strategic build-up of the 1960s, had already been made in articles by Albert Wohlstetter, then a leading figure in the American strategic studies community.[50] Team B took the Wohlstetter analysis a stage further, arguing that the failure of the estimators could be traced to a misappreciation of Soviet doctrine born out of a reluctance to acknowledge the truly menacing nature of this doctrine.[51]

The basic failure was to concentrate on so-called hard data which it then interpreted 'in a manner reflecting basic US concepts while slighting or misinterpreting the large body of "soft" data concerning Soviet strategic concepts.' A basic source of misinterpretation they claimed, was 'mirror-imaging' – that is assuming that Soviet decision-makers would behave as if they were American acting under analogous circumstances, and that, as in the American view, nuclear war was seen 'as an act of mutual suicide that can be rational only as a deterrent threat.' Rather:

> The NIEs' focus on the threat of massive nuclear war with the attendant destruction and ignore the political utility of nuclear forces in assuming compliance with Soviet will; they ignore the fact that by eliminating the political credibility of the US strategic deterrent, the Soviets seek to create an environment in which other instruments of their grand strategy, including overwhelming regional dominance in conventional arms can be brought to bear; they fail to acknowledge that the Soviets believe that the best way to paralyze US strategic capabilities is by assuring that the outcome of any nuclear exchange will be as favorable to the Soviet Union as possible; and, finally they ignore the possibility that the Russians seriously believe that if, for whatever reason, deterrence were to fail, they could resort to the use of nuclear weapons to fight and win a war. *The NIEs' tendency to view deterrence as an alternative to a war-fighting capability rather than as complementary to it,* is in the opinion of Team 'B', a grave and dangerous flaw in their evaluations of Soviet strategic objectives.[52]

The flaws in the estimates were put down to political pressures in favour of detente, strategic arms negotiations, as well as being too aware of the policy issues at stake in individual estimates.

The two cases were argued in front of the PFIAB, and although reports vary there does not appear to have been a great meeting of minds. In practical terms the episode had few consequences. The new administration of Jimmy Carter did not adopt the Team B perspective, and the PFIAB itself was soon disbanded. Some members of Team B provided the nucleus of the Committee on the Present Danger, a group which lobbied against the strategic arms limitation talks, and became a thorn in the side of the Carter administration.[53] Their moment of greatest influence came later when some of the team moved on to influential positions in the Reagan administration.

VI

In retrospect also the numerical error in the estimates of Soviet ICBM construction during the 1960s was of moderate importance strategically, although it was undoubtedly important politically, largely because of the high salience of crude comparisons of missiles. The SS-9 was assessed correctly in both quantitative and qualitative terms, in that it never became a hard-target killer. SS-11 numbers were underestimated as was the durability of the second-generation ICBMs, but this was hardly the basis for a first-strike threat.

It is also evident that Soviet plans in the late 1960s were increasingly influenced by new developments such as the American ABM and MIRV programmes and the promise of arms control negotiations. The patterns of influence were not of the mechanical sort suggested by a simple arms race model but that does not mean to say that they were absent.

Problems did arise as a result of the estimators using American criteria, such as assured destruction and damage limitation capabilities, when assessing Soviet forces. These must have been misleading because they did not reflect categories in use in Moscow. It probably was the case that there was a lack of appreciation of Soviet strategic thinking, its respect for raw indicators of strength and presumption that these could make all the difference to security and political influence.

On the other hand this doctrine was clearly misconceived. Team B may have had a better feel for Soviet strategic thinking but they suspended their critical faculties when it came to assessing its validity and feasibility. Team B criticized the notion that 'Soviet doctrine is primarily exhortative in character and possess little of any operational significance.'[54] In retrospect much Soviet doctrine does seem to have had exactly this exhortative character. While it may well have been the case that the CIA, and the rest of the US defence establishment, had assumed too readily that Soviet strategic practice would follow that of the United States, in their own way Team B were also imposing an American framework in an attempt to understand Soviet behaviour. The difference in this case was that the perspective was more conservative, informed by a keen sense of American vulnerabilities. Team B raised important questions on Soviet doctrine and objectives but did not provide an answer of any sophistication.[55] It is also quite unfair to suggest that the CIA did not produce studies of Soviet strategic thinking.[56]

At the time the importance of the episode was mainly to confirm the loss of authority of the national estimates on the most crucial question they were asked to address. This loss had begun with the Nixon administration in 1969 and gathered pace in the subsequent years. It had been reflected in a continual challenge to the validity of the NIEs on Soviet strategic forces from the Pentagon and combined with an assault on the estimating process itself, including the disbanding of the Office of National Estimates in 1973 after almost a quarter of a century of service. The problem was that a fragmented intelligence community was struggling to produce an estimate that was subject to inherent uncertainties at a time when great political issues appeared to turn on its content. If the community had been more coherent, if the evidence had been more sure, then the intelligence professionals might have been able to exercise more influence even when the issues were more than trivial.

NOTES

1. Albert Wohlstetter, 'Is there a Strategic arms Race?', *Foreign Policy*, No. 15 (Summer 1974); idem, 'Rivals but no "race"', ibid. No.16 (Fall 1974); idem, 'Optimal Ways to Confuse Ourselves, *Foreign Policy*, No.20 (Fall 1975). For an early critique see Michael Nacht, 'The Delicate Balance of Error,' ibid. No.19 (Summer 1975).
2. Lawrence Freedman, *US Intelligence and the Soviet Strategic Threat* (London: Macmillan 1986); John Prados, *The Soviet Estimate: U.S. Intelligence Analysis and Russian Military Strength* (NY: Dial Press 1982); David Sullivan, 'Evaluating US Intelligence Estimates,' in Roy Godson (ed.) *Intelligence Requirements for the 1980s: Analysis and Estimates* (Washington DC: National Strategy Information Centre 1980).
3. Barry H. Steiner, 'American Intelligence and the Soviet ICBM Build-up: Another Look', *Intelligence and National Security* 8/2 (April 1993) pp.172–98.
4. As Steiner reports, the portions of the Secretary of Defense's annual posture statements that included information derived from the NIEs were declassified on 25 June 1975. He notes that they were published in microfiche form in *Declassified Documents Qtly*, 1 (July–Sept. 1975). The actual NIEs have now been declassified and have been published in National Security Archive, *The Soviet Estimate* (London: Chadwyck–Healey 1996). All references to intelligence documents are from this source.
5. Kent's philosophy was set out in his *Strategic Intelligence for American World Policy* (Princeton UP 1966).
6. W. Bruce Berkowitz, 'Intelligence in the Organizational Context: Coordination and Error in National Estimates, *Orbis* 29 (Fall 1985) pp.571–96.
7. *Ibid.*, p.581. See Chester Cooper, 'The CIA and Decision-Making,' *Foreign Affairs* 50/2 (Jan. 1972) p.224.
8. For background on McNamara's attitudes and personality see Deborah Shapley, *Promise and Power: The Life and Times of Robert McNamara* (Boston: Little, Brown 1993).
9. The view on the CIA's Vietnam estimates appears to be that they were generally accurate but too hedged to have the impact required to challenge policy makers.
10. On the missile gap see Freedman (note 2) Ch.4.
11. National Intelligence Estimate [hereafter NIE], Number 11-8-64, *Soviet Capabilities for Strategic Attack*, 8 Oct. 1964, pp.2, 3. The only dissent came from USAF intelligence which expected more ICBMs and an intensive R&D effort 'toward achievement of an effective first-strike counter-force capability before the close of this decade'. (p.4). Interestingly the only area where the USAF considered Soviet capabilities were being exaggerated was in the hardness of their missile silos. The ability of these silos to withstand a direct hit was central to prospects for an American first strike.(p.5).
12. 'Is Russia Slowing Down in Arms Race', *US News & World Report*, 17 April 1965.
13. This missile was the SS-11. Up to this point it had been assumed that a missile known as the SS-10 was soon to be deployed, but test firings of this stopped abruptly in Oct. 1964. USIB, *Memorandum to Holders of National Intelligence Estimate, Number 11-8-64, Soviet Capabilities for Strategic Attack*, 10 May 1965.
14. NIE, Number 11-8-65, *Soviet Capabilities for Strategic Attack*, 7 Oct. 1965. Navy Intelligence agreed with DIA but the Air Force still pushed for a higher overall number. This DIA dissent is discussed in Daniel Graham, 'Estimating the Threat: A Soldier's Job', *Army* (April 1973).
15. Made up of 1,000 Minuteman ICBMs and 54 of the larger but older Titans.
16. NIE, Number 11-8-66, *Soviet Capabilities for Strategic Attack*, 20 Oct. 1966 p.7, 19–20.
17. USIB, NIE, Number 11-3-66, *Soviet Strategic Air and Missile Defenses*, 17 Nov. 1966, p.3.
18. Ibid. p.2. This debate is discussed in Freedman (note 2) Ch.5.

19. US Arms Control and Disarmament Agency, *Documents on Disarmament 1966*, McNamara News Conference of 10 Nov. 1966, pp.728–33.
20. The flavour of this debate is well conveyed by Morton Halperin, 'The Decision to deploy the ABM', *World Politics* 25 (Oct. 1975).
21. Although the term, with the acronym MAD, was invented by Don Brennan, a critic of McNamara working for the Hudson Institute, it does capture the essence of McNamara's position. For a discussion of the origins of assured destruction as a concept see Lawrence Freedman, *The Evolution of Nuclear Strategy*, (London: Macmillan 1989) Ch.16.
22. On the use of these concepts in force planning see Alain C. Enthoven and Wayne Smith, *How Much is Enough?* (NY: Harper & Row 1972).
23. It is important to note that MIRVing would have gone ahead even if there had been no Soviet ABM. Its virtue was to allow him to meet USAF demands for increased coverage of Soviet targets without expanding the number of ICBM launchers or SSBNs.
24. See John Newhouse, *Cold Dawn: The Story of SALT* (NY 1973). For background on Soviet strategic thinking at this time see Christoph Bluth, *Soviet Strategic Arms Policy Before SALT* (Cambridge UP 1992).
25. USIB, NIE 11-3-68, *Soviet Strategic Air and Missile Defenses*, 31 Oct. 1968.
26. See John Clearwater, 'The Origins of SALT in the Johnson Administration', PhD thesis, King's College London, 1996.
27. Harold P. Ford, 'The US Government's Experience with Intelligence Analysis: Pluses and Minuses', *Intelligence and National Security* 10/4 (Oct. 1995) pp.39–40.
28. NIE, Number 11-8-68, *Soviet Capabilities for Strategic Attack*, 3 Oct. 1968.
29. USIB, National Intelligence Estimate 11-8-69, *Soviet Strategic Attack Forces*, 9 Sept. 1969, p.18. The State Dept. and the Pentagon agencies, however, all seem to have agreed that 1,800 represented the upper limit.
30. Freedman, *US Intelligence* (note 2) Ch.8.
31. Laird's speculation on the potential vulnerability of SLBMs appeared in a letter to Senator Fulbright, dated 1 July 1969, published in the preface to Senate Foreign Relations Committee, *Intelligence and the ABM* (Washington DC: US GPO 1969) p.x. Rear Adm. Levering Smith, of the USN's Special Project's Office, commented that the Russians 'had no specific new anti-submarine warfare methods the Navy knows of that would make the Polaris fleet vulnerable to attack.' *Washington Post*, 12 July 1969. It is apparent from the declassified NIEs that Air Force intelligence did occasionally push the contrary line.
32. Freedman, *US Intelligence* (note 2) pp.121–2.
33. Senate Foreign Relations Committee (91st, Congress, 1st session), *Hearing: Intelligence and the ABM* (Washington DC: 1969).
34. Prados (note 2) p.211. Kissinger, *The White House Years* (Boston: Little, Brown 1979), describes how in this debate he 'leaned towards the more ominous interpretation' of the SS-9 triplet and adopted a 'procedure much resented by traditionalists who jealously guarded the independence of the estimating process' by gathering the experts together in the White House and playing 'the Devil's advocate.' He notes that the DCI, Richard Helms, stood his ground and adds 'he was later proved right', p.37.
35. NIE 11-8-68 (note 28) p.12.
36. NIE 11-8-69 (note 29) p.15.
37. USIB, NIE, Number 11-4-68, *Main Issues in Soviet Military Policy*, 19 Sept. 1968. See also USIB, Special NIE, Number 11-16-68, *The Soviet Approach to Arms Control*, 7 Nov. 1968. On the influence of expectations of an American response, and the assumption that Moscow must have learned a lesson from the missile gap experience and the stimulus this gave to American strategic forces see Berkowitz (note 6) p.586. See also his *American Security: Dilemmas for a Modern Democracy* (New Haven/London: Yale UP 1986) p.243.
38. NIE 11-8-69 (note 29) p.9. The incident is discussed in US Senate, Select Committee to study Governmental Operations with Respect to Intelligence Activities, *Final Report, Book I, Foreign and Military Intelligence* (Washington DC: 1976) p.78 and Prados (note 2) pp.217–18.
39. With some justice Jackson complained during the ratification hearings on START 1 that: 'You can't come up here when you are demanding a weapons system with one line and then

when you are trying to justify a treaty take an opposite line.' Senate Armed Services Committee, *Military Implications of the Treaty on the Limitations of Anti-Ballistic Missile Systems and the Interim Agreement on Limitations of Strategic Offensive Arms* (July 1972) pp.470–3.

40. The tensions within the community can be sensed even in the title of a Special NIE of 10 Sept. 1973, *Soviet Strategic Arms Programs and Detente: What Are They Up To?*. This picked up on an apparent contradiction between Soviet detente policies and military policies that was recognized might not appear as such to the Soviet leadership. The conclusion was that the Soviets were largely opportunistic, but were unlikely

> to curb new programs unless they are persuaded both that US reactions to such programs would jeopardize their minimum objectives and that Soviet restraint would be reciprocated. But precisely what price, in terms of strategic limitations, the Soviets will prove willing to pay for detente remains to be tested.

This was exactly the sort of conclusion that exasperated policy makers as well as hawks (Air Force intelligence offered a sharper conclusion that the Soviets 'must view detente as a principal means of forestalling US advances in defense technology while enhancing their own relative power position', (p.4) A KGB analysis of US objectives at the same time could have reached the same conclusion!

41. Kissinger, *White House Years* (note 34) pp.36–8. See also Commission n the Organization of the Government for the Conduct of Foreign Policy (Murphy Commission) *Report*, (Washington DC: 1975) p.103.
42. Rhodri Jeffreys-Jones, *The CIA and American Democracy* (New Haven, CT: Yale UP 1989).
43. PFIAB can be traced back to the Eisenhower administration. It had a brief revival during the Kennedy administration after the Bay of Pigs fiasco but was barely used during the Johnson years. Nixon gave it more authority under Executive Order 11460 dated 22 March 1969. See Stephen J. Flanagan, 'Managing the Intelligence Community', *Int. Security* 10/1 (Summer 1985) p.70.
44. William Colby, *Honorable Men* (London: Hutchinson 1978) pp.351–2.
45. Flanagan (note 43) p.90.
46. US President, Commission on CIA Activities Within the United States, *Report to the President* (Washington DC: June 1975).
47. Robert Ellsworth and Kenneth L. Adelman, 'Foolish Intelligence,' *Foreign Policy* 36 (1979); Prados (note 2) pp.248–57.
48. A critical analysis of the episode was produced after a Congressional investigation. Report of the Senate Select Committee on Intelligence Subcommittee in Collection, Production, and Quality, Together with Separate Views, 95 Cong. 2 session, *The National Intelligence Estimates A-B Team Episode Concerning Soviet Strategic Capability and Objectives* (16 Feb. 1978). For the Chairman's reminiscence see Richard Pipes, 'Team B: The Reality Behind the Myth', *Commentary* 82 (Oct. 1986).
49. NIE, 11-3/8-76, *Soviet Forces for Intercontinental Conflict Through the Mid-1980s* (21 Dec. 1976). The real Team A/Team B contest is in fact contained within this report. No important judgement is left unchallenged. All the Pentagon agencies developed their view that

> the Soviets do, in fact, see as attainable their objective as achieving the capability to wage an intercontinental nuclear war, should such a war occur, and survive it with resources sufficient to dominate the postwar period(p.23).

The difference is that a more liberal alternative view is also available, courtesy of the State Dept. Its dissent stated that the Soviet leaders:

> do not entertain, as a practical objective in the foreseeable future, the achievement of what could reasonably be characterized as "war-winning" or "war-surviving" (p.22).

The line taken in the text is that the Soviets were striving for some meaningful superiority which might give them useful political advantages if not quite a first strike capability.
50. See note 1. Wohlstetter died in Jan. 1997.

51. Thus validating Team B's conclusions, which Harald Ford believes to have been achieved by 'subsequent evidence' (note 27, p.42) involved the underlying objectives that the build-up was supposed to be supporting rather than the actual force levels. Here Ford seems to be giving too much to Team B. Read with hindsight it seems tendentious and crudely overstated. As Bruce Berkowitz and Allan Goodman note, there were 'B teams' on Soviet air defenses and missile accuracy which were generally constructive in their input. *Strategic Intelligence for American National Security* (Princeton UP 1989) p.132. For commentaries see article by Anne Hernig Cahn and John Prados, 'Team B: The Trillion Dollar Experiment', *Bulletin of the Atomic Scientists* 49 (April 1993) pp.22–31.

52. Report of 'Team B,' *Intelligence Community Experiment in Competitive Analysis: Soviet Strategic Objectives An Alternative View*, Dec. 1976, p.2.

53 See Charles Tyroler II (ed.) *Alerting America: The Papers of the Committee o the Present Danger* (Washington DC:Pergammon-Brassey's 1984).

54. Ibid. p.13.

55. For useful collections of essays illustrating the range of views on Soviet strategy at this time see John Baylis and Gerald Segal (eds.) *Soviet Strategy* (London: Croom Helm 1981) and Derek Leebaert (ed.) *Soviet Military Thinking* (London: Allen & Unwin 1981). For a masterly overview of the whole period see Raymond l. Garthoff, *Detente and Confrontation: American-Soviet Relations from Nixon to Reagan* (Washington DC: Brookings 1994).

56. E.g. Directorate of Intelligence, CIA, *Soviet Nuclear Doctrine: Concepts of Intercontinental and Theatre War*, June 1973. This played down the prospects of a Soviet drive to a first-strike capability.

8

National Intelligence and the Iranian Revolution

MICHAEL DONOVAN

While 1997 will mark Central Intelligence Agency's 50th anniversary, 1998 will mark the 20th anniversary of what many believe to be one of that agency's greatest predictive and reporting failures, the Iranian Revolution. Senior American policy makers in particular have cited a lack of intelligence to explain their own belated and limited response to the crisis.[1] However, a wealth of now declassified documentation has allowed historians to make a more complete evaluation of this theory of intelligence failure. What can be deduced from the flow of information in national intelligence channels and from the subsequent policy response to events as they unfolded in Iran? The argument here is that there was accurate and, in part, timely intelligence at the disposal of policy makers, but the availability of this information did not redirect the long-standing policy predispositions in Washington.

On the last day of 1977, President Jimmy Carter declared Iran to be 'an island of stability in one of the more troubled areas of the world'.[2] A week after Carter's speech the government-controlled press in Iran published an article entitled 'Iran and Red and Black Colonialism' which ridiculed the Ayatollah Ruhollah Khomeini. In response to the article, violent demonstrations were staged in the holy city of Qom, marking what is generally acknowledged as the beginning of the Iranian Revolution.[3] Not a month passed thereafter without significant anti-regime riots throughout Iran.[4] This tide of popular dissent would unseat the regime of Muhammad Reza Shah Pahlavi in January 1979. Yet only in November 1978, did the foreign policy establishment in Washington become aware that the regime in Tehran was faltering. There were, however, plenty of danger signals from the outset.

Contrary to influential official accounts of the Carter years, American foreign intelligence did observe and report on these danger signals. On 29

January 1978, a Bureau of Intelligence and Research (INR) analysis of the Qom riots demonstrated considerable sensitivity to the gravity of the situation:

> The recent incidents of violence in Iran are the most serious of their kind in a decade. Though they are not an immediate threat to the Shah's regime, they have put his traditionalist Islamic opponents in their strongest position since 1963. If he crushes the dissidents, he will damage Iran's relations with the US; if he does not, they will be encouraged to step up their actions against him. So far, the Shah has demonstrated considerable uncertainty about how to face the challenge.

INR described those taking part in the demonstrations as, 'a broad range of traditional dissidents (Islamic conservatives, student progressives, dissatisfied intellectuals, and terrorists) and some new and potentially powerful elements (judges, lawyers, and businessmen)'.

The analysis was a timely warning. The violence at Qom was indeed the worst since 1963, but more importantly, the composition of those who took part in the demonstrations represented the degree to which disaffection had spread, infecting the professional middle class. This class was counted among those who supported the Shah's modernization program and their alliance with traditional dissident groups should have set off alarm bells in Washington. The analysis concluded with the ominous and prescient prediction that, 'the greatest potential danger to the Shah is that he may lose control over the religious elements and their adherents, leading to the inherently more dangerous confrontation of secular modernizers against fundamentalist religious leaders — a problem that has been avoided for almost 15 years.'[5]

From January to May 1978 there was a stream of embassy reporting that also could have alerted the policy establishment to the gravity of the situation. This reporting was reflected in the above INR analysis and noted the high quality of organization among the opposition and their improved position *vis-à-vis* the government after the incident in Qom. This information failed to have any substantial impact on policy makers for two reasons. First, American ambassador William Sullivan tightly controlled the reporting from the embassy and was himself only gradually convinced of the magnitude of the crisis. Second, the traffic that did contain alarming information was given such a low classification that attention was not forcefully drawn to its contents in Washington.[6]

During the spring and summer the intelligence community began to focus on the religious community in Iran and its political significance. In

March, the Defense Intelligence Agency (DIA) detailed the religious hierarchy which has 'in modern times played a prominent role in anti-government activities,' and outlined their demands for constitutional rule.[7] On 11 May, the National Intelligence Daily (NID) observed:

> There appears to be little room for compromise between the Shah and conservative Muslim opponents, who believe that reforms instituted by the Shah and his father threaten the future of Islam in Iran. The Shah is gambling that his program of modernization has enough popular support to allow him to take measures against conservative Muslims – a community that, in his opinion, wants to turn the clock back to the Middle Ages.

Widespread disturbances occurred in 34 cities over a three-day period starting on 8 May.[8] On 10 May, in Qom, police forced their way into the home of Ayatollah Kazem Shariatmadari, the most prominent religious figure in Iran, killing two theological students. Given this pervasive violence and the provocative act of the security forces in Qom, it is little wonder that the CIA saw the differences between the Shah and his opponents as intractable.

A month later, another NID article predicted continued violence at the end of the last 40-day mourning period. More importantly, the article argued that the opposition was not 'limited to the large conservative Muslim community. Moderate left-wing critics of the government, who are united with the dissident Muslim clergymen only in their opposition to the Shah, may encourage their followers to swell the ranks of conservative religious demonstrators.' Attention focused on the widening power base of the 'politicized clergy', who were successfully exploiting popular socio-economic grievances among students and the urban working class. The article concluded that an alliance between the moderate left and the extreme Muslim right was possible and would be 'a dangerous development for the regime'.[9]

Prior to fall 1978, there was considerable division in the intelligence community, not about the makeup of the opposition in Iran, but rather about how the Shah might best deal with the continuing crisis. At the State Department, the Iran desk officer Henry Precht, backed by INR, favored continued political liberalization in order to blunt the demands of the opposition. This argument, however, betrayed the predisposition at State that the radicals did not maintain significant influence over other opposition elements.[10] The events of June and July seemed to justify this view. These two months passed with relatively little disorder. Shariatmadari and the moderate clergy encouraged their followers to avoid demonstrations. While Khomeini continued his call for the overthrow of the monarchy,

Shariatmadari declared that he could live with the Shah as long as there was a return to the 1906 constitution. By June, demonstrators seemed to be aligning themselves with Shariatmadari rather than Khomeini, engendering a false sense of calm.[11] Indeed, there appeared to be such a lull in events that Ambassador Sullivan left Iran for home leave in June returning in late August.

DIA, and to a lesser extent the CIA, continued to see the regime's staying power in the context of the loyalty of the armed forces and security services.[12] This view also seemed to be justified given the comparative calm of the summer. That INR, CIA and the DIA differed in their interpretation of events is not hard to understand given the regime's own vacillation, as it initiated contradictory policies of repression and cosmetic reform designed for mass consumption.[13] Predicting continued violence in August, the DIA characterized the Shah's circumstances as follows: 'The government will probably be able to handle the situation, but the Shah is still faced with a dilemma: How to continue liberalizing Iranian society and maintain order at the same time without cracking down too harshly on the dissidents.'[14]

The calm of June–July was short-lived. In response to increasingly deteriorating economic conditions and apparent government confusion, the urban working class began to take to the streets in late June, swelling the ranks of the demonstrators, and further debilitate the economy through general strikes. By August, what had been a traditional and professional middle class protest had grown into a revolutionary movement that transgressed class boundaries.[15]

The differences between Khomeini and Shariatmadari did not go unnoticed in Washington. In a memo to Secretary of State Cyrus Vance, Harold Saunders reported:

> The Shah's strongest opponents come from the Shia religious leadership, split in two apparently cooperating factions, one an ultra-conservative group headed by Khomeini (exiled in Iraq) and the other by the more moderate Shariatmadari of Qom, Iran. Drawing their support from the poorer classes, the traditional bazaar merchants, single men who have been uprooted from their villages for work in the cities, and underemployed youths, the mullahs probably are also helped by covert left-wing groups.[16]

Though the memo concluded that, 'an early end to the disorders in not a prospect', the conclusion missing from the above analysis was that as the urban working class (who were more susceptible to the exhortations of Khomeini) took more of a role in the demonstrations, the opposition would become increasingly radicalized, elevating the uncompromising Khomeini to an even more prominent position.

On 1 June, the NSC ordered a National Intelligence Estimate (NIE) on Iran, but production of the estimate became bogged down over the summer. Though the NIE has been pointed to as evidence that the intelligence community failed to grasp the situation in Iran, debate over the substance of the estimate seems to have helped coalesce opinion in the community. INR had become increasingly pessimistic over the summer. By the fall, CIA was beginning to gravitate to the INR position.

The NIE placed the causes of the unrest in the rapid social and economic changes that had outpaced Iran's political development. It defined the broad based composition of the opposition which included two cooperating components: the successors to the National Front of the 1950s,[17] supported by the urban middle class and upper class intelligentsia, and the Shia religious community, supported by lower and lower middle classes.

The NIE was by no means optimistic, though the varying views of the contributors were evident in the draft. For the first time since the crisis began the continued loyalty of the military was questioned. Yet the estimate prescribed the same contradictory response to the crisis that the regime had employed through the first half of 1978:

> Even sweeping concessions will not ensure continued calm, however, for there is an almost universal tendency among Iranians, and certainly among the political and religious opposition, to interpret any concessions as signs of weakness that should be exploited rather than as positive elements of a political settlement. The Shah and the government therefore will need to couple well timed and well defined concessions with the judicious exercise of sufficient authority and force to intimidate those who, equating lenience with weakness, would further challenge the regime.

The draft did not 'foresee any likely circumstances in which a government controlled by religious leaders would come to power'. Its outlook for the future seems strangely contradictory given its prediction: 'If the Shah does not remain in power, we will see one or more alternative regimes, most likely a rightist military junta, but perhaps a civilian government dominated by Shia religious leaders.'[18]

There are a number of explanations for the contradictions inherent in the draft NIE and the debate surrounding the product. The work on the NIE had actually begun in April and did not reflect current research.[19] As of April, there was considerable confusion as to the true nature of events in Iran. Throughout the spring, INR became increasingly pessimistic about the Shah's grasp on power. By September, when the unfinished draft was shelved by DCI Admiral Stansfield Turner, INR analysts believed that it was now a question of institutional collapse.[20] Over the summer, the CIA remained somewhat more sanguine about the situation, which it did not view as revolutionary.[21] These differences led INR on 1 August, to state in a dissenting footnote that the Shah's prospects were 'somewhat less favorable than portrayed in some parts of this NIE'.[22]

Another explanation for the confusion surrounding the NIE has to do with the production process itself. A House of Representatives' evaluation on intelligence found the production of an NIE to be inherently cumbersome and time consuming. In this case there had been differences over the length and focus of the product. As the pace of events in Iran quickened, the estimate became more of a distraction for analysts and consumers alike, given the need for current intelligence.[23]

Finally, Iran analysts in the CIA subscribed to what James Bill calls the Pahlavi Premise — the premise that the Shah, who had weathered so many challenges to his authority in the past, could do so again.[24] By contrast, INR had no full time Iran analyst during 1978.[25] This absence may have been an advantage. Given the lack of any 'old Iran hands' at INR, area specialists, though handicapped to a certain extent by their lack of firsthand experience, were more willing to question the durability of the Shah. The director of INR, agreed with his analysts that the tone of the estimate did not adequately reflect the gravity of the crisis. He went to DCI Turner, who was also uncomfortable with the tone, and the unfinished draft was shelved in mid-September.[26]

The dispute over the NIE, though embarrassing for the intelligence community, may have been more valuable than previously supposed. By the time the draft was shelved, opinion in the community was beginning to coalesce. On 7 September, an NSC staffer, Commander Gary Sick, argued in a memo to the President that the reaction by Iran specialists both inside in the government and in academic circles was 'universally pessimistic' and that Iran may be ripe for full-scale revolution.[27] The next day, 'Black Friday', the Jalah Square Massacre confirmed the danger the Shah now faced.[28] In place of the disputed NIE, INR composed an Interagency Intelligence Memorandum (IIM) published on 29 September. The IIM stated that while the situation had quietened, 'there was still considerable question ... of his [the Shah's] ability to survive in power over the next 18 to 24 months'.[29] Given these pronouncements, more than a month before the first NSC meeting on Iran, it is difficult to understand the lack of attention the crisis was receiving at higher levels in Washington. True, the intelligence community had substantial differences of opinion during the early months of 1978, but these had been put to rest by 'Black Friday'.

By 20 October, the CIA's National Foreign Assessment Center (NFAC) reported that 'the possibility of a complete collapse of government authority and the likely emergence of a military dictatorship has encouraged them [the moderate opposition] to talk to the government'. However, the report continued, 'those who see in the present situation an opportunity to eliminate the monarchy will continue to carry out violent action'.[30]

For those in the US government, the crisis could not have occurred at a worse time. Secretary of State Vance was heavily preoccupied with both the Camp David peace process and the SALT II negotiations. Meanwhile, a policy feud developed between the Secretary of State and National Security Advisor Brzezinski over the US *rapprochement* with China. Once the crisis in Iran received high level attention in Washington, the existing institutional rivalry did anything but abate. Given Vance's heavy workload, Brzezinski was able to monopolize the crisis.

That the crisis in Iran was being dealt with inside the Old Executive Office Building (OEOB) is significant. The National Security Advisor was intensely conscious of the role Iran under the Shah played in the peripheral containment of the Soviet Union, and continued to view events within this myopic context. Brzezinski's staffer responsible for Iran was Commander Sick, an expert on Soviet and Chinese policy in the Indian Ocean. Sick was put into the unenviable position of becoming an Iran specialist overnight. The NSC, as an advisory and coordinating body, is dependent on other agencies and departments for information. In addition, expertise on Iran at the OEOB was extremely low relative to State and the CIA, who were becoming increasingly alienated by the National Security Advisor. Despite Sick's former intelligence experience in the Navy, neither he nor Brzezinski, himself highly critical of the CIA's analytical capabilities, maintained close relationships with the intelligence community. During the entire Iranian crisis, Sick spoke only 'two or three times' with CIA analysts.[31] Brzezinski, on the other hand, relied heavily on back channel communications with the Iranian ambassador in Washington, Ardeshir Zahedi, the Shah's former son-in-law.

The first high-level meeting in Washington on Iran was held on 2 November. The Special Coordinating Committee (SCC) chaired by Brzezinski included Deputy Secretary of State Warren Christopher; Secretary of Defense Harold Brown; Chairman of the Joint Chiefs General David Jones; DCI Turner; Brzezinski's deputy David Aaron, and Commander Sick. Brzezinski argued forcefully that the US should offer unrestricted support for the Shah, and that a military government would be the best option for restoring order in riot-torn Iran.[32] But neither Christopher nor Turner felt that a military government would resolve the fundamental problems facing the Shah.[33] This meeting set up the lines for a policy feud that would continue throughout the crisis.

The same day, INR produced the most hard-hitting analysis of the Shah's fortunes to date. 'Fast breaking events in Iran', the memo argued, had placed the Shah in a very tenuous position. The memo continued:

> The Shah's attempts to appease his opponents have failed. The opposition is coalescing and gaining momentum, while he loses the initiative. The Shah himself has admitted in a conversation with Ambassador Sullivan that immediate action is needed to quell the turmoil, but he seems unable to make up his mind what to do...So far, the Shah cannot see beyond half-measures designed to defer hard decisions. If he has convinced himself that his ideas to date represent bold gestures or sweeping changes, then he is seriously out of touch with the current scene. His reversion to the moods of depression and vacillation he displayed in the early 1950s make it doubtful that he can move to salvage what remains of national unity, unless others intervene on his behalf.

In INR's view, the Shah faced two choices: he could try to remain in Iran as a constitutional monarch with severely limited powers, or he could abdicate. Should the Shah choose the latter course, the probable outcome would be a military takeover. Regardless of the choice, the memo asserted, 'the Shah's powers will be reduced. If he does nothing to channel the course of events, he is likely to be ousted'. The memo also highlighted the dilemma facing both the Shah and American policy makers. No matter how the transition of power unfolded, short term repression would probably be necessary to end the disorder. Repression would in turn lead to continued violence, risking a total collapse of authority, and radicalizing Iranian politics.

INR was skeptical about the viability of a coalition government. Khomeini, now exiled in Paris, held 'almost mystical' sway over protesters. This power would prevent other political and religious leaders of a more moderate disposition from arriving at any accommodation with the Shah. The memo concluded with two ominous points: '... only drastic measures by the Shah hold any promise for staving off a descent into chaos...Unless the Shah acts very soon, the chances of a military intervention are high. Order imposed by the Army probably would not last more than six months.'[34]

Given this analysis, it is not difficult to understand the opposition to a military government by Turner and Christopher. The time when the Shah could have brought out the troops to crush the demonstrations, as he had done in 1963, had passed. Implicit in the analysis was the grassroots, popular nature of the revolution. The State Department began to lobby for a transition to a broadly-based coalition government. By early November, the CIA, the State Department, the American ambassador to Iran, and even the Shah saw the futility of a repressive response to the crisis. The greatest proponent for this solution continued to be Brzezinski.[35]

Meanwhile, attention in Washington turned to the quality of intelligence on Iran. On 6 November, a Policy Review Committee meeting (PRC) chaired by Vance dealt with the subject. Both Brzezinski and Sick believed that a fundamental intelligence failure had occurred. In Sick's view, Iran had been, 'an intelligence disaster of the first order. Our information has been extremely meager, our resources were not in a position to report accurately on the activities of the opposition forces, on external penetration... or the basic objectives and political orientation of the demonstrators.'[36]

Conscious that valuable time had been lost, policy makers argued that their limited options were the result of an intelligence failure. On 11 November, a handwritten, eyes only note from the President was delivered to Turner:

> To Cy, Zbig, Stan: I am not satisfied with the quality of our political intelligence. Assess our assets and as soon as possible give me a report concerning our abilities in the most important areas of the world. Make a joint recommendation on what we can do to improve your ability to give me political information and advice. J.C.[37]

Turner correctly assumed that the note was the brainchild of Brzezinski who had already restricted DCI's access to the President.[38] Carter had written the note at the request of his National Security Advisor.

The story surrounding the now infamous note is a strange one. The note was immediately leaked to the press, embarrassing Turner whose management of the intelligence community had become a subject of controversy. As Gary Sick notes, whoever leaked the note was motivated to do so in order to further undercut Turner's relationship with the President.[39] According to Turner, the note had come as a complete surprise given that just a week before the President had complemented him on the excellent work of the intelligence community.[40] The resulting debate over the 'intelligence failure' in Iran alienated the President's chief intelligence officer at a time of acute crisis for the sake of a bureaucratic end-run. For Brzezinski, the controversy surrounding the note was fortunate. With Turner either unwilling or unable to assert himself with Carter, and Vance preoccupied with the Camp David negotiations, Brzezinski was able to pursue his own policy agenda relatively free of opposition on the NSC.

Unable to reach a compromise with the moderate opposition, the Shah declared a military government on 6 November in the aftermath of widespread, violent demonstrations the day before. A CIA article reported that senior Iranian military officers had been pressing the Shah for firm action for some time and concluded:

Most observers – and the Shah – doubt that military rule will solve Iran's political crisis. A tough crack-down on demonstrations at this juncture could as easily provoke new violence as preclude it. The Shah expects exiled Muslim fundamentalist Khomeini now to call for a holy war, with further bloodshed the result. In such a situation the loyalty of the troops – most of them drawn from the same social class as the demonstrators – will be severely tested.[41]

In declaring a military government, the Shah was playing what many thought was his last card. In fact, little changed with the new government, which maintained the divide and co-opt strategy of past months. On 13 November, the CIA reported that the National Front had joined Khomeini in his demand for a national referendum concerning the monarchy.[42]

From the administration's point of view, the intelligence community was providing nothing but bad news. Intelligence reports became increasingly skeptical of the military's cohesion. In addition, they saw little chance of accommodation between the Shah and the moderate opposition. On November 20 the CIA reported that 'Khomeini is determined to overthrow the Shah and is unlikely to accept any compromise... His influence is now so strong that neither other clerics nor civilian opposition leaders will take actions he opposes.' The report continued: 'The eloquent and charismatic Khomeini has amassed wide support among Iran's 35 million people, and has so intimidated the moderate opponents of the Shah that they have accepted his veto over their activities.' Concluding, the memo stated that Khomeini 'is determined to see the Shah and the Pahlavi monarchy abolished even at the cost of throwing Iran into chaos and anarchy'.

Clearly, the CIA was not optimistic about any compromise that would include a role for the Shah. Given Khomeini's uncompromising demands, his influence over the rest of the opposition by virtue of his mass popularity precluded any accommodation. In retrospect, the CIA analysis seems astute. Though the agency recognized that the ulema was by no means monolithic, it argued that these differences and rivalries worked against the Shah as each faction attempted to outdo the other in appealing to the demonstrators.[43]

Various reports throughout 1978 had noted the Shah's mood swings and vacillation. On 22 November, a psychological profile of the Shah concluded: 'That he [the Shah] moves in one way and then the other should not be considered surprising. It is his way of grappling with pressure from all sides in a situation that has no clear solution'. Brzezinski later cited this report as further evidence that the CIA did not adequately understand events.[44] Years later, James Bill echoed this analysis: 'In late 1978, he [the Shah] stood in the path of millions of Iranian citizens in revolt against him.

He did take actions, both forceful and accommodating. Nothing worked. It is no wonder that his grip weakened and his mind wavered.'[45] Indeed, history had shown that the Shah was capable of great indecision in moments of crisis. He had acted similarly in 1953.

At a later date, frustrated policy makers dealt with intelligence that did not support their distorted views by ignoring it. The failure of intelligence occurred in Washington rather than in Tehran, Qom, Isfahan, or any other part of Iran. At the heart of the situation was doctrinal support for the Shah among some of the President's key advisers who saw in the Iranian crisis, a venue for extending their control over American foreign policy.[46] The National Security Advisor and his staff became a filter through which information had to pass. Given the agenda that existed in the OEOB, the balance of the end product is questionable.

By late November, the time for any tenable option, either for the 'iron fist' or a compromise between the Shah and his opponents, had passed. Yet the State Department and the CIA were still unable to educate the White House to the political realities in Iran. The Islamic holy month of Moharram in December would prove to be the zenith of the revolution. During Moharram, Iranians would take to the streets in the millions. Yet Brzezinski still maintained that a forceful response to the crisis would restore order and save the Shah.

On 29 November, two important intelligence reports highlighted the looming crisis of Moharram.[47] These reports were the most grave to date and it is useful to examine them in some detail.

Entitled 'The Meaning Of Moharram', the first report by the NFAC described the historical and religious background to the period, and its political significance. Ceremonies in the past, it was noted, had often been used to express political opposition. The symbolism of a 13-century-old battle between Hussein, a founder of Shia Islam, and Yazid, his rival, would be exploited by opposition members. The Sermons of Moharram would be explicit in their call for the Shah's downfall. The report concluded that 'many of the faithful will see themselves as warriors for Hussein against the tyrant'.[48]

This memorandum supplied the background for a second 'Alert Memorandum' of the same day. 'Iran – Prospects for Moharram' carried an attached cover letter from the DCI highlighting its importance: 'The following analysis is useful for the critical nature of the period up to and around Ashura (11 December); the key factors that will determine the direction events will go; and the likely near-term political ramifications if the Shah survives or does not survive.'

Despairing in its thrust, the memorandum once again placed little hope on the possibility of either a military or political solution to the crisis.

Moharram was,

> likely to put the Shah and Iran's new government to a test more severe
> than any they have faced to date ... Even in calm times these
> observances emphasize the clerical challenge to secular authority that
> is integral to Shia Islam. In the current very difficult political
> circumstances there is a good chance that the civil unrest will develop
> on a scale sufficiently serious to threaten the survival of the monarchy
> itself.

In the view of the CIA, there was widespread expectation that Moharram
would precipitate a decisive test of power between the opposition and the
Shah. The report continues:

> This in effect challenges the opposition to demonstrate its strength,
> and the Shah and the military government to counter any such display.
> With both sides apparently unable to find the flexibility to reach a
> political settlement in the near term to avert such a confrontation, we
> will see a serious test of the ability of the military and the security
> services to keep order, of their ability to maintain discipline and
> morale, and of the leadership and determination of the Shah.

The CIA placed the greatest significance on Khomeini, upon whom the
legitimacy of other opposition members was dependent and who held veto
over the actions of these groups. Consequently, the CIA saw 'almost no
chance' of a political accommodation between the Shah and the moderate
opposition. The latter would be immediately discredited by Khomeini
should they compromise. As the report stated:

> Compromise with the more moderate clergy might have been possible
> until recently. In the earlier stages of the crisis the religious moderates
> helped to limit destructive public demonstrations; they cannot be
> counted on to do so now. In recent demonstrations religious leaders
> have in fact been unable to control their followers even when they
> have wanted to do so.

The report was succinct in its review of the Shah's political options.
Given the influence of Khomeini, any settlement would require his seal of
approval. Yet the CIA saw 'no evidence to suggest that a settlement between
the Shah and Khomeini is possible even in principle'. Nor could the Shah
rely on his past strategy of repression mixed with concessions. Reviewing
this approach, the report concluded:

> Despite these steps, neither the opposition nor the population
> generally is convinced that the Shah has the will and the strength to

defend himself. He is perceived as weak, and has lost his credibility almost completely ... The popular impression that the Shah is alternating between concessionaire and authoritarian responses to the current crisis serves to undermine rather than promote a political settlement.

With hindsight, the analysis demonstrates considerable understanding of the Shah's position. By late November, only the most hardline loyalists could have held any hope that the Shah would weather the revolution. The CIA saw Moharram to be the final test before the Shah, a test he was unlikely to pass, even if he survived the month. The outlook for the future was no less pessimistic:

The Shah's survival of Moharram would not change the views of Khomeini ... nor would it substantially affect the extent of Khomeini's influence over the masses of Iranians. In such a situation it would remain very difficult to persuade National Front leaders to compromise with the Shah and participate in a coalition government. And it is only such a government that would have a reasonable chance of re-establishing public trust.[49]

The DIA, too, saw the Moharram crisis as a critical test of the Shah's staying power. Yet the DIA position was somewhat more optimistic. That the Shah might survive Moharram was questionable. Should he do so however, he would 'increase his chances of reaching an accommodation with the moderate opposition elements'.[50]

Moharram began on 2 December 1978 with widespread violence and deaths. Thousands violated the night curfew wearing white shrouds symbolizing the willingness to die. On 5 December, a CIA update saw 'no reason to alter our conclusions that civil unrest may threaten the survival of the monarchy'. 'Well orchestrated' demonstrations conveyed an 'overwhelming national consensus against the Shah'. Reinforcing its prior outlook, the report stated:

The National Front has refused to compromise their demands; moreover, they do not control the demonstrators and concessions on their part would not break the impasse. Khomeini holds sway over the demonstrators and he will not relent on his demand to end the monarchy. His call to his followers to shed their blood to overthrow the Shah and his appeal to the military to desert will only increase pressure on the military by the demonstrators. There appears little chance between now and Ashura of a political solution short of the Shah's removal.[51]

The above reporting had little impact at the OEOB where a coherent assessment and response to the crisis still did not exist. Faced with well organized demonstrations on a massive scale, Brzezinski became convinced that the Soviets were orchestrating events. Brzezinski's evidence for this was outlined in an article in the *New Republic* entitled 'Whose Meddling in Iran?'[52] The CIA found no evidence of any foreign involvement: 'There is no evidence to substantiate the claim voiced periodically by moderate opposition leaders and members of the government that behind the pattern of events lies the guiding hand of "foreign elements", '"leftists", or more specifically, the Tudeh Party.'[53] Brzezinski reproduced the article and distributed it to the President and other top policy advisors, where apparently, it was well received. According to Gary Sick, at a critical moment the article attained the status of a key policy document.[54] Faultlines in Washington continued to be defined. Now backed by Energy Secretary James Schlesinger and Defense Secretary Harold Brown, Brzezinski continued to lobby for a military crackdown.

Futile debate of this kind finally brought about a long overdue reappraisal in the White House. At the urging of Treasury Secretary Blumenthal, former Under Secretary of State George Ball was brought in to make an independent appraisal of the situation. Rather than dashing off to Tehran, Ball spent a frantic two weeks talking to the Pentagon, the State Department, and the CIA. On 12 December, Ball presented his report to the President. Entitled 'Issues and Implications of the Iranian Crisis', the report confirmed the views of State and the CIA. Ball was not optimistic about the use of force: 'The Shah has been irreparably damaged by recent events. He cannot regain his absolute power position except through violent repression that could turn Iran into another Lebanon.' Any attempt to use the military to preserve the Shah would run the risk of a complete breakdown of loyalty among the troops.

Ball recommended two courses of action. First, the Shah should transfer unconditional power to a Council of Notables that represents the will of the people and would be capable of negotiating with Khomeini. Second, the CIA should 'begin exploring immediately the possibility of establishing a disavowable channel of communication to Khomeini and his entourage. At some point we will probably need to send and receive messages; if the mechanism is to be in place when it is needed, we should start now.'[55]

Both proposals were anathema to Carter and Brzezinski, neither was accepted. At the heart of the Ball report was the reality that the Shah had no future governing Iran. Yet even at this late date, this was a reality Carter and his National Security Advisor were unprepared to accept. An independent review had confirmed what Iran specialists at both State and the CIA had argued since late September; the destiny of Iran lay with an aging religious populist exiled in Paris. Yet any proposal to contact Khomeini provoked a knee-jerk reaction from senior policy makers in Washington.

Ball's short experience had been a frustrating one. By his own admission, his proposals had been too little, too late. In September or October, there might have been a chance for compromise. By the time he had been asked to make his assessment, this possibility had disintegrated. Moreover, Ball was aghast at the bureaucratic imperialism of Brzezinski. Ball had reviewed CIA reports, talked to their analysts, and relied on the agency for the 'intellectual background' for the Council of Notables. In his view, the agency had been performing perfectly well. Yet, 'Brzezinski cut the CIA pretty much out of the whole process ... Brzezinski was his own intelligence source.'

Unbeknown to Vance, Brzezinski's distorted views continued in part to be the product of his back channel communication with Zahedi. For his part, the Iranian ambassador had his own agenda which was dependent on maintaining the Shah, and colored his interpretation of events accordingly. On the other hand, like Ball, the CIA's chief analyst, Robert Bowie, believed that the Shah had to go.[56] Given his own disposition, it is little wonder that Brzezinski found Zahedi to be a more attractive source of information.

Brzezinski later related that he came to regret the Ball exercise.[57] Rather than consolidating opinion, the report exacerbated differences in the cabinet. On 13 November, a SCC debated the merits of the report. Brzezinski, Brown, and Schlesinger felt that an authoritarian military government that would progressively liberalize was the most favorable option. Ball replied that repression could precipitate a civil war. Warren Christopher sided with Ball, and added that in his view, perhaps less than two weeks remained in which to take decisive action.[58] DCI Turner also believed that the use of force was not an option.[59] Implicit in the 'iron fist' option was the idea that millions of Iranians could be controlled by a military standing aloof from the disaffection of the masses. The information existed in Washington that could have confirmed this option to be untenable. Iranian specialists in the government were unanimous. Yet, one month and three days before that Shah would depart Iran for the last time, the seriousness of the situation was still a matter of debate in the NSC.

In the meantime, conditions in Iran continued to deteriorate in the midst of mass demonstrations, strikes, and riots. The country's economy had come to a standstill, as had its production of petroleum. The opposition was gaining more momentum as political options evaporated. On 21 December, the CIA reported:

> The protest marches in Tehran on 10 and 11 December 1978, which brought as many as a million demonstrators into the streets were

masterfully organized and controlled...The ability of these local community leaders to bring out large numbers of the people in response to directives from members of the Islamic clergy gives the religious opposition in Iran an organizational strength which distinguishes it from any other group within the opposition. National Front politicians have benefited politically through cooperation with the leaders of the religious opposition, but the National Front has neither the independent mass following nor any significant ability to mobilize and orchestrate demonstrations.

The report observed that Khomeini was the 'focal point' for the loyalty of the religious movement that acts in his name. The significance of the report was obvious. The continued hope that some kind of accommodation between the Shah and the moderate opposition could be achieved had lost credibility. Khomeini's 'constant and pervasive influence' over millions of Iranians was radicalizing the opposition. It was also noted that while the relationship between the National Front and the religious opposition was one of cooperation only, 'the religious opposition does not appear to be susceptible to specific direction by the National Front or any other political leaders.'[60]

In the end, the agency proved to be remarkably accurate. In late December, in a last ditch effort to develop a moderate government, the Shah once again reopened negotiations with National Front leaders. The negotiations were short-lived. Older, more experienced leaders refused to form any government of which the Shah would still be the titular head. However, Shapour Bakhtiar accepted the Shah's invitation and became prime minister on 30 December.[61]

Predictably, the Bakhtiar government was immediately discredited. The National Front expelled him from the movement, Khomeini declared his government illegal and encouraged a street referendum. Millions poured onto the streets in protest. Significantly, the Bakhtiar government was besieged despite the support of Shariatmadari, whose influence continued to pale next to that of Khomeini. According to the CIA, the religious leadership continued to be 'predominate' in the opposition to the Bakhtiar government.[62]

Concurrently, the deadlock in Washington had been reduced to one policy option: should the US support the 'iron fist' to preserve the Shah. Upon his return from the Middle East, Vance had taken the view that the US should not. Torn between his two foreign policy advisors, Carter authorized a policy directive that appealed to both. Ambassador Sullivan was to convey to the Shah that if he thought a moderate government could be sustained, that was preferable. However, if the Shah felt the military was beginning to fragment, he should institute the military option to end disorder. Ironically, the Shah broke the deadlock. To his credit, the Shah responded on 29 December that he felt the 'iron fist' option to be 'unrealistic' and in any case, he simply 'did not have the heart.'[63] Just 18 days later, the Shah's 37-year reign came to an end with his departure from Iran.

Did the Iranian Revolution represent a failure for the intelligence community? The record is mixed. Prior to 1978, there was no intelligence that predicted the fall of the Shah. Certainly, all the information was there. An economy in the midst of a sharp retrenchment, political underdevelopment, and other cracks in the edifice of the Shah's power had been observed. Yet few in the intelligence community, or anywhere else, managed to draw the proper conclusions.

Iran was a very hard case to get right. In 1976–77, to have concluded that the Shah of Iran would fall to millions of Iranians rallied by an aging cleric in exile, one would have needed the Oracle of Delphi. To a great extent, these problems were complicated by the nature of the US-Iranian relationship. Though the Shah was an ally, Iran remained very much a 'hard target' for intelligence analysts. The dilemma was clear to the intelligence community. The nature of the Iranian power structure tended to obfuscate sources of information that might have been available in other countries.[64]

In the early stages of the crisis, the intelligence community was deeply divided over events in Iran, and this may go a long way in explaining the belated response of the policy establishment in Washington. Each of the community members displayed varying degrees of skepticism. Yet INR awakened early to the dangers facing the Shah, and produced timely and important warnings. Indeed, INR was consistently more willing to question the traditional pedestals of the Shah's power base than either the CIA or DIA. DIA products tended to be more optimistic than those of CIA or INR, in part because of a reliance on these pedestals. On 1 September, the DIA had stated: 'Despite the clear danger to the Shah's position posed by the continuing unrest, we believe that since he has the support of Iran's military leaders and much of Iran's educated elite that his regime will survive.'[65]

CIA also tended to focus on the traditional pedestals of the Shah's regime early in the crisis. Consequently, the CIA was generally optimistic of the monarch's ability to weather the crisis. In August 1978, the CIA produced a 23-page Assessment entitled 'Iran after the Shah'. 'Not an assessment of what will happen', but 'an examination of persons, institutions, and other factors', the report was found to be useful in its intended purpose. Yet the preface of the report included the now famous assertion; 'Iran is not in a revolutionary or even "prerevolutionary" situation.'[66] By late September, however, a discernible shift in mood could be observed in CIA reporting. CIA began to focus on the level of popular disaffection, and the influence of Khomeini over the demonstrators. Through November and December, the agency cited Khomeini's pervasive influence over the mass of Iranians and the disparate opposition groups, and the unlikely possibility of a political settlement given this influence. Moreover, the CIA maintained a healthy skepticism about the loyalty of the Iranian military.

In the final analysis, American policy was dependent on the Shah and, therefore, bad news was unwelcome. Policy makers tended to disregard intelligence that did not substantiate their preferred view of the situation. As the House evaluation on intelligence states: 'In the case of Iran, long-standing US attitudes toward the Shah inhibited intelligence collection, dampened policy makers' appetite for analysis of the Shah's position, and deafened policy makers to the warning implicit in available intelligence.'[67] In the words of the former head of the National Foreign Assessment Center, Robert Bowie, 'I think certainly by September '78 we [CIA] had a better grasp of the situation than the policy establishment, but we were providing intelligence they were not necessarily interested in using.'[68] Thus, the nature of the US-Iranian relationship and bureaucratic maneuvering limited Washington's policy options, not a lack of intelligence. Those who advocate the elevation of the DCI to cabinet rank, as is the case currently, may find support for their argument in the lessons of 1978.

By 1978, after a decade of scandals, reorganizations, public skepticism and partisan ideological debate about the Agency's work, value, and methods, there existed no broad based consensus in Washington that would allow the intelligence community, particularly the CIA, to challenge longstanding policy attitudes about Iran. This situation was exacerbated by the initial confusion of the community itself and by the inability of intelligence officials, particularly the DCI, to assert themselves. If there was an intelligence failure with regard to Iran, it lay in the relationship between policy and intelligence. As one scholar points out, the efficacy of intelligence at times depends as much on the power to persuade as on accuracy.[69]

NOTES

1. Jimmy Carter, *Keeping Faith: Memoirs of a President* (NY: Bantam Books 1982).
2. Carter, *Keeping Faith*, p.436. Gary Sick, *All Fall Down: America's Tragic Encounter With Iran* (NY: Random House 1985); Zbigniew Brzezinski, *Power And Principle: Memoirs of the National Security Advisor, 1977-1981* (NY: Farrar, Straus, and Giroux 1983).
3. Gary Sick, *All Fall Down* (note 1) p.34. Two mullahs were among the dead in Qom. Shia Islamic tradition requires a mourning period after a death. The incident set of a recurring cycle of demonstrations at 40-day intervals that culminated in the departure of the Shah on 16 Jan. 1979. See John D. Stempel, *Inside the Iranian Revolution* (Bloomington: Indiana UP1981) p.91.

4. James A. Bill, *The Eagle and the Lion: The Tragedy of American-Iranian Relations* (New Haven, CT: Yale UP 1988) p.236.
5. US Dept of State (DOS)/Bureau of Intelligence and Research (INR), 'Iranian Dissidence on the Increase' 29 Jan. 1978 in 'Making of US Policy in Iran 1977-1980', microfiche collection at the National Security Archives, Washington DC, doc. 3568. Hereafter cited as 'Making of US Policy'.
6. Zachary Karabell, '"Inside the US Espionage Den": The US Embassy and the Fall of the Shah', *Intelligence and National Security* 8/1 (Jan. 1993) pp.43–59.
7. US Defense Intelligence Agency (DIA), Intelligence Appraisal, 'Iran: Religious Inspired Opposition' 29 March 1978 in 'Making of US Policy', doc. 01350.
8. US CIA, National Intelligence Daily Article, 'Iran: Civil Disturbances' 11 May 1978 in 'Making of US Policy', doc. 01385. The report also notes that 'The Shah is frustrated with his failure to contain the unrest, and seems baffled as to how to deal with the underlying causes of Muslim fundamentalist dissidence.'
9. US CIA, National Intelligence Daily Article, 'Iran: Increased Religious Dissidence', June, no day, 1978 in 'Making of US Policy', doc. 01404.
10. US DOS, Memo., NEA-Harold Saunders to the Secretary, 'Assessment of Internal Political Scene in Iran' Aug., no day, 1978, in 'Making of US Policy' doc. 01476'
11. Everand Abrahamian, *Iran Between Two Revolutions*, (Princeton UP 1982) p.510.
12. US House of Representatives, Subcommittee on Evaluation, Permanent Select Committee on Intelligence, Staff Report, *Iran: Evaluation of U.S. Intelligence Performance Prior to November 1978* (Washington DC: GPO 1979) p.5.
13. Abrahamian, *Iran Between Two Revolutions* (note 1) pp.508–9.
14. US DIA, Intelligence Appraisal, 'Iran: Renewal of Civil Disturbances', 16 Aug. 1978 in 'Making of US Policy', doc. 01472.
15. Abrahamian, *Iran Between Two Revolutions* (note 11) p.511.
16. US DOS, Saunders to the Secretary, 'Assessment of Internal Political Scene in Iran'.
17. In the 1950s the National Front was a coalition of liberal, secular opposition groups championed by Dr. Muhammad Musaddiq. Prime Minister Musaddiq fell from office in a coup in 1953 in which the CIA and the British intelligence service played active roles.
18. US CIA, Unpublished draft 'Iran NIE' in *Documents From the U.S. Espionage Den*, Vol.34, pp.97–103. *Documents* is a collection of official documents pieced together by Iranian students after the seizure of the US embassy in Tehran. Hereafter cited as DUSED.
19. Michael Ledeen and William Lewis, *Debacle: The American Failure in Iran* (NY: Knopf 1981) pp.132–3.
20. Author's interview with Philip Stoddard, 5 Jan. 1994, Bethesda, Md. As of 1 Sept., INR had taken a definitive view of the Shah's predicament: 'We expect that violent dissent from the Shah's rule will continue to disrupt Iranian Society, despite his efforts at political liberalization and other reforms. We are dubious that the Shah, in the near term, can suppress urban violence without substantial use of force. That, in turn, would further aggravate his difficulties by enlarging the circle off opposition against him and possibly calling into question the loyalty of the armed forces and security services.' The analysis also noted the pervasive 'cynical distrust' with which the Shah's regime is viewed and concluded that 'This attitude could also infect the armed forces – the mainstay of the Shah's power.' US DOS, White Paper, 'The Strength and Durability of the Shah's Regime', 29 Jan. 1980 in 'Making of US Policy', doc. 03568.
21. US House Staff Report, *Iran: Evaluation of U.S. Intelligence* (note 12) p.5.
22. US DOS White Paper, Political/Intelligence Issues, 'Strength And Durability Of The Shah's Regime: Assessments of the Bureau of Intelligence and Research,' n.d., in 'Making of US Policy', doc. 3570.
23. US House Staff Report, *Iran* (note 21) p.5.
24. Bill, *The Eagle and the Lion* (note 4) pp.379–424. In DCI Turner's view, 'some of the CIA's key analysts were hung up on the durability of the Shah.' Stansfield Turner, *Secrecy and Democracy: The CIA in Transition* (Boston: Houghton Mifflin 1985), p.115.
25. US House Staff Report, *Iran* (note 12) p.6.
26. Author's interview with Philip Stoddard.

27. Sick, *All Fall Down* (note 1) p.58.
28. Stempel, *Inside The Iranian Revolution* (note 3) pp.115–17. Up to 20,000 Iranians gathered in Julah Square in Tehran. Troops opened fire on the crowd. Estimates of casualties vary from 122–1000 deaths. Doctors tending the wounded estimated 300–400 dead, and ten times that number wounded.
29. US DOS, 'Strength and Durability of the Shah's Regime'.
30. US CIA, Report, 'Middle East and South Asia Review' 20 Oct. 1978 in 'Makings of US Policy' doc. 01604. The report also cited the apparent rejection by the National Front and the religious opposition of a united front with the Iranian communist Party.
31. Author's Interview with Gary Sick, 1 Aug. 1993, NYC.
32. Sick, *All Fall Down* (note 1) pp.78–79. As a result of this meeting, Brzezinski telephoned both Ambassador Zahedi and the Shah to express the US' unequivocal support.
33. Brzezinski, *Power And Principle* (note 1) pp.363–4.
34. US DOS/INR, Briefing Memo, David E Mark, Acting Director to the Secretary, 'The Gathering Crisis in Iran', 2 Nov. 1978 in 'Makings of US Policy', doc. 01666.
35. Bill (note 1) p.236 also argues that the Shah was aware of the futility of the use of force.
36. Sick, *All Fall Down* (note 1) pp.90–106. Brzezinski wrote in his diary on 5 Nov. that Turner's comments at the 2 Nov. SCC had been 'inept and vague'. *Power and Principle* (note 1) p.367.
37. Quoted in Turner, *Secrecy and Democracy* (note 24) pp.113–14.
38. John Prados, *Keepers Of The Keys: A History of the National Security Council form Truman to Bush* (NY: Morrow 1991) p.438.
39. Sick, *All Fall Down* (note 1) p.91.
40. Turner, *Secrecy and Democracy* (note 24) pp.113–14.
41. US CIA, National Intelligence Daily Article, 'Iran: Military Government', 6 Nov. 1978 in 'Makings of US Policy', doc. 01693.
42. US CIA, National Intelligence Daily Article, 'Iran: Shah's Strategy', 13 Nov. 1978 in 'Making of US Policy', doc. 01728.
43. US CIA, Intelligence Memorandum, 'The Politics Of Ayatollah Ruhollah Khomeini' 2 Nov. 1978 in 'Makings of US Policy', doc. 01778.
44. Brzezinski, *Power And Principle* (note 1) p.368.
45. Bill, *The Eagle and the Lion* (note 4) p.242.
46. Scott Armstrong, 'Carter Held Hope Even after Shah Had Lost His', *Washington Post*, 25 Oct. 1980, p.A12.
47. Moharram, the first month of the Islamic year, is a month of mourning commemorating the death of Hussein, one of Shia Islam's most revered founders. Hussein, the grandson of Muhammad, disputed the claim of the Caliph of Islam, Yazid, to his position. In 680 CE, two armies met in battle on a plain called Kerbala, south of present day Baghdad. Yazid's forces vastly outnumbered those of Hussein. On the 10th day of the confrontation, Yazid's troops were victorious, and Hussein was killed. The 'Tragedy at Kerbala' is at the center of the Moharram mourning period.
48. US CIA, Intelligence Memo., 'Iran: The Meaning of Moharram', 29 Nov. 1978 in 'Making of US Policy', doc. 01819.
49. US CIA, Alert Memo., 'Iran – Prospects for Moharram', 29 Nov. 1978 in 'Making of US Policy', doc. 01818.
50. US DIA, Intelligence Appraisal, "Iran: The Month Of Moharram'" 29 Nov. 1978 in 'Making of US Policy', document 1820.
51. US CIA, Alert Memorandum, 'Iran – Update on Moharram', 5 Dec. 1978 in 'Making of US Policy', doc. 01865.
52. Robert Moss, 'Who's Meddling in Iran?', *New Republic*, 2 Dec. 1978, pp.15–18. Moss was described to Sick as a 'professional anti-Communist polemicist'. Sick, *All Fall Down* (note 1) p.124. These tenuous allegations of Soviet involvement are based on very little evidence indeed.
53. US CIA, Intelligence Memo., 'Opposition Demonstrations In Iran: Leadership, Organization, And Tactics', 21 Dec. 1978 in 'Making of US Policy', doc. 01952.
54. Sick, *All Fall Down* (note 1) p.124.

55. George Ball, Secret Paper, 'Issues And Implications of the Iranian Crisis', 12 Dec. 1978. Personal copy provided to the author by George Ball.
56. Author's interview with George Ball, 5 April 1994, Princeton NJ. It should be noted that the CIA was not the only casualty of the back channel with the ambitious Zahedi. As the views of Brzezinski and Ambassador William Sullivan diverged, the National Security Advisor found in Zahedi a convenient excuse to undermine Sullivan's credibility with the President. According to Zahedi, the Shah was losing confidence in the ambassador.
57. Brzezinski, *Power And Principle* (note 1) pp.370–1. Brzezinski wrote of the exercise: 'In selecting Ball I violated a basic rule of bureaucratic tactics: One should never obtain the services of an 'impartial' outside consultant regarding an issue that one feels strongly about without first making certain in advance that one knows the likely contents of his advice.'
58. Sick, *All Fall Down* (note 1) pp.135—6.
59. Author's interview with Gary Sick.
60. US CIA, Intelligence Memorandum, 'Opposition Demonstrations In Iran'.
61. Abrahamian, *Iran Between Two Revolutions* (note 11) p.524. Bakhtiar's conditions included that the Shah should promise to 'reign' rather than 'rule', exile 14 hardliners in the military, and take a vacation abroad.
62. US CIA, Intelligence Memo., 'Iran: The Radicals in the Opposition', 12 Jan. 1979 in 'Making of US Policy', doc. 2074.
63. Sick, *All Fall Down* (note 1) pp.147–8.
64. US CIA, David H. Blee, National Intelligence Officer for the Middle East, to Ambassador Edward S. Little, Chairman of Human Resources Committee, Central Intelligence Agency 'Reporting Assessment – FOCUS Iran', 4 Nov. 1976, in DUSED, 8, p.140
65. US DIA Report, 'Assessment of the Political Situation in Iran' 1 Sept. 1978 in 'Making of US Policy', doc. 01497.
66. US House Staff Report, *Iran* (note 12) p.5.
67. Ibid. p.7.
68. Author's telephone interview with Robert Bowie, 6 April 1994, Washington DC.
69. Rhodri Jeffreys-Jones, *The CIA & American Democracy* (New Haven, CT: Yale UP 1989) p.1.

9

American Economic Intelligence: Past Practice and Future Principles

PHILIP ZELIKOW

This essay uses the term, 'intelligence', in a broad sense, to mean information collected by the government, overtly or covertly, to inform its international policy judgments. Economic intelligence is information about how those outside of the United States develop, produce, or manage their material goods, services, and resources. The term, as it is used here, encompasses the interpretation and presentation of raw information or data to produce finished reports or analyses offered to inform policy making consumers.

THE ORGANIZATION OF ECONOMIC INTELLIGENCE GATHERING

The US government has always collected economic intelligence. In late 1776 the first US intelligence agency, the Committee of Secret Correspondence of the Continental Congress, sent one William Carmichael to Europe, in the guise of a merchant, to report on a variety of economic topics of interest to the new government. Worried, for example, about foreign tobacco competition, Carmichael was to monitor foreign competition in European markets from tobacco grown in Ukrainian provinces of the Russian Empire. In a November 1776 secret dispatch from Amsterdam, Carmichael reported reassuringly that, 'You have been threatened that the Ukraine would supply Europe with tobacco. It must be long before that time can arrive. I have seen some of its tobacco here, and the best of it is worse than the worst of our ground leaf.'[1]

Once executive departments of the US government were created, they began to satisfy their own needs for intelligence. No intelligence agency existed outside of these departments until World War II. As needed, these departments did collect and analyze information on supply and demand of critical materials, the economies of particular countries, trade issues, or scientific and technological concerns. During World War I an economic intelligence section within the army's military intelligence operation was headed by John Foster Dulles. Preparing for the Versailles peace conference, President Woodrow Wilson turned to a collection of private experts, the 'Inquiry', which gathered economic intelligence from its headquarters at the American Geographical Society in New York.

In World War II the traditional departments were supplemented by the Board of Economic Warfare, which studied the Japanese economy, for example, or analyzed the role of critical commodities.[2] Other vital economic intelligence work was performed by the Office of Strategic Services (OSS). OSS collected information on key commodities, like tungsten, or on diamond smuggling, or on production of ball bearings. Its analytical talents roamed from formidable historical analysis of the German state to the employment of the then-novel methods of operations research in order to plot ways to attack German industry. The USSR division of OSS, directed by Abram Bergson and Wassily Leontief, offered prescient appraisals of the Soviet Union's postwar economic condition.[3]

In 1945 OSS was dissolved. Whenever a successor organization was contemplated the he traditional departments resisted surrendering any of their responsibilities for collection and analysis of information. Every department head insisted on the right to provide the intelligence affecting their department's issues. Even the Postmaster General declared that, 'it must be clear that any government intelligence service outside the Post Office Department must operate through the Post Office Department and recognize the absolute jurisdiction of the Department.'[4] One important exception was evaluation of scientific intelligence, a job turned over to the CIA's forerunner, the Central Intelligence Group, during 1946 and 1947.

The Central Intelligence Group (CIG) soon began coordinating provision of adequate economic intelligence to top officials. In June 1946 a progress report to cabinet offcials then constituting the 'National Intelligence Authority' reported on success in gathering intelligence on 'foreign industrial establishments' and ongoing work in foreign petroleum extraction. The CIG compiled comprehensive geographic information and utilized the services of overseas-stationed attachés to gather data on strategic minerals. The then-Director of Central Intelligence (DCI), Lt General Hoyt Vandenberg, used economic intelligence to illustrate the need for coordinated assessments:

> ... as regards a given steel plant, State is studying what products are made there and the rate of production. War Department, however, is interested in the construction and physical details of the plant, the railroads serving it, and other data required for target information.

State Department, if it broadened the base of its studies, might well be able to furnish at least part of that type of economic intelligence. It is the job of CIG, therefore, to find out the needs of all the departments and to meet them, either by recommending that one department expand its activities or by performing the necessary research in CIG.[5]

When the Central Intelligence Agency (CIA) was established by the National Security Act of 1947, its roles were limited. The State Department had primary responsibility for 'political, cultural, sociological' intelligence; the uniformed services were responsible for military intelligence; and 'economic, scientific, and technological intelligence' was assigned to 'each agency in accordance with its respective needs'.[6] The CIA's only role was to provide 'national intelligence' on transcendent issues, and to do this by coordinating the information collected by the various departments of government.

But there was growing recognition that while some economic intelligence did not fall into the dominant interest of any particular department, it might still have great value for the US government as a whole. Following the 1949 recommendations of a review group chaired by Allen Dulles, the CIA created a new Office of Research Reports to collect and examine more economic information.[7]

This office was important because it was the only truly analytical office in the new CIA, separate from the retail work of preparing and coordinating national estimates or providing daily or weekly intelligence summaries. In other words, most of the large analytical establishment of CIA today can trace its lineage to the work on economic intelligence in the early days of the Cold War. In a 1951 NSC directive the US government held the CIA responsible for determining the overall requirements for 'foreign economic intelligence'. The CIA was to insure that 'the full economic knowledge and technical talent available in the Government' was brought to bear on issues involving national security. The agency was also ordered to evaluate the 'pertinence, extent, and quality of the foreign economic data available bearing on national security issues, and develop ways in which quality could be improved and gaps could be filled.' Finally, as a service of 'common concern' to various departments the CIA was itself to conduct 'such foreign economic research and produce such foreign economic intelligence' as was required to supplement work being done by other agencies.[8]

By 1952 the DCI, then General Walter Bedell Smith, was able to inform the National Security Council that his new Office of Research and Reports (ORR) was in full operation. Smith commented that 'although accurate appraisal of an enemy's economic potential is a most important factor in estimating his military capabilities, this crucially important task had previously been scattered among twenty-four separate agencies of the Government.' An interdepartmental Economic Intelligence Committee was also put in place, chaired by the assistant director of ORR.[9]

The allocation of responsibility for economic intelligence over the next 20 years was, in large part, a story of the shifting roles of the CIA and the Department of State. CIA and State had worked closely together during the Truman administration. These were years when economic issues received great attention and enjoyed high prestige in State, supervised by powerful and capable officials like Will Clayton and Paul Nitze and harnessing the talents of economists like Edward S. Mason, Walt Rostow, Charles P. Kindleberger, and John Kenneth Galbraith. Over the years, however, as CIA's capabilities grew, the State Department retreated from its position as the primary center in the US government for both the collection and the analysis of economic data.

For a time State officials felt confident that they could collect and analyze foreign economic data, trends, and other related intelligence without CIA's help. The Department conceded, however, that its diplomats could offer little help in evaluating the economies of countries in the Soviet bloc. The economies of these communist countries therefore became the special responsibility of CIA.[10] The bargain was clearly established, in writing. The State Department would produce 'economic intelligence on countries outside the Sino-Soviet Bloc' and CIA 'shall produce economic intelligence on the Sino-Soviet Bloc and scientific and technical intelligence as a service of common concern'.[11]

The job of coordinating economic intelligence by the US government, assigned to CIA in 1951, was a substantial challenge. The Economic Intelligence Committee, chaired by the head of CIA's Office of Research Reports (ORR), worked to establish priorities and publish interdepartmental economic estimates. Since the various agencies still worked for their own bosses, this new committee's work often did little more than add to the flow of paper.[12]

It was the CIA's economic work on the Soviet bloc, though, that propelled its ascent to the status of a major source of intelligence analysis to the US government. ORR's new head, a brilliant, young economics professor from the Massachusetts Institute of Technology, Max Millikan, 'had an electric effect' on the office and helped recruit a number of bright economics graduate students before he returned to Massachusetts. (He remained an influential consultant to ORR). In 1955 there were nearly 500 analysts in ORR, more than the other offices of CIA's analytical side, the Directorate of Intelligence, put together, and almost all these ORR analysts were working on Soviet bloc economies.[13] They had a formidable task, since there was little information available on any aspect of the Soviet economy.

(Moscow did not begin publishing even basic economic statistics until 1957.) The office was generally credited with composing the first good pictures of Soviet economic capabilities – its transport system, current production, plant capability, and so on.[14]

This economic analysis became CIA's route to challenging the military services' monopoly over the provision of broader strategic intelligence. In the mid-1950s the Agency was embroiled in a major controversy with the Air Force over Soviet bomber production. CIA argued that because of limited economic production capacity, the USSR could not possibly have built a force of the size claimed by the Air Force. The CIA was generally perceived to have won this fight. Its analysis was valued by the Kennedy administration and it added to its luster by establishing dominance in the interpretation of the new photo imagery taken from aircraft and satellites. During the 1960s the CIA became the government's leading provider of strategic intelligence.[15]

The CIA also began expanding the scope of its economic analysis to cover 'Free World' economies, partly in response to specific requests and partly under the rubric of examining Soviet bloc economic activity in the developing world. In 1961 State's Bureau of Intelligence and Research, faced with severe budget constraints, cut the majority of its economic research in order to maintain its capabilities for political analysis. CIA picked up most of State's responsibilities for providing regular economic inputs to national intelligence documents and also picked up substantial new demands from policy makers, especially for information on developing countries.[16] CIA director John McCone struck a new bargain with Secretary of State Dean Rusk in 1965, formally authorizing CIA to pursue worldwide economic intelligence.[17] Relatively few policy officials were deeply interested, however, in economic information about the developed world.

By 1967–68 a growing sense of European and Japanese competition sparked new interest in those economies, while the devaluation of Sterling at the end of 1967 also created a demand to know more about international monetary problems. The CIA replaced ORR with a new office, the Office of Economic Research, which began receiving its first formal requests for intelligence from the Treasury Department in 1968. The President's Foreign Intelligence Advisory Board (PFIAB) reported to the White House on economic intelligence in December 1971. The State Department, the Board concluded, had not carried out its assigned responsibilities for collection and analysis on free world economic activity; only CIA's Office of Economic Research could do the job. The PFIAB urged that the CIA get more resources to produce intelligence for the US government's entire international economic agenda. As another sign of growing attention being given to economic intelligence, the Treasury Department became a formal member of the intelligence community, represented on the US Intelligence Board, in 1972.[18]

As in the early 1990s, after the end of the Cold War, economics was suddenly the fashionable priority for international policy in the early 1970s. A 1974 issue of *Foreign Affairs* announced the 'Year of Economics'.[19]Close attention to various economic developments was ranked as one of the top five 'substantive objectives' in guidance issued to the intelligence community for fiscal year 1976.[20]

These new demands stretched CIA's economic capabilities more thinly. Diversion of analysts to studying Vietnam or other crisis spots drained away a significant part of the effort that had been devoted to the Soviet economy. Demand for analysis from CIA grew, as other economic agencies such as Treasury and Commerce increasingly challenged State's views on foreign economic policy. These agencies, along with the White House-organized Council for International Economic Policy (CIEP) sought information gathered or interpreted from outside of the State Department. CIA built up its abilities to follow world commodity markets, especially gold, oil, and agriculture (working closely with the Agriculture Department on problems like Soviet grain import requirements). CIA became the most important producer of intelligence for policy makers responding to the oil shocks of the 1970s. Meanwhile the CIA remained a crucial source of information about communist economies, especially China, a country which released no economic statistics at all between the late 1950s and the late 1970s.

Yet the CIA's overall importance in the provision of economic intelligence diminished during the 1980s. There was still little competition from the State Department. The analytical capabilities in its Intelligence and Research Bureau (as many as 100 analysts in the 1950s) were never rebuilt and remain at a small fraction of the former effort. But other policy agencies substantially bolstered their in-house expertise during the 1970s. The Treasury Department and the Federal Reserve Board both took steps to improve their monitoring of international financial issues. During the 1980s the Commerce Department built up a staff of hundreds of industry and country analysts.

The CIA's most important new competition, though, has come from the new wealth and sophistication of international economic analysis available to policy makers from the private sector. Dramatic increases in international capital flows and international trade have naturally been accompanied by a greater market interest in international economic information. Complementing this, the international financial institutions such as the International Monetary Fund (IMF) and the World Bank have become strong, knowledgeable, providers of the kind of information about the developing world that was once almost the exclusive province of CIA. The net result is a far greater volume of private information and analysis available to government officials, enhanced by more sophisticated information-processing. On-line services now give private analysts access to a tremendous array of reports and data; their products in turn raise the general level of discussion in newspapers and trade publications.

COLLECTION AND ANALYSIS: HOW IS IT PRODUCED?

While alternative sources of information and analysis, often produced outside of the US government, have proliferated, the CIA's reservoir of experts has remained more or less constant for many years. The number of Agency analysts working on economic topics was at an all-time high in the 1950s, when creating a database for the Soviet economy was such a labor-intensive task. Work on economic topics now extends beyond the Directorate of Intelligence's economic office, renamed once again as the Office of Resources, Trade, and Technology (RTT), to analysts concerned with particular regions, with day-to-day intelligence briefings, or with special topics like export control and nonproliferation. But the total number of analysts working on economic topics throughout the Directorate of Intelligence has been fairly constant since the 1970s, with about 250–270 professionals.[21]

Overt government collection of economic information overseas, whether by State Department economic officers of the Foreign Service or by the Commerce Department's foreign commercial officers or by the Treasury's financial attachés, has also remained at roughly the same level for decades. The end of the Cold War may have stimulated new interest in economic intelligence, but it has not had a dramatic effect on the resources available to perform the mission in any of the relevant agencies. The situation at the State Department has actually deteriorated.

The quality of CIA's effort has been undermined by turbulence in the assignment of its analysts, as groups of people are moved from one hot topic to another. The quality has also been undermined by the rise of private sector activity. Talented economic analysts are hired away to lucrative private work and 20 per cent turnover a year among the trained economists is not unknown.

The main sources of economic intelligence are, in approximate order of importance, open sources, 'overt' reporting, and clandestine reports. Open sources may range from official statistical publications, newspapers, radio broadcasts, and trade publications to IMF country studies. 'Unclassified sources generally constitute the foundation of any economic analysis, even on the USSR and other communist countries, and provide an essential context to interpret classified material and how it fits into the overall picture.'[22] The volume of records is massive, and the intelligent synthesis of material – in both English and foreign languages – is no mean feat. The bulk of documents and transcripts are practically valueless without high-quality information processing.

The CIA is reluctant to acknowledge how much it relies upon open sources. Some officials fear that Congress will not appropriate money for experts who 'just read the newspapers'. But all agencies performing economic intelligence must admit the obvious: the world economy functions on the basis of publicly available information. In general, the CIA does more to aggregate and interpret open-source literature than any other government agency. The Agency has developed and applied new computerized tools for sorting through open data, tools that are unrivaled in the US government or even in the private sector.

Though it may seem that many agencies, including the Library of Congress, could do this job of sorting open data equally well, these other entities are not staffed or equipped to digest such a diverse quantity of data, match it against classified information, and provide a synthesis tailored to the needs of executive branch officials. To say, as some do, that this task is little more than 'reading the newspapers', is like saying that the US Navy's multibillion dollar acoustic signal processing technology just 'listens to the ocean'. The CIA's ability to process open literature can become an overexploited resource, since it is effectively free to users in the executive departments and since no gatekeeper now sorts out which requests really merit extra attention from the CIA.

The second major source of economic intelligence are the reports from America's embassies and consulates, penned by State Department economic officers, Treasury attachés (in some embassies), and officers of the Foreign Commercial Service. Since Foreign Commercial Service officers usually attend to aiding American businesses rather than systematic analysis of the local economy, the State and Treasury reports are most important. Unfortunately, the quality of these overseas reports vary greatly from post to post and from officer to officer.

Few economic officers in the State Department are trained economists. The entry examination for the Foreign Service 'is almost obsessively neutral with regard to specialized qualifications'.[23] Though mid-career economic training has improved, the State Department does not always provide the interested and critical audience needed for adequate development and reward of outstanding work or analytical talent. Instead economic officers are often burdened by 'low-priority, even trivial, requests', stemming from State's own 'lack of coordination and parochialism' in the economic field, promoting 'a reactive, issue-specific focus'.[24] The total number of economic officers in the Foreign Service actually declined between 1985 and 1992 by 7.5 per cent, from 931 to 861 (about 600 of them stationed overseas).[25] Limits on the deployment, training, and tasking of overt collection and analysis by State's economic officers are one of the most important constraints on the potential of American economic intelligence work.

Other overseas collectors also present a mixed picture. Treasury attachés are fewer in number (about 400 American staff overseas worldwide) and have a narrower focus, though the general standard of reporting is regarded somewhat more highly than that coming from State. Commerce and Agriculture each employ about 250 Americans overseas, but Commerce does little mainstream economic reporting or analysis and Agriculture obviously concentrates on its relatively narrow portfolio.[26]

Clandestine information is data obtained without either the knowledge or consent of foreign governments. It can come from satellites, from intercepted communications, or from secrets stolen by a foreign national employed by the United States. Such information rarely contributes vitally to the daily stream of economic intelligence flowing through government offices, but it often adds a special strategic insight or a tactical tip that instantly can catch the attention of top officials.

The economic information arriving in Washington from these various sources is then processed, analyzed, and disseminated principally by the CIA, Treasury, and State. The other agencies tend to consume far more economic intelligence than they produce. As mentioned earlier, CIA's base of economic analysts has remained roughly constant for decades while demands upon it have grown, and it is getting harder for the Agency to recruit and retain the best and most experienced analysts. Treasury was once considered to have an outstanding staff of economists in its Office of International Affairs, but the quality of their labors is widely believed to have suffered from benign neglect during the 1980s. The State Department has never recovered the economic expertise or mandate it sacrificed more than 30 years ago. Its Bureau of Economic Affairs has been hard hit by budget cuts in the 1990s, with declines in staffing, even while total domestic employment at State has remained stable. On the brighter side, the staff of the International Trade Commission and the Federal Reserve Board's Division of International Finance have, within their narrower areas of responsibility, established excellent reputations for interpretation and presentation of economic information.

Overall, however, despite the louder rhetoric about new challenges to American competitiveness, there is no evidence of any significant change in the methods or resources devoted to the collection of economic intelligence in recent investments in recruiting, developing, or retaining the people needed to present such intelligence effectively to policy makers.

The CIA's role in providing economic intelligence to the US policy community is now substantial. Hundreds work in the RTT office, parceled out among divisions working on (1) international transactions (including sanctions enforcement and illicit finance); (2) international economic and environmental problems (including trade and finance and competition); (3) defense markets and logistics; (4) geographic resources (including demographics and commodities); (5) civil technology (including aerospace, advanced manufacturing, and emerging technologies); and (6) energy resources.

These analysts join others, including those assigned to particular regions or countries, in preparing papers for policymaking officials. The Clinton administration's creation of the National Economic Council (NEC) has established an active new primary consumer of intelligence in the White House and has stimulated publication of a *Daily Economic Brief* distributed to top officials around the government. CIA analysts personally brief senior NEC, Treasury, Commerce, and USTR (Office of the US Trade Representative) officials almost every day.

WHEN TO RELY ON GOVERNMENT: FOUR PRINCIPLES

The growing availability of economic information from the private sector, international organizations, and the international financial institutions raises the question: Should the government be in this business at all? If an entity outside of the US government can do the same work nearly as well as government agencies, or even better, why not let harried budget-strapped agencies settle comfortably into the saddle of a free rider, using the products already produced for the marketplace at someone else's expense?

This essay presumes the agencies should do just that; they should take full advantage of the enlarged, more sophisticated flow of outside information and avoid duplicating tasks already performed adequately by others. The word 'adequately' is especially important. The government may believe that it can do a better job at collecting or analyzing certain information. The burden, though, is on government to show why taxpayers should be obliged to pay for this added increment in performance (if in fact the increment really exists outside the minds of those asking for the government money).

However, the government does have some unique responsibilities in the collection and preparation of economic intelligence. Here are four principles proposed as a guide for reflecting on the duties the US government should perform on behalf of its citizens.

First, the United States should decide whether the collection or interpretation of the information is a public good that the private sector will not provide. There are certain kinds of information for which there is little market demand but significant public need. The CIA's economic intelligence function grew in response to the underserved need for more reliable estimates about Soviet bloc economies and then the economies of the less developed and newly independent nations of the Third World, decades before the international financial institutions (IFIs) began to accumulate impressive data about such problems. North Korea is still an example of an economy America needs to understand better but which offers little interest either to the private sector or to the IFIs. There are many other gaps in private sector coverage of economic issues which justify public concern: the export efforts of the Ukrainian arms industry might be one; the finances of the Cali cocaine cartel might be another. US government production of such intelligence is therefore an expenditure in the public interest.

Second, the US government has unique intelligence collection capabilities which can be applied to some economic questions. The government has both unique collection assets and unique legal privileges. Washington has invested enormous sums of money in systems deployed, from outer space to the bottom of the sea, to collect imagery, communications, electronic emissions, and many other detectable physical phenomena. Private citizens cannot afford to do most of these things, and they would go to jail for doing some of them.

The US government also sponsors clandestine intelligence collection by intelligence officers overseas or, more bluntly, 'it employs secret agents to perform acts that break foreign laws'.[27] Further, US intelligence agencies have a variety of 'liaison' relationships with the intelligence agencies of other countries. 'Indeed, we have created whole national services, internal and external, from one end of the world to the other, trained them, vetted them, funded them, in order to be able to conduct liaison in their countries, and to get them to do work that we, though expending vast sums in training and subsidy of operations, thought we were too small or too poor to handle ourselves.'[28]

Government officials unanimously praise the value of economic intelligence gathered by such means, even if the flashes of special insight are unpredictable or episodic. These unique methods, as well as the craft that accompanies their use, are also essential attributes of indispensable counterintelligence (including countering some of the services with whom the US also has liaison relationships).

Third, there may be issues or questions where the US government does not wish to rely solely upon available outside sources of information. Outside information can be biased. The marketplace produces information in response to commercial interest. These interests may not coincide with the way the government has defined the public interest. The mining industry may not be an objective source on the US need to enlarge its strategic stockpile of manganese. Motorola might not be the most objective judge of its competitors' pricing practices. Outside information can even be distorted. The Soviet Union never accurately reported its true defense spending. The United Nations might be obliged to rely on Iraq's reported GNP statistics because it would be impolitic to challenge a member state's veracity. The United States cannot afford to be so tolerant.

Outside information may also be too opaque to be useful. An institution might have a model for calculating China's use of fossil fuels, one so complex (or proprietary) that the crucial assumptions are invisible to all except the model's operators. Or construction company X reports that it lost a public building contract due to an unfair import restriction when actually that was just the excuse the overseas executive gave to his home office to conceal his mishandling of the bidding process. The government has no way of ascertaining the true provenance of such information.

Fourth, and finally, the US government may want to mold information to fit its own special requirements. A policy-maker might read several different forecasts for Japan's economic future. Which forecast is best?, he asks. I need to know by next week, he adds. A quick check of the literature reveals a good article in an economic journal, but it was written two years earlier. It does not reflect on the newly announced changes in Japanese fiscal policy. There is no time to wait for another, better academic paper or brokerage firm analysis to turn up. An answer must be provided, and it must take the latest developments into account as well as the fate of the new proposals in the Japanese Diet (a political factor wholly ignored in the journal article). Another policy maker wants to know how the European Union's latest carbon tax proposal would affect the American coal mining industry. The literature yields good treatments of the aggregate effect of alternative carbon tax regimes, but none of the alternatives match up exactly with the EU proposal and the work does not break the impact out into specific sectors, like coal. In each of these hypothetical cases, the government needs to add some value to the available information. Even where information is abundant and on point, perhaps on a topic like predictions for world oil supplies, government analysts might need to process a variety of judgments or methodologies into a terse, plausible synthesis.

NOTES

This essay is a revised version of a chapter from a monograph, 'American Intelligence and the World Economy', that was included in Report of the Twentieth Century Fund Task Force on the Future of US Intelligence, *In From The Cold* (NY: Twentieth Century Fund Press 1996). It appears here with the permission of the Twentieth Century Fund. The report of this task force also includes some policy recommendations suggested by the author that encompass and transcend the specific recommendations offered here.

1. Quotation provided from CIA's Historical Intelligence Collection, Langley, Virginia.
2. For the memoir of an intelligence officer who studied the Japanese economy for the Board of Economic Warfare, see Shannon McCune, *Intelligence on the Economic Collapse of Japan in 1945* (Lanham, MD: UP of America 1989).
3. The best available overview of this work is Barry M. Katz, *Foreign Intelligence: Research and Analysis in the Office of Strategic Services, 1942–1945* (Cambridge, MA: Harvard UP 1989).
4. Arthur B. Darling, *The Central Intelligence Agency: An Instrument of Government, to 1950* (Univ. Pk: Pennsylvania State UP 1990) p.35. This declassified history by the CIA's first historian was written in 1952–53.
5. See memo from Rear Adm. Sidney W. Souers to the National Intelligence Authority, 'Progress Report on the Central Intelligence Group', 7 June 1946, pp.5–6; minutes of fourth meeting of the National Intelligence Authority, 17 July 1946, p.1; both repr. in Michael Warner (ed.), *CIA Cold War Records: The CIA Under Harry Truman* (Washington, DC: CIA 1994) pp.41–52, 55–62.
6. National Security Council [hereafter NSC] Intelligence Directive No.1, 'Duties and Responsibilities', 12 Dec. 1947 (declassified); National Security Council Intelligence Directive No.3, 'Coordination of Intelligence Production', 13 Jan. 1948 (declassified).
7. Darling, *CIA* (note 4) p.336.
8. NSC Intelligence Directive No.15, 'Coordination and Production of Foreign Economic Intelligence', 13 June 1951 (declassified).
9. Memo from Walter Bedell Smith to the National Security Council, 'Report by the Director of Central Intelligence', 23 April 1952, pp.1–2, repr. in Warner, *CIA Cold War Records* (note 5) pp.457–8.
10. Ludwell Lee Montague, *General Walter Bedell Smith As Director of Central Intelligence: October 1950-February 1953* (Univ. Pk: Pennsylvania State UP 1992) pp.149–50. This recently declassified internal history was actually completed in 1971.
11. NSC Intelligence Directive No.3, 'Coordination of Intelligence Production', 21 April 1958 (declassified); see also Maurice Ernst, 'Economic Intelligence in CIA', *Studies in Intelligence* 28/4 (Winter 1984) pp.1, 3 (declassified).
12. See William M. Leary (ed.) *The Central Intelligence Agency: History and Documents* (Tuscaloosa: U. of Alabama Press 1984) (repr. historical work written by Anne Karalekas for the Church Committee in the 1970s) pp.33–4; Montague, *Smith* (note 10) pp.152–4.
13. Montague, *Smith* (note 10) pp.151–2; Leary (Karalekas) *CIA* (note 12) p.69. Millikan was succeeded by another effective and energetic head of ORR, Robert Amory, who in 1953 became CIA's deputy director for intelligence.
14. Ernst, 'Economic Intelligence in CIA' (note 11) pp.2–3.
15. Leary (Karalekas) *CIA* (note 12) pp.68–70. Robert McNamara was an appreciative and demanding consumer of CIA's work and he helped reduce Defense Dept. resistance to sharing its information. In 1965 CIA director McCone and deputy defense secretary Cyrus Vance formally agreed that CIA had primary responsibility for studies related to the cost and resource impact of foreign military and space programs.
16. Ernst (note 11) pp.4–5.
17. The State Dept's former general mandate in economic intelligence was revised to extend only to 'countries of the Free World' and CIA's limited mandate for the 'Sino-Soviet Bloc' was replaced by with general authority to 'produce economic, scientific, and technical intelligence'. NSC Intelligence Directive No.3, 'Coordination of Intelligence Production', 17

Feb. 1972 (declassified). See also Leary (Karalekas) *CIA* (note 12) p.91. The State Dept retained primary responsibility for *overt* collection of foreign economic information. NSC Intelligence Directive No.2, 'Coordination of Overt Collection Activities', 17 Feb. 1972 (declassified).

18. See Ernst, 'Economic Intelligence in CIA' (note 11) p.7; NSC Intelligence Directive No.1, 'Basic Duties and Responsibilities', 17 Feb. 1972 (declassified).
19. 'The Year of Economics', *Foreign Affairs* 52/3 (April 1974).
20. US Intelligence Board, 'Key Intelligence Questions for FY 1976', quoted in William R. Johnson, 'Clandestinity and Current Intelligence', *Studies in Intelligence* 20/3 (Fall 1976) pp.15, 45 (declassified).
21. Ernst, 'Economic Intelligence in CIA' (note 11) p.13.
22. Ibid. p.16.
23. Edward A. Casey Jr, 'Annex C: State's Economic Role', in Report of the US Department of State Management Task Force, *State 2000: A New Model for Managing Foreign Affairs* (Washington DC: Dept of State 1992), p.169.
24. US Dept of State Management Task Force, *State 2000* (note 23) pp.38–9.
25. Casey, 'Annex C: State's Economic Role' (note 23) p.164.
26. A less formal but very important source of overseas 'reporting' comes from private US citizens and organizations. The CIA's domestic contact unit, its its various forms, has a leading role in debriefing Americans who have learned about significant foreign economic activities. 'The domestic contact units have been highly responsive to the needs of economic intelligence analysts who in turn often took the trouble to provide very detailed guidance and requirements because the pay-off was evident and quick.' Ernst, 'Economic Intelligence in CIA' (note 11) p.16.
27. Johnson, 'Clandestinity and Current Intelligence' (note 20) p.64.
28. Ibid. p.56.

10

The CIA and The Question of Accountability

LOCH K. JOHNSON

THE SHARING OF GOVERNMENTAL POWER

By Constitutional design, the executive branch of government in the United States is required to share its powers with the legislative and judicial branches. While this can lead to frustrations and inefficiencies, its virtue lies in the accountability that sharing provides – including a continuous look over the shoulders of bureaucrats and even presidents by congressional watchdogs. This legislative monitoring or review is usually referred to by the awkward term 'oversight'.

The concept of power-sharing has roots that run deep into American tradition. 'If angels were to govern men, neither external nor internal controls on government would be necessary', James Madison observed in 1788. Perhaps unable to recollect any angels he had meet in public life, he advised the adoption of precautions for obliging the government to control itself. 'A dependence on the people' would be paramount, especially a cycle of open elections. Yet, while necessary, voting in itself would not be sufficient. 'Experience has taught mankind the necessity of auxiliary precautions', Madison added; in between elections, the three branches of government would have to keep a close watch on one another. In his most famous dictum, 'Ambition must be made to counteract ambition.'[1]

Thomas Jefferson eloquently resonated this concern, widespread in the new Republic, about the dangers of concentrated power. He scoffed at the notion that loyal citizens should exhibit an obsequious confidence in their leaders. Instead, he recommended a form of eternal vigilance directed inward toward those serving in high office. 'Confidence is everywhere the parent of despotism', he warned. 'In questions of power, then, let no more be heard of confidence in man, but bind him down from mischief by the chains of the Constitution.'[2] The preeminent link in these chains was the

First Article, which enumerated the powers of Congress and made it clear that legislators would have a major say over the war, treaty, and spending powers (along with an opportunity to impeach an executive or judicial official who violated the public trust).

Into every crevice of America's most famous document, the founders worked the philosophy that became their most notable contribution to the art of governance: the doctrine of the separation of powers. Contemporary political scientists have refashioned that well worn phrase to read 'separate institutions *sharing* powers', considering this expression a more accurate portrayal of the day-to-day reality of how the Constitutional framework operates in practice.[3]

Enshrined in the civics books simply as 'checks and balances', this idea of power-sharing was forcefully endorsed in modern times by Supreme Court Justice Louis Brandeis. In a ringing affirmation of Madisonian restraints, he reminded a new century of Americans that the founders had sought 'not to promote efficiency but to preclude the exercise of arbitrary power. The purpose was not to avoid friction, but, by means of the inevitable friction incident to the distribution of the governmental powers among three departments, to save the people from autocracy'.[4]

Down through the years, the governing arrangements envisioned by the founders have never worked perfectly. Institutional struggles over the war and the treaty powers have been particularly heated.[5] Sometimes the powers of the president have expanded to alarming proportions, as when Abraham Lincoln assumed the status of an autocrat during the early phases of the Civil War, when Andrew Johnson acted capriciously in the Era of Reconstruction, when Lyndon B. Johnson escalated the war in Vietnam without meaningful congressional debate, and when Richard M. Nixon engaged in the coverup of a White House espionage operation against the opposition party (the Watergate scandal).

On other occasions, the powers of Congress have grown too large, as when Joseph McCarthy (Republican, Wisconsin) grossly misused the Senate's investigative powers to harass the Truman and Eisenhower administrations. Occasionally, too, the judiciary has overreached, as in 1936 when Justice George Sutherland issued a sweeping *dicta* in favor of expanded presidential powers in foreign affairs.[6]

For the most part, though, the government has abided by the founding principle of power-sharing, though its precise form has always been dependent on the personalities and conditions of the times. Some personalities have been forceful in their interpretation of inherent Constitutional powers (consider Franklin D. Roosevelt versus William Howard Taft). Some events have compelled a greater concentration of power in the hands of the executive, for the sake of swift action and secrecy.

The Depression, World War II, and the Cold War have been the major centralizing forces of the modern era that encouraged an aggrandizement of power in the executive branch.

Yet almost always (the Civil War excepted), dialogue and accommodation have burnished the sharp edges of dispute between the departments of government, albeit with plenty of verbal scrapes, strained emotions, and, in the cases of Andrew Johnson and Nixon, near impeachment. At the end of the day, those in high office have been willing to display (however begrudgingly) a spirit of comity upon which power-sharing depends. Always at the heart of these arrangements has remained the idea of vigorous checks against power imbalances – oversight. Yet, one policy domain has stood out as a conspicuous exception to the rule: the nation's secret intelligence operations.

THE EXCEPTIONAL CASE OF INTELLIGENCE

Throughout America's early history, intelligence operations eluded serious supervision by Congress and the courts.[7] Even in the modern era with all the growth of congressional oversight capabilities (budgets, staff, frequency of hearings, strengthened subpoena and other investigative authorities), the Central Intelligence Agency (CIA) and its 12 companion agencies that comprise the 'intelligence community' have never really been a part of the government's usual checks and balances – until recently. Members of Congress deferred to the expertise of intelligence officers in this arcane realm, and preferred anyway to avoid responsibility for controversial secret operations like the Bay of Pigs fiasco (1961).[8]

A Director of Central Intelligence (DCI), James R. Schlesinger, has recalled a meeting he had in 1973 with John Stennis (Democrat, Mississippi), the chairman of the subcommittee dealing with intelligence on behalf of the Senate Armed Services Committee. 'I went up to the [Capitol] Hill and said, 'Mr Chairman, I want to tell you about some of our programs'. To which the Senator quickly replied: "No, no, my boy, don't tell me. Just go ahead and do it – but I don't want to know!"'[9] With little scrutiny, the leaders of the Armed Services committees in both chambers quietly folded funds for the CIA into the Defense Department's annual appropriations bill.

Nor did the Executive Office of the Presidency (EOP) offer reliable accountability over the intelligence establishment that sprawled beneath the White House in the organizational charts of the federal government. Key members of the National Security Council (NSC) rarely – in some cases, never – even saw the Agency's budget.

'I never saw a budget of the CIA, although I was a statutory member of the National Security Council', Dean Rusk once recalled, looking back over his long tenure as secretary of state during the Kennedy and Johnson administrations. 'The CIA's budget apparently went to two or three specially cleared people in the Bureau of the Budget, then run briefly by the President, turned over to Senator [Richard Bevard] Russell [Democrat, Georgia], and that was the end of it. He would lose the CIA budget in the Defense budget and he wouldn't let anybody question it. There were no public hearings on it. So again his judgment, his word on that, was the last word.'[10]

Many of the CIA's activities (including aggressive covert action, collection, and counter-intelligence operations) never received a thorough examination – or, in some cases, even approval – by the NSC.[11] Even when the NSC did initially approve a CIA covert action proposal, an adviser to several presidents from Truman onward has commented on the slipperiness of the decision process:

> I believe on a number of occasions a plan for covert action has been presented to the NSC and authority is requested for the CIA to proceed from point A to point B. The authority will be given and the action will be launched. When point B is reached, the persons in charge feel it is necessary to go to point C, and they assume that the original authorization gives them such a right. From point C, they go to D and possibly E, and even further. This has led to some bizarre results, and when an investigation is started the excuse is blandly presented that authority was obtained from the NSC before the project was launched.[12]

Mindful of the need for improved supervision over the CIA and its companion agencies, legislators attempted from time to time to craft new congressional controls (particularly in the wake of intelligence flaps, such as the Bay of Pigs and the CIA's infiltration of the National Student Association[13]). These initiatives were always defeated, as a majority of legislators remained content to abide by the rule of exceptionalism for America's secret agencies. They were persuaded by the argument that intelligence operations were too delicate for oversight-as-usual; and they remained wary, too, of being drawn into the circle of consent for operations that might prove embarrassing.

Some of the oversight proposals were modest efforts to strengthen the review of CIA programs and they could have helped stem later intelligence scandals.[14] Other proposals were more extreme, including one to abolish all covert actions regardless of type or circumstance.[15] Whatever the merits of the various oversight proposals, Congress remained unwilling to extend the doctrine of power-sharing into the darker recesses of American government.

In December 1974, this attitude changed abruptly. In a series of articles, reporter Seymour M. Hersh of the *New York Times* revealed that the CIA had spied on American citizens during the Vietnamese War era (Operation 'Chaos'), and had also attempted to topple the constitutionally elected president of Chile (Salvador Allende). While the revelations about covert action in Chile may have been ignored by the Congress as just another necessary chapter in the Cold War against Soviet interference in the developing world, spying on American citizens – voters – was an allegation difficult for legislators to dismiss. Blazing newspaper headlines demanded oversight, not the usual overlook. Both the executive and legislative branches immediately launched investigations, in what became known as the 'Year of Intelligence' (or the 'Intelligence Wars', in the view of some embittered CIA officers).[16]

At these inquiries, a parade of horrors emerged from the hidden vaults of the intelligence agencies, from murder plots against foreign leaders to widespread espionage operations against American citizens (whose crimes had been to protest the war in Vietnam or join the civil rights movement). The stage was set for an infusion of genuine accountability into the invisible side of American government. The Ford administration revived the President's Foreign Intelligence Advisory Board (PFIAB) and created a complementary Intelligence Oversight Board (IOB), both part of the EOP and now expected to keep a close watch on secret government activities for the president. By way of executive order, President Gerald R. Ford also banned assassination plots against foreign leaders, and tightened CIA and NSC approval procedures for the use of covert actions. His successor, Jimmy Carter, further codified and strengthened the NSC's intelligence procedures by way of another executive order and supporting intelligence directives.[17]

The zeal for reform was most evident, however, on Capitol Hill. Indeed, President Ford's initiatives were widely considered more of an attempt to preempt congressional action than bold steps to rein in the intelligence agencies. On the last day of the legislative session in 1974, Congress enacted the first-ever statute to place some controls on the use of covert actions (the secret interference in the affairs of other nations or factions). The landmark Hughes-Ryan Amendment wrought two profound changes: first, before a covert action could be carried out, the President would have to authorize the operation through a special approval called a 'finding'; and, second, the finding would have to be reported to the appropriate committees of Congress 'in a timely fashion', thereby alerting overseers that a covert action proposal had been accepted by the White House.[18] A few legislators had been admitted into the 'witting circle' – not to the extent of requiring their approval, but at least permitting them to know about these sensitive operations and (by implication) have an opportunity to object.

As the Year of Intelligence unfolded, legislators raised the ante. In televised hearings, they hung out for display a sampling of dirty laundry from the intelligence agencies. Members of Congress cross-examined – and sometimes humiliated – leading intelligence officials unaccustomed to a public scrutiny of their work. Errant officers were reprimanded; questionable programs terminated (including covert action in Angola, through passage of the Clark Amendment); and new standards of accountability introduced.

When the sound and fury finally subsided in 1976, senators had established a permanent committee on intelligence oversight, entitled the Senate Select Committee on Intelligence (SSCI) and designed to provide a close monitoring of intelligence budgets and day-to-day operations. The following year the second chamber of Congress followed suit, establishing the House Permanent Select Committee on Intelligence (HPSCI) with comparable duties and expectations.[19]

Between then and now, the Congress continued its experiment with power-sharing over intelligence activities. Sometimes legislators tightened the reins, most notably with passage of the Intelligence Oversight Act of 1980, the Boland Amendments to curtail covert action in Nicaragua during the Reagan administration, the Intelligence Oversight Act of 1991, and, in the same year (both responses to the Iran-Contra scandal), the creation of a CIA inspector general's office confirmed by and accountable to Congress.[20] Sometimes legislators loosened the reins when they proved too restrictive (as with the repeal of the Clark Amendment in 1985), or Congress otherwise aided the intelligence agencies in the protection of their legitimate programs (as with passage of an Intelligence Identities Protection Act in 1982 to prohibit the exposure of intelligence officials under cover). While the pulling and tugging continued, one conclusion was clear: the CIA had become a part of America's system of shared powers.

ON THE MERITS OF ACCOUNTABILITY

Was the new accountability for better or for worse? The house remains divided on this question, as reflected in two recent studies of intelligence.[21] For one author, Kathryn Olmsted, the answer is for better – but by no means good enough. According to her critique, the movement to introduce accountability into this secret world has largely failed, however well intended and proper the effort. Despite the year-long investigations by three separate panels – one in the Senate led by Senator Frank Church (Democrat, Idaho), one in the House led by Representative Otis Pike (Democrat, New York), and a third in the White House led by Vice President Nelson Rockefeller (Republican, New York) – the end result was 'little reform'.[22]

The Congress was 'ultimately unwilling to shoulder its responsibilities for overseeing the intelligence community'.[23]

In an attempt to discover why this was the case, Olmsted begins with an observation (laced with heavy sarcasm) from Richard Helms, a former DCI pilloried by Senate investigators: 'Where is the legislation, the great piece of legislation, that was going to come out of the Church Committee hearings? I haven't seen it.'[24] Though for quite different reasons (Helms would have legislative overseers imitate the dodo bird[25]), Olmsted, too, is unimpressed by the will of legislators to monitor the secret government. Their preference is 'to maintain their basic deference' to the intelligence agencies, she maintains, rather than hold them to high standards of accountability. On another front – accountability from outside the government – she finds the nation's media equally feckless.

While much of Olmsted's criticism of legislative oversight is compelling, she too easily discounts the improvements that have come about as a result of the investigations in 1975. The contrast in the degree of accountability before and after the Year of Intelligence is remarkable. She (and Helms) have the wrong benchmark: it is not the number of laws or their sweep that matters the most, but rather the day-to-day supervision of the secret agencies by legislators and their staff. By this measure, the creation of the two intelligence oversight committees – the vital legacy of the investigations – has led to an infinitely closer check on America's secret government than existed earlier.

Moreover, the oversight laws that have been passed should not be so easily discounted, especially their reporting requirements. The Intelligence Oversight Act of 1980, though less than three pages long, considerably improved accountability and included a provision for *advanced* notice to Congress of every important covert operation (not just covert actions). Significant, too, are the Foreign Intelligence Surveillance Act (FISA) of 1978, which brought the judiciary into the ambit of intelligence oversight by requiring a special court review of requests for national security wiretaps; and the Intelligence Oversight Act of 1991, which insists on a prior, written presidential finding for important covert actions – not *ex post facto* oral approval, as once given by President Ronald Reagan.[26] These initiatives are not shadows on the wall but (like the new inspector general statute) tough laws that have given genuine meaning to intelligence accountability. This is particularly evident when compared to the statutory void that existed before passage of the Hughes-Ryan Act.

The media also deserves a little more slack than Olmsted allows. Clearly some American reporters went too far in the past when they accepted secret stipends from the CIA for intelligence work, blurring the line between journalism and espionage.[27] Moreover, reporting on intelligence matters has often been superficial (Olmsted's central point). Yet, the reason for the thin coverage is understandable. The secret agencies are surrounded by towering walls, just as daunting for journalists as for scholars and other outsiders; expectations that the media will be able to break down these walls with any frequency is unrealistic. Nor would most citizens want the nation's secrets so easily breached.

Further, on occasion the media have behaved in a manner that has been not so much deferential as wildly irresponsible. Although columnist Jack Anderson has had his moments of laudable reporting in the public interest, his disclosure of Operation 'Guppy' (US wiretapping of Soviet limousines in Moscow) and the *Glomar Explorer* story (when the CIA attempted to salvage a sunken Soviet submarine in the Pacific) undermined two valuable intelligence-collection operations.[28] Several members of the media with access to these stories prudently decided against printing them, on grounds that the best interests of the United States might be harmed. There are times (however few) when the media should restrain itself in the national interest.

In Olmsted's opinion, the 'secret agencies clearly emerged the winners of their long battle with the investigators [in 1975]', for the inquiries resulted 'only in restoring the CIA's credibility'.[29] Yet consider the whole new set of arrangements for closer intelligence supervision on Capitol Hill, including the establishment of SSCI and HPSCI by lopsided votes (even though the White House and the CIA lobbied strongly against them). The two committees enjoy line-by-line budget authorization, competent staffs, subpoena powers, and a mandate to prevent further abuses. Consider, too, the exposés on assassination plots, domestic spying, covert action in Chile, and drug experimentation. Some 'winners'. True, the CIA was not dismantled, as some feared (including then DCI William E. Colby[30]); but the end result was nonetheless a significant tightening of legislative control over the secret agencies.

As for restoring the CIA's credibility (which Olmsted seems to view as a dubious outcome), it was never the intention of the Church Committee to undermine the Agency's ability to perform its legitimate work. Rather, Senator Church hoped to improve American intelligence by rooting out its rotten branches – just as a police department grows stronger, not weaker, when the corrupt practices of a few misguided officers are dealt with firmly. Frank Church's most important speech during the inquiry concentrated on lauding the CIA for its analytic skills and solid reporting to policy officers over the years – the Agency's most important mission.[31] His purpose was to extol the virtues of a valuable government agency, giving it a renewed legitimacy even as he criticized its excesses.

Olmsted ends her study with a troubling question about the evolution of intelligence oversight in the United States: Have the legislative committees caved into the very agencies they were created to supervise? Once more the author discerns a pattern of deference toward the agencies by overseers, citing as an illustration a journalist's observation that within a decade after the Year of Intelligence the House intelligence committee 'was staffed largely by former CIA officers'.[32]

The oversight committees have been disappointing since their creation two decades ago; yet, at times they have also demonstrated tough resolve, depending on the mix of members and how seriously they have taken their oversight responsibilities. Representative Edward P. Boland (Democrat, Massachusetts) stood up to the covert-action chicanery in Nicaragua directed by the NSC staff during the Reagan years, as did Iran-Contra investigators in 1987. Throughout 1995–96, both intelligence committees engaged in a wide-ranging, constructive review of intelligence reform proposals.[33] Again, the contrast with the pre-1975 period is stark.

The presence of former intelligence officers on the congressional oversight staffs should not in itself be alarming. Some of these individuals have approached their new assignments with integrity and seriousness of purpose. They have become stalwart advocates of congressional prerogatives. Moreover, they bring with them a good sense of what programs need closer attention, and when the agencies are being forthright. A few intelligence officers transplanted to Capitol Hill have been less vigorous (to put it politely); and, obviously, it is foolhardy to have too many of them monopolizing the task of supervision over their erstwhile agencies. The real problem, however, lies less at the staff level than in convincing members of Congress – harried as they are – to spend more time on their oversight duties.

'For a brief moment', Ms Olmsted concludes, '[investigators] forced the nation to debate the perils of secrecy in a democracy'.[34] On the contrary, this has not been a debate 'for a brief moment'; it has been ongoing. It continued throughout the Carter years, and heated up during the Reagan-Bush administrations. It was revived during the Clinton years with the report of a Presidential-Congressional Intelligence Commission in 1996, along with concomitant efforts by Congress and scholars in the private sector to draft reform legislation.[35] How much intelligence is enough, what is the proper balance between liberty and security, when should legislators and the media be supportive or openly critical of sensitive intelligence operations – these are questions without final answers. A free people must debate them persistently.

If Ms Olmsted is dismayed by the lack of robust intelligence oversight, a second recent study takes quite the opposite view. Steven F. Knott is aghast over the stifling degree to which oversight has choked America's secret agencies. He usefully reminds us that some of the gods in the

American pantheon – Washington, Jefferson, Lincoln – resorted to unsavory covert practices. He derives from this history lesson a more normative brief, namely, that a reliance on executive discretion over intelligence activities served the nation well in the past. These operations are frequently delicate and perishable; they rely on secrecy, flexibility, timeliness, and efficiency – all lost when Congress enters the picture.

Knott is impressed by precedents set in the nation's early history and rightly so, for the accomplishments of the founders are impressive. The enthusiasm, though, can be carried too far. During the Watergate scandal, defenders of the Nixon administration insisted that the President had done nothing more than happened in earlier administrations. 'I do not share this view', responded a House member during the impeachment proceedings, 'or the view of those who hold that all presidents have lied, have broken the law, have compromised the Constitution. And if George Washington accepted bribes, it would not make bribery a virtue, nor would it be grounds for overlooking such acts by his successors.'[36] Similarly, Knott's finding that earlier presidents engaged in intelligence operations without serious accountability should not condone the practice.

Knott is a fervent critic of the post-Watergate rebellion against the imperial presidency. He laments the 'myth of innocence' that befell Frank Church and his band of reformers in Congress. Indeed, he views his book as a reminder of how America's most venerated leaders were willing to engage in operations that today would send pantywaist legislators to the press room crying foul. He encourages America to put on its covert fighting gloves again and, at the same time, dismiss Congress as a ringside manager.

'The most important reform that should be made to the current system', he writes, 'would be the elimination of the intelligence committees and the restoration of the system that existed from 1947 to 1974'.[37] The system he prefers is one of overwhelming executive dominance in decisions about how the United States will fight secret wars, spend billions of dollars on spy machines, and develop clandestine relationships with American journalists, scholars, and clergy. As well, he recommends repeal of President Ford's 'ludicrous' executive order prohibiting the assassination of foreign leaders.[38]

Despite the value of his historical research, Knott is on less firm ground when he turns to the modern era. His first misstep is to assume that congressional reformers in 1975 failed to appreciate the early evolution of intelligence activities – indeed, they 'distorted' and 'misrepresented' this history.[39] He quotes a passage from the report released by Senate investigators, stating that covert action had been used 'for the past twenty-eight years'.[40] Yet, as even a cursory reading of the multi-volume report indicates, this phrase was used simply because legislators elected to focus their remarks (in volume 1 of their final report) on the CIA and the modern era; in a supplementary volume, they issued a history of early American intelligence.

The Committee members were certainly aware of early covert action precedents. Senator John Tower (Republican, Texas), the panel's vice chairman, regaled colleagues with stories (provided to him by the CIA) of covert actions carried out by Washington, Jefferson, and even Benjamin Franklin; so did DCI Colby.[41] In the midst of the inquiry, the CIA sent to every member a slickly printed in-house history of covert action in the nation's early days. So the notion that legislators suffered 'historical myopia'[42] about earlier intelligence practices is the real myth, not their presumed 'innocence'.

What disturbed legislators in 1975 was the extent to which many of the modern intelligence agencies had violated the law and their charters. Most legislators were shocked by the discovery of assassination plots and the hiring of mob hitmen to dispatch Fidel Castro; the creation of over a million intelligence files on US citizens; illegal mail openings, wiretaps, and cable interceptions; drug experiments against unsuspecting citizens; illegal sequestering of chemical-biological materials; a master White House spyplan against American citizens; an intelligence scheme to promote the suicide of Dr Martin Luther King Jr; the infiltration of this country's media, universities, and church groups; the incitement of violence among African-Americans; covert harassment against Vietnamese War dissenters and civil-rights activists; and covert actions directed against not just autocracies.

Despite this chilling record, Knott insists that the presidency is the office 'best suited' to deal with covert operations.[43] Yet, the wisdom of the founders lies not in their use of covert action (although this instrument may be necessary from time to time), but in their understanding of the corrupting nature of power. Their enduring gift to the art of governing was the establishment of a system that incorporated safeguards against the concentration of power.

Throughout most of the Republic's history, secret operations remained small and peripheral. Now – the central point dismissed by Knott – the intelligence establishment has grown vast, beyond the capacity of the president alone to monitor. The Congress would have to help. In Knott's opinion, this legislative supervision ('micromanagement', he calls it, in the preferred put-down of oversight critics) has only stymied the secret agencies. Most of the intelligence directors since 1975, however, take a different view; they have welcomed the opportunity to share their burdensome responsibilities with Congress.[44] And no administration has sought to repeal the core set of laws and procedures that presently guide intelligence activities.

Nor do legislators wish to see a recurrence of the Orwellian nightmares uncovered in 1975. They understand as well that this nation continues to possess, when needed, a viable covert action capability – and one that can still move swiftly. According to the author, the new oversight has caused the CIA to shy away from this option; but, in fact, its most extensive use occurred during the Reagan years, well after the reforms were in place.[45]

Knott does the Congress a further disservice by blaming it for the unauthorized disclosure of classified information. Studies on the subject of leaks consistently trace the overwhelming majority back to the executive branch.[46] If the author insists on charging the oversight committees with leaking the nation's secrets, he should provide evidence – not innuendo – to support the claim.[47] The members and staff of these committees, on both sides of the aisle, have been individuals of the highest integrity and deserve better than this.

The author also maintains that the oversight exercised by Congress from 1947–74 was sufficiently vigorous.[48] Every other credible study disagrees.[49] He then goes from the improbable to the impossible: a defense of the relations between DCI William J. Casey of the Reagan administration and the Congress. The fact is that Casey's standing on Capitol Hill reached rock bottom. He had nothing but disdain for the legislative branch and even managed, in a Herculean feat, to alienate the CIA's arch-defenders (including SSCI chairman Barry Goldwater, Republican, Arizona). Knott states, too, that legislative reforms have suffered from an air of superiority, based on a belief that Congress is wiser than the executive branch.[50] In truth, the model of government envisioned by reformers since 1975 has not been one of legislative supremacy over intelligence, but rather one in which both branches cooperate together to avoid the disquieting excesses disclosed by investigators in the past. The choice does not have to be between executive or legislative sovereignty over intelligence; the challenge is to tap into the best attributes of both branches in the service of the national security. The Congress brings to the table a strong sense of what the American people will support, plus a large amount of foreign policy expertise in its own right. It provides a second opinion, carefully tendered in the executive (closed) sessions of the oversight committees by a small group of legislators in each chamber.

During the Iran–Contra investigation, Vice Admiral John M. Poindexter (President Reagan's National Security Advisor) conceded that he had bypassed the intelligence committees to avoid 'outside interference'.[51] This extreme form of executive discretion is evidently what Knott seeks as well. Secrecy and efficiency are his ideals, less the preservation of safeguards against abuse. What riles him the most are the presumed 'ill effects' democracy brings to intelligence decisions.[52] Granted, in this domain, debate must often remain hidden behind closed doors; the new system of oversight, though, provides an opportunity for some degree of independent review. The alternative is covert operations by executive fiat. The unfortunate consequences of that approach, well documented by investigators in 1975 and again in the wake of Iran-Contra, remain seared in the memory of many observers – if not Knott.

ADAPTING TO THE NEW ERA OF ACCOUNTABILITY

Regardless of whether one likes the idea of greater intelligence accountability, the fact remains that 1975 was a critical turning point in the history of American intelligence.[53] In the years to follow, oversight has fluctuated from this high point of legislative attention according to the degree of commitment displayed by individual overseers toward their supervisory responsibilities and how often (and persuasively) the media have reported incidents of intelligence impropriety.[54] Generally, though, the level of oversight has remained *relatively* high, compared to its near absence in the earlier era of benign neglect. Legislative overseers slacked off during the first half of the Reagan administration; but the Iran–Contra affair (revealed by a Middle East newspaper) jolted them back to the job.

Despite the ups-and-downs of legislative attention to intelligence review, the overall trend during the latter stages of the Cold War was unmistakable: Congress and the executive branch had entered into a new era of partnership in the conduct of intelligence activities. As a recent DCI has put it, the CIA now found itself poised equidistant between the two branches – 'responsible and accountable to both, unwilling to act at presidential request without clearance from Congress'.[55] In the 1986–90 period, the number of CIA briefings to the congressional oversight committees, individual members, and staffers shot upward from a few hundred a year to 1,040 in 1986; 1,064 in 1987; 1,044 in 1988; 947 in 1989; 1,012 in 1990; and 1,000 in 1991. The number of written reports sent to Congress (most of them classified) has also increased sharply since 1986. In 1991 alone, 7,000 intelligence reports went to Capitol Hill.[56]

The frequency of contact between the CIA and Congress has accelerated in the post-Cold War era. In 1993, 1,512 meetings took place between members of Congress and the CIA's legislative liaison staff, along with 154 one-on-one or small-group meetings between legislators and the DCI, 26 congressional hearings with the DCI as a witness, 128 hearings with other CIA witnesses, 317 other contacts with legislators, and 887 meetings and contacts with legislative staff – a 29 per cent increase over 1992. In 1993, the Agency also provided 4,976 classified documents to legislators, along with 4,668 unclassified documents and 233 responses to constituency inquiries.[57]

Another sign of a more serious effort to monitor the CIA and keep American citizens informed of at least some of its activities was the series of hearings in Congress held from 1991–94 in which CIA witnesses testified in public – a rarity during the Cold War.[58] President Bill Clinton's first DCI, R. James Woolsey, appeared in eight open hearings in 1993, whereas in previous years – even after the congressional investigations of 1975 and calls for greater openness – DCIs often never appeared in public hearings during an entire session of Congress or, if testifying, never more than once or twice. The upshot: the Agency would now have two masters: the president and the Congress – and sometimes a third, as the courts increasingly adjudicated intelligence-related litigation and regularly examined requests for electronic-surveillance warrants against national-security targets (mandated by FISA).

The degree of CIA openness should not be overstated. That Congress was still kept in the dark on key aspects of intelligence policy was startlingly underscored in 1994. Legislators learned only through a chance audit that the National Reconnaissance Office (NRO, the most secretive member of the intelligence community, responsible for the supervision of satellite manufacturing and launching) had engaged in cost overruns amounting to $159 million dollars for its new headquarters in the Virginia countryside. Subsequent reports in 1995–96 revealed further that the NRO had concealed from Congress a $4 billion hidden slush fund of accumulated appropriations.[59] In 1995, it also came to light that the CIA had failed to report to Congress its ties with a controversial military colonel in Guatemala (Julio Roberto Alpirez) suspected of involvement in the murder of an American citizen there, as well as the death of a Guatamalan man married to an American citizen.[60] 'Guatemala's most important lesson', concluded the *New York Times*, 'is that the CIA cannot be trusted to police itself'.[61]

The CIA's degree of openness and cooperation with legislative over-seers, then, has been uneven in recent years. What about other overseers inside and outside the government with responsibilities for ensuring that intelligence remains accountable?

The White House

During the Reagan years the Agency enjoyed a close relationship with the White House, mainly because DCI Casey was a personal friend of the President and had served as his national campaign manager. Casey became the first DCI ever appointed to the Cabinet. Further, Reagan was entirely supportive of Casey's enthusiasm for secretly countering the influence of the Soviet Union (which the President in the middle of his tenure labeled the 'evil empire'). Unfortunately, the free rein given to the Agency and the NSC staff led to the Iran–Contra excesses. Under former DCI Bush, the CIA had the luxury of a chief executive who understood and appreciated intelligence as well as anyone to have served in the nation's highest office.[62] Bush was also sympathetic to most of the Agency's funding requests, though he did wind down covert action.[63]

The Clinton administration was quite a different matter, with its relative inattentiveness to foreign policy (at least in its early years). Intelligence deficiencies in Somalia during the administration's first significant foreign policy crisis – among them, a failure to understand the intentions, or even the whereabouts, of the Somalia tribal leader General Muhammad Farah Aideed – raised doubts among NSC officials about the usefulness of the CIA.[64]

In 1994, President Bill Clinton focused on a proposal from his former Secretary of Defense Les Aspin, Vice President Al Gore, and National Security Adviser Anthony Lake to establish a presidential reform commission on intelligence – the President's first expression of interest in the direction the CIA should take during his tenure.[65] Events in Somalia were not the only consideration. Criticism over the CIA's failure to have forecast the fall of the Soviet Union abounded inside and outside the government. Senator Daniel Patrick Moynihan (Democrat, New York) called for a dismantling of the CIA, and reporter Seymour Hersh soon joined the abolition movement.[66]

Critics further excoriated the intelligence agencies for underestimating the nuclear-weapons programs in Iraq and North Korea. Others simply argued that with the end of the Cold War America no longer needed a large intelligence establishment; and its reported $26–28 billion annual budget was an inviting target for budget cutters concerned about the spiraling national debt.[67] Above all, the discovery in 1994 of a highly placed Soviet/ Russian mole inside the CIA – Aldrich H. Ames – threw gasoline on the smoldering coals of reform.[68]

President Clinton understood that something had to be done. Senator John Warner (Republican, Virginia) had in mind, though, quite a different commission: a legislative probe whose main objective would be to reassure the American people – historically, the purpose of most commissions[69] – that the CIA (based in his constituency) was an effective organization and needed to be preserved, not abolished or even substantially reduced. The SSCI, of which Warner was a senior member, accepted the Virginian's view and pushed for a purely congressional panel of inquiry.

The eventual compromise between the branches was a law passed in 1994 that created a joint presidential-congressional Commission on the Roles and Capabilities of the United States Intelligence Community. It authorized the President to select nine members (which he drew from PFIAB, including its chair and therefore the Commission's chair, Les

Aspin), and congressional leaders from both parties picked the remaining eight members (Senator Warner among them). The Commission began its work in March 1995 and, when Aspin tragically died three months later, he was replaced by another former secretary of defense, Harold Brown (of the Carter administration).

The report issued by the Commission in March 1996, largely met Warner's objective.[70] Rather than recommending major reforms, the blue-ribbon panel – the first significant probe into intelligence policy in 20 years – extolled the good work of the secret agencies, kept their budgets intact, offered a few modest suggestions for improvement, and disappeared as a footnote to history.

Perhaps the Commission's boldest initiative was an attempt to help President Clinton's second intelligence chief, John M. Deutch, expand his powers by recommending that the DCI have joint approval (along with the relevant department secretaries) over all intelligence agency directors. The Commission further advocated greater DCI authority over community-wide budget decisions. The individual intelligence agencies – and especially the military – laid siege immediately against these proposals, however, drawing upon the assistance of the Armed Services committees and other powerful allies in the Congress. As Deutch himself conceded in a private memorandum for the President, 'Not surprisingly, the Secretary of Defense, the Secretary of State, the Attorney General and the Director of the FBI offer arguments, many cogent, against broadening the DCI's authority over appointments.'[71]

Interest Groups

Just as the CIA stood aloof from government overseers for most of the Cold War, its effort to keep secrets from foreign adversaries (manifested most obviously in the barbed-wire fences and guardhouses around its perimeter) also kept it insulated from the other usual forces of pluralism in American society. A graph registering the presence of interest groups advocating specific intelligence policies, or one that traced CIA lobbying on its own behalf, would run practically flat – until 1975, when the Agency found itself under attack by government and media investigators.

In that year, a senior intelligence officer resigned from the CIA to establish the Association of Retired Intelligence Officers (ARIO).[72] The purpose, embraced by many former intelligence officials who quickly swelled ARIO's ranks, was to lobby legislators and the American people on behalf of the secret agencies. Other pressure groups came into existence soon thereafter, some for and some against the CIA. In yet another way, the CIA had become a part of the government and politics-as-usual. Still, compared to the extensive outreach and large war chests of most successful lobbying groups in the United States, those concerned with intelligence policy remained relatively few in number and modestly funded throughout the Cold War.

As the Pentagon's budget began to ebb after the Soviet collapse, industrial leaders cast an eye toward ongoing government requirements for espionage hardware – especially expensive satellites – as supplements for dwindling tank, ship, and aircraft contracts.[73] Members of Congress in districts with weapons plants – and jobs at risk – have been solicited for assistance in procuring intelligence-hardware deals, in the manner they once were for Department of Defense acquisitions and the forestalling of base closures. The end of the Cold War had ushered classic interest-group politics into the once pristine domain of intelligence policy.[74]

With respect to the CIA's own lobbying efforts (known in Washington euphemistically as 'legislative liaison'), in the wake of the searing investigations of 1975 intelligence managers began to understand a lesson already well learned by the FBI and the Pentagon, namely, the importance of defending (read selling) one's programs on Capitol Hill. The number of attorneys in the Agency's Office of General Counsel soared from 2 in 1974 to 65 in 1994; and the Office of Congressional Affairs expanded as well, from two staffers in 1974 to over a dozen in 1994. Forced (somewhat) out into the open by the *New York Times* allegations of improprieties in 1974, the CIA started to devote additional resources to its public defense, like most other government agencies.

Scholarly Groups

The same forces that led to the creation of an Intelligence Commission in 1994 also stirred various non-government groups to study intelligence reform, including panels at Georgetown University, the Council on Foreign Relations (CFR), and the Twentieth Century Fund. Their recommendations have been knowledgeable and thoughtful, adding to the national debate on the future of intelligence. They have also been somewhat disconcerting because, together with the various government recommendations, they reveal a wide discrepancy in opinion over how the nation ought to improve its intelligence performance.

Perhaps most controversial of the views expressed by members of these outside panels came from the project director for the CFR report, Richard N. Haass, who would turn back the clock on 20 years of bipartisan intelligence reform.[75] He recommended the restoration of assassination plots; using the Peace Corps as a cover for CIA officers abroad (which has never been done); allowing intelligence officers to pretend they are American journalists, academics, or clergy traveling overseas; and a more aggressive participation in *coups d'état* against regimes deemed unfriendly to the United States – proposals rejected by every major government panel of inquiry from Church, Pike, and Rockefeller through Aspin-Brown. (The Aspin-Brown Commission concluded that covert actions 'should be initiated only in the most compelling circumstances'.[76])

The Debate Continues

As in the 1974 exposé that initiated the Year of Intelligence, journalists sometimes provide the public with the most telling and timely information on the abuse of power by the CIA, whether based on leaks or skillful investigative probing – usually a combination of both. Yet, even though the media has served as an indispensable safeguard for democracy over the years, its reporters have hardly been an infallible check on improprieties. The Agency's fortress has proven largely inviolable to all outsiders, including the media corps. This has changed little since the end of the Cold War, although CIA officials have been slightly more forthcoming in their public release of selected documents from the organization's early history (including analytic papers on the USSR in the 1950s and documents on the Cuban Missile Crisis[77]).

With its subpoena powers, budget review, control of the CIA's purse strings, and a capacity to focus public attention with open hearings, the Congress remains the strongest *potential* intelligence overseer in the post-Cold War era. This potential rests, though, on the question of whether its members have the will to perform these vital duties – a mixed record so far.[78] For the most part, intelligence accountability has rested on the shoulders of a few dedicated legislators and their staff aides (a pattern common for other policy domains as well).

Even if the SSCI and HPSCI members concentrated on their oversight duties with Sisyphean determination, they could never hope to monitor – or even understand – US intelligence in all its entirety. The community is too vast and complex. Few people in the country, let alone on Capitol Hill, truly understand the technological aspects of satellite imaging or the intricacies of electronic eavesdropping. Much of what goes on in the world of intelligence depends upon the skills and integrity of experts; the system spins along largely free of outside scrutiny, just as the earth continues to turn on its axis without attention from legislators.

Accountability from Congress and other entities remains important, though, for the selective examination of ongoing programs they provide; for the questioning of intelligence officers – not on everything but on enough to keep people more honest; for their latent capacity to punish those who do violate their oath of office, if only by embarrassing them in the public light; for the guidance overseers can provide to bureaucrats about what the public expects from its secret agencies. As former DCI Robert Gates has observed:

' . . . some awfully crazy schemes might well have been approved had everyone present [in the White House] not known and expected hard questions, debate, and criticism from the Hill. And when, on a few occasions, Congress was kept in the dark, and such schemes did proceed, it was nearly always to the lasting regret of the Presidents involved.'[79]

Democracy's success will continue to depend on these checks, along with – vitally – the attitudes of people in high office. One of the most thoughtful DCIs, the late William Colby, once expressed a sense of strong optimism about the new era of intelligence accountability that had come to pass on his watch:

> With today's supervision, and with the command structure trying to keep things straight, the people in CIA know what they should do and what they should not do – as distinct from the 'fifties, in which there were no particular rules. If CIA people today are told to violate their limits, or if they are tempted to violate those limits, one of the junior officers will surely raise that question and tell the command structure, and, if not satisfied there, he will tell the Congress, and, if not satisfied there, he will tell the press, and that is the way you control it.[80]

Yet, the Iran–Contra scandal erupted soon after, throwing cold water on this roseate view (however true it is up to a point). We were reminded again of how critical a commitment to law and integrity is for those who govern – a lesson handed down from the venerable Greek philosophers.

The greatest cause for celebration in this year of the CIA's 50th birthday is the realization that the overwhelming majority of those who serve in the intelligence agencies have been, and continue to be, men and women of enormous talent and integrity – among the best anywhere. Jefferson's eternal vigilance will remain necessary, though, for a few who from time to time lack honor and violate the rule of law and the principle of power-sharing.

Scholars and practitioners are likely to carry on the debate over the proper degree of intelligence accountability. Proponents will cite Madison, Jefferson, and Brandeis; opponents, Jefferson again (this time his exercise of covert action in simpler days), *Curtiss-Wright*, and Admiral Poindexter. Proponents will warn of Big Brother intrusion at home and tampering with democratic regimes abroad; opponents will point to the paralysis of micromanagement and the foolishness of turning the CIA into a nunnery.

The champions of oversight want reliable safeguards to preserve liberty; its critics seek more effective secret operations to shield the United States from enemies at home and abroad. The rub comes from this obvious fact: the nation needs both civil liberties and a shield against danger. So the search continues to find the right formula for power-sharing in this most difficult of government domains – knowing full well that no formula exists, only the hope that in a spirit of comity Congress, the executive, and the courts will continue the quest for a *modus vivendi* that takes into account both values.

NOTES

1. James Madison, *Federalist Paper No.51*, 8 Feb. 1788, repr. in *The Federalist* (NY: Modern Library 1937), p.337.
2. Thomas Jefferson, Draft of the Kentucky Resolutions, Oct. 1798, in *Jefferson* (NY: Library of America 1984) p.455.
3. Richard E. Neustadt, *Presidential Power and the Modern Presidents* (NY: Free Press 1990) p.29, original emphasis.
4. *Myers v. United States*, 272 US 52 293 (1926).
5. Louis Fisher, *The War Making Powers* (Manhattan: UP of Kansas 1996); Loch K. Johnson, *The Making of International Agreements: Congress Confronts the Executive* (NY: NY UP 1984).
6. *United States v. Curtiss-Wright Export Corporation* 299 US 304 (1936).
7. See Stephen F. Knott, *Secret and Sanctioned: Covert Operations and the American Presidency* (NY: OUP 1996).
8. See e.g. Loch K. Johnson, *A Season of Inquiry: The Senate Intelligence Investigation* (Lexington: UP of Kentucky 1985); Jerrold L. Walden, 'The CIA: A Study in the Arrogation of Administrative Powers', *George Washington Law Review* 39 (Oct.1970) p.95.
9. Loch K. Johnson, interview with James R. Schlesinger, Washington DC, 16 June 1994.
10. Richard B. Russell Library, Richard B. Russell Oral History No.86, taped by Hughes Cates, 22 Feb. 1977, U. of Georgia, Athens, GA.
11. 'Foreign and Military Intelligence', *Final Report*, Select Committee to Study Governmental Operations with Respect to Intelligence Activities (hereafter, the Church Committee), US Senate, Sen. Rept. No.94–755, Vol.I, 94th Cong. 2d Sess. May 1976, Washington DC, US GPO, p.157.
12. Clark Clifford, ibid. p.158 (based on testimony given to the Church Committee on 4 Dec. 1975).
13. See Rhodri Jeffreys–Jones, *The CIA and American Democracy* (New Haven, CT: Yale UP 1989); John Ranelagh, *The Agency: The Rise and Decline of the CIA* (NY: Simon & Schuster 1986); Peter Wyden, *The Bay of Pigs: The Untold Story* (NY: Simon & Schuster 1979); and Sol Stern, 'NSA and the CIA' *Ramparts* 5 (March 1967) pp.29–38.
14. These more moderate initiatives, sponsored by Mike Mansfield (Democrat, Montana) are found in the *Congressional Record* at 11 April 1956, p.6068, and 14 July 1966, p.15699.
15. On the Abourezk Amendment (after its sponsor James Abourezk, D, South Dakota), see *Congressional Record*, 2 Oct. 1974, p.33482.
16. See Johnson, *Season of Inquiry* (note 8); Kathryn Olmsted, *Challenging the Secret Government: The Post-Watergate Investigations of the CIA and FBI* (Chapel Hill: U. of N. Carolina Press 1996); Frank J. Smist Jr, *Congress Oversees the United States Intelligence Community, 1947–1989* (Knoxville: U. of Tennessee Press 1990).
17. The Ford executive order is No.11905, signed on 18 Feb. 1976 (*Weekly Compilation of Presidential Documents* 12, Washington DC, GPO 1976, pp.234–44); the Carter order, No.12036, signed on 24 Jan. 1978 (*Public Papers of the Presidents of the United States: Jimmy Carter, 1978*, Book I, Washington DC, GPO, 1979, pp.194–214).
18. Section 662 of the Foreign Assistance Act of 1994 (22 USC. 2422).
19. SSCI was established by S. Res. 400 on 19 May 1976; and HPSCI by H. Res. 658 on 14 July 1977.
20. On these statutes, see William E. Conner, *Intelligence Oversight: The Controversy Behind the FY 1991 Intelligence Authorization Act*, Intelligence Profession Series, No.11 (McLean,

VA: Assoc. of Former Intelligence Officers 1993); Louis Fisher, 'How to Avoid Iran-Contras: Review Essay', *California Law Review* 76 (1993) pp.919–29; Loch K. Johnson, 'The CIA: Controlling the Quiet Option', *Foreign Policy* 39 (Summer 1980) pp.143–52, and 'Legislative Reform of Intelligence Policy', *Polity* 17 (Spring 1985) pp.549–73; and Frederick M. Kaiser, 'Impact and Implications of the Iran-Contra Affair on Congressional Oversight of Covert Action', *Int. Jnl of Intelligence and Counterintelligence* 7 (1994) pp.205–34.

21. Olmsted (note 16); Knott (note 7).
22. Olmsted, ibid. p.3.
23. Ibid. p.5.
24. Ibid. p.3.
25. Loch K. Johnson, interview with Richard Helms, Washington DC, 12 Dec. 1990.
26. See US Senate Select Committee on Secret Military Assistance to Iran and the Nicaraguan Opposition and US House of Representatives Select Committee to Investigate Covert Arms Transactions with Iran (hereafter the Inouye-Hamilton Committees), *Report on the Iran-Contra Affair*, S. Rept. No.100–216 and H. Rept. 100–433, Nov. 1987, Washington DC, US GPO p.379.
27. See Loch K. Johnson, 'The CIA and the Media', *Intelligence and National Security* 1/2 (May 1986), pp.143-69.
28. See Jack Anderson, 'How the CIA Snooped Inside Russia', *Washington Post*, 10 Dec. 1973, p.B17; on the *Glomar Explorer*, see the *New York Times*, 20 and 26 March 1975.
29. Olmsted (note 16) pp.169–70.
30. See William E. Colby and Peter Forbath, *Honorable Men: My Life in the CIA* (NY: Simon & Schuster 1978).
31. Frank Church, 'An Imperative for the CIA: Professionalism Free of Politics and Partisanship', *Congressional Record*, 11 Nov. 1975, pp.35786–88.
32. Olmsted (note 16) p.180, citing Leslie Gelb, 'Overseeing of CIA by Congress Has Produced Decade of Support', *New York Times*, 7 July 1986, p.A1.
33. See e.g. IC21: Intelligence Community in the 21st Century', *Staff Study*, Permanent Select Committee on Intelligence, US House, 104th Cong. Washington DC, GPO 1996.
34. Olmsted (note 16) p.189.
35. *Preparing for the 21st Century: An Appraisal of US Intelligence*, Report of the Commission on the Roles and Capabilities of the United States Intelligence Community (the Aspin-Brown Commission), 1 March 1996. For a brief summary of this and the other reports (and how to acquire copies), see John Macartney, 'Reform: Bonanza for Scholars', *Intelligencer*, Assoc. of Former Intelligence Officers (AFIO) Academic Exchange Program Newsletter 7 (Summer 1996) pp.3–5.
36. Rep. Jack Brooks (Democrat, Texas), video from the impeachment hearings, Judiciary Committee, US House of Representatives, Washington DC 1974, in 'Congress: We the People', Program 20, WETA Television, Washington DC 1983.
37. Knott (note 7) p.184–5.
38. Ibid. p.184.
39. Ibid. p.5.
40. Ibid.
41. Johnson, *Season of Inquiry* (note 20) p.101.
42. Knott (note 7) p.169.
43. Ibid. p.6.
44. Among the nine DCIs from Richard Helms forward, the two dissenters would be Helms (1966–73) and William J. Casey (1981–87).
45. See Robert M. Gates, *From the Shadows* (NY: Simon & Schuster 1996); and Loch K. Johnson, *Secret Agencies: US Intelligence in a Hostile World* (New Haven, CT: Yale UP 1996).
46. See Loch K. Johnson, *America's Secret Power: The CIA in a Democratic Society* (NY: OUP 1989) p.295, n. 63.
47. Knott (note 7) p.177.
48. Ibid. p.163.

49. See Church Committee *Report* (note 11) Vol.1, esp. pp.133, 150, 157; Jeffreys-Jones (note 13) p.80; Loch K. Johnson, 'Legislative Reform of Intelligence Policy', *Polity* 17 (Spring 1985) pp.549–73 (esp. pp.558–9, 567); Frederick M. Kaiser, 'Congress and the Intelligence Community: Taking the Road Less Traveled', in Roger H. Davidson (ed.) *The Postreform Congress* (NY: St Martin's Press 1992) pp.279–300; Ranelagh (note 13) p.284; Smist (note 16) and Walden (note 8).

50. Knott (note 7) p.164.

51. Testimony of Vice Adm. John M. Poindexter, the Inouye-Hamilton Committees, *Hearings*, Vol.8, 100th Cong. 1st Sess. (1987) p.159.

52. Knott (note 7) p.179.

53. Gregory F. Treverton, 'Intelligence: Welcome to the American Government', in Thomas E. Mann (ed.) *A Question of Balance: The President, the Congress and Foreign Policy* (Washington DC: Brookings Instn. 1990) pp.70–108.

54. Smist distinguishes between 'institutional oversight', on the one hand, in which the legislative and executive branches cooperate together in pursuit of improved intelligence policies, and, 'investigative oversight', on the other hand, in which the two have adversarial relationship, (note 49) pp.21–4. Most of the time, in my experience, oversight is of the institutional variety; when scandal occurs, however, or when the media uncovers what may be an impropriety, the adversarial side of the relationship comes to the fore. As in all aspects of oversight, this also depends upon the personality of the overseers; some like publicity more than others and an adversarial relationship is bound to attract more media attention than routine institutional oversight. On the relationship between intelligence scandal and the decline in the CIA's credibility and clout in Washington, see Jeffreys-Jones (note 13).

55. Gates (note 45) p.61.

56. Senior official, CIA, letter to Loch K. Johnson, dated 21 Sept. 1991; see, also, Loch K. Johnson, 'Smart Intelligence', *Foreign Policy* 89 (1992–93) p.67.

57. Deputy director for Congressional Affairs, briefing to Loch K. Johnson, Langley, Virginia, 1 April 1994.

58. Johnson, *Secret Agencies* (note 45).

59. Unsigned editorial, 'The Keys to the Spy Kingdom', *New York Times*, 19 May 1996 p.E14.

60. Tim Weiner, 'A Guatemala Officer and the CIA', ibid. 26 March 1995, p.6.

61. Unsigned editorial, 'Making the CIA Accountable', *New York Times*, 18 Aug. 1996 p.E-14.

62. Christopher Andrew, *For the President's Eyes Only: Secret Intelligence and the American Presidency from Washington to Bush* (NY: HarperCollins 1995).

63. Former president George Bush, letter to Loch K. Johnson, dated 23 Jan. 1994.

64. Loch K. Johnson, interview with Les Aspin, Washington DC, 8 July 1994.

65. Ibid.

66. Daniel P. Moynihan, 'Do We Still need the CIA? The State Department Can Do the Job', *New York Times*, 19 May 1991, p.E17; Seymour M. Hersh, 'Spy vs. Spy', *New Yorker*, 8 Aug. 1994, pp.4–5.

67. See e.g. Tim Weiner, 'CIA Chief Defends Secrecy, in Spending and Spying, to Senate', *New York Times*, 23 Feb. 1996, p.A5.

68. On Ames, see David Wise, *Nightmover* (NY: HarperCollins 1995).

69. See David Flitner Jr, 'Presidential Commissions', in Leonard W. Levy and Louis Fisher, *Encyclopedia of the American Presidency*, Vol.1 (NY: Simon & Schuster, 1994), pp.266–9.

70. Aspin-Brown Commission Report (note 35).

71. John M. Deutch, Memo for the President, 5 April 1996, p.3.

72. This group has been renamed the Association of Former Intelligence Officers (AFIO).

73. Robert Kohler, 'The Intelligence Industrial Base: Doomed to Extinction?' Monograph, Working Group on Intelligence Reform, Washington DC 1994.

74. John Mintz, 'Lockheed Martin Works to Save Its Older Spies in the Skies', *Washington Post*, 28 Nov. 1995, p.D1.

75. Richard N. Haass, 'Don't Hobble Intelligence Gathering', *Washington Post*, 15 Feb. 1996, p.A27. For the broader and less extreme views of the Council's report, see Council on Foreign Relations, 'Making Intelligence Smarter: The Future of US Intelligence', *Report of an Independent Task Force*, New York, 1996.

76. Aspin-Brown Commission Report (note 35) p.19.
77. See John M. Deutch, 'CIA, Bunker Free, Is Declassifying Secrets', letter to the editor, *New York Times*, 3 May 1996, p.A10; John Hollister Hedley, 'The CIA's New Openness', *Int. Jnl of Intelligence and Counterintelligence* 7 (Summer 1994) pp.129–42; and 'US Spy Satellite Photos Go Public', *New York Times*, 25 Feb. 1995, pp.1, 8.
78. Loch K. Johnson, 'Congress and the CIA: Monitoring the Dark Side of Government', *Legislative Studies Qtly* 5 (1980), pp.477–99; and Johnson, *Secret Agencies* (note 45).
79. Gates (note 45) p.559.
80. William E. Colby, 'Gesprach mit William E. Colby', *Der Spiegel* 4, 23 Jan. 1978, p.114.

11

The CIA's Own Effort to Understand and Document Its Past: A Brief History of the CIA History Program, 1950–1995

GERALD HAINES

Not unlike other segments of the vast CIA bureaucracy, the fortunes of the CIA historical program have been closely tied to the personal interest paid to them by the DCI and senior management officials.[1] Since its origins the CIA history program experienced brief periods of DCI concern and attentiveness and suffered through long periods of inattentiveness and neglect. When directors and senior staff promoted and nourished the program it flourished. When they ignored or were unaware of the program it atrophied and became moribund. CIA History Staff leadership also played a major role in determining the fortunes of the CIA history program. If it aggressively protected and promoted the program and the importance of history, and had the ear of senior officials, the program prospered. If it remained passively in the background and produced little, the program suffered.[2]

Moreover, what becomes strikingly clear in this brief study of the origins and development of the CIA history program is the general ignorance and misunderstanding on the part of most CIA officials of history's value to the Agency. Most CIA officers and decision makers, although they use historical analogies every day, are basically ahistorical. They believe they have no time or need for history. Caught up in current crisis management and day-to-day intelligence producing activities, they fail to appreciate history's value not only as a preserver of the 'Agency's memory' (what did it do in the past, how did it react?), but as an important training mechanism, and as a tool in the overall policy making process. For many CIA officials, resources and personnel were and are better placed in other areas. Generally, history *per se* has a very low Agency priority, as this study will reflect.

The study traces the development of the CIA history program from its origins under Director of Central Intelligence (DCI) General Walter Bedell Smith in 1950 to its status under DCI Judge William Webster in 1991. It examines the changing Agency attitudes toward the program and its evolution from a small, but valuable part of management, to a period of neglect, to a resurgence and the creation of a large Agency-wide history structure to help capture and document its past, to the decline and abolition of an official CIA history program, to its resurrection in the 1980s and expansion in the early 1990s.

THE EARLY YEARS

The new Central Intelligence Agency was only three years old when some of its top officials met to discuss recording its history and documenting its successes and failures. Meeting in recently-appointed DCI General Walter Bedell Smith's office on 26 December 1950, Deputy Director William H. Jackson, Executive Assistant Lyman B. Kirkpatrick, and Chief of the Office of Intelligence Coordination (OIC), James Q. Reber, proposed that a historical study of CIA and its origins be undertaken to accurately portray the activities and development of the Agency. It was not to be simply a 'history for history's sake', but a serious analytical work which would be circulated among top Agency officials, members of the National Security Council, the Intelligence Advisory Committee (IAC), and the President's top national security advisers.

Keenly interested in the subject and drawing on his military experience in which historians had been attached to General Dwight D. Eisenhower's Supreme Headquarters, Allied Expeditionary Forces, to record the history of the war and major command decisions, DDCI Jackson sought out Assistant to the Director, Colonel Chester B. Hansen, for advice. Hansen, who had helped draft the memoirs of General Omar N. Bradley, also saw the value in preserving an accurate record of CIA activities. On 29 January 1951, Jackson reported at the daily staff meeting that Hansen had agreed to head a DCI Historical Staff located in OIC. By design or coincidence, Jackson's remarks followed President Harry S. Truman's praise the very same day of government agencies for keeping their history in order, especially in crisis situations.

Officially appointed in May 1951, Hansen was to compile a complete history of CIA. He was also to coordinate all presentations of CIA officials to other government agencies, handle CIA press relations, and conduct Congressional liaison functions. Addressing Hansen's historical function, DCI Smith directed Hansen to undertake a historically critical and objective study of the Agency as a whole for the use of the President, the NSC, and the IAC.

In his budget justification for the historical study of CIA, Hansen stressed that a 'historical audit' of CIA and the peacetime intelligence system would allow officials a better understanding of the evolution of the centralized intelligence concept and apprise them of the effectiveness of the system. Hansen also believed that policy makers would profit from studying the detailed evolution of intelligence successes and avoid repeating major failures by studying history. The study of Agency history had the attention of major CIA officials.

Hansen's duties as Assistant to the Director, however, soon overwhelmed him. He proposed a staff which included six historians and two research assistants to help him carry out his historical duties. On the recommendation of Harvard historian, William Langer, a long time friend of DCI Smith and head of the National Board of Estimates, the Agency approached Arthur J. Marder to help write the history. When Marder was unavailable Arthur Darling head of the history department at Phillips Academy, Andover, Massachusetts, and a former professor of history at Yale, received a one year appointment in October 1951 to help out. Darling was a close friend of Sherman Kent, the new chief of the National Board of Estimates and former professor of history at Yale. Darling had taught Kent at Yale. (Darling also taught future President George Bush at Andover).

Hansen still intended to write an annual historical report for circulation to top officials. (It became the precedent for the DCI's annual and semi-annual progress reports to NSC.) In 1952, however, Hansen turned the writing of the report over to OIC and later to the Office of National Estimates (ONE). Hansen also instructed Darling to prepare a detailed study of the early postwar period of the Agency and the evolution of the concept of the national intelligence system. The finished study was to be circulated to members of the National Security Council (NSC), IAC, and future DCIs. Darling was also to 'pay close attention to historical perspective, to any weaknesses in the organization, and defects of administration which might emerge from the evidence'. He was to cover all aspects of the Agency, including the Clandestine Service. Darling set to work examining documents and interviewing top officials. By November 1951 Hansen renewed his request for additional historians increasing it from six to nine professional historians. Although Hansen's suggestion was never fully implemented, by June 1952 the Historical Staff numbered six: four historians and two researchers. It was to be the high-water mark for the History Staff until the late 1960s.

DCI Smith continued to follow the program closely. At a 14 May 1952 morning staff meeting, for example, Smith expressed his strong support for the Agency's historical efforts. What he wanted was a dispassionate, chronological type; history which laid out all the facts. When Hansen informed the Director that Professor Darling would be returning to Andover in 1953, Smith told him to hire another top historian and suggested S.L.A.

Marshall who had just written the history of the Supreme Headquarters Allied Expeditionary Force (SHAEF). The history of the Agency had to be written.

In August 1952 Colonel Stanley J. Grogan replaced Hansen as the Assistant to the Director. Although Grogan professed to 'believe in history' and continued to oversee the program until 1963, under his overall direction the program began a long, gradual decline. The decline was not evident at first. Darling completed a 12-chapter study of the early postwar Agency in December 1953.

Entitled *The Central Intelligence Agency: An Instrument of Government to 1950,* Darling's work laid out in detail the legal and legislative problems faced by policy makers in creating a central intelligence service and carefully documented the bureaucratic squabbles over who was to control it, especially the military's resentment over losing part of 'its turf' to a civilian intelligence agency. George S. Jackson also began a study of DCI Smith's administration. The program, although small, appeared healthy.

THE DULLES ERA

When Allen Dulles replaced Smith as DCI in February 1953, the atmosphere for the historical program began to change. Dulles disliked the tone of Darling's study, which carefully documented the continuing problems between the military and the civilians over control of the centralized intelligence apparatus. Dulles did not wish to disturb the delicate relationship between the Agency and the other members of the intelligence community, especially the military. Accordingly, he had Darling's manuscript classified Top Secret and placed under the Director's privileged seal. It was not to be circulated and was to be withheld from review by anyone inside or outside of the Agency and released only with his personal approval.

Darling left the Agency in the fall of 1953 to return to Andover. By 1954 the History Staff consisted of two professionals and two clerical. It appeared to be in a caretaker status. The CIA then invited Forrest Pogue, a well-known respected military historian and later General George C. Marshall's biographer, to succeed Darling in early 1954. Unfortunately, Pogue declined the offer to become senior CIA historian.

Instead of instituting another search, Grogan selected in-house historian George Jackson, to assume the duties of the senior historian. Under Jackson and Grogan, the program began to slip even further. There was now little interest from the top. Dulles never had the same feeling for history and its benefits that Smith had. The program directors, Grogan and Jackson, were not strong enough to push an aggressive program. The program languished. It lacked real direction and suffered from benign neglect.

Ironically, Darling himself contributed to the program's decline. Upon his departure, Darling recommended that Jackson's study covering Smith as DCI from October 1950 to February 1953 be postponed indefinitely as 'it was too soon to write an historical analysis of the period'. Instead of continuing to write history, Darling suggested that the staff begin an archival project of selecting significant documents and attempting to fill in the gaps in the record. Darling's position reflected a long-standing argument among historians as to when sufficient time had elapsed to enable historians to gain sufficient to write balanced history.

Jackson, although continuing to work on his Smith manuscript, in general perspective he supported Darling's recommendations. In his Proposed Plans for the Director's Historical Staff of 15 January 1954, Jackson asked how best the History Staff could serve the interests of the Agency and concluded that it was 'Too early to continue the chronology of the Agency since it would lack historical perspective and because', quoting Chairman of the Board of Estimates, Sherman Kent, 'problems of the first five years are likely still to be, in one form or another, the problems of the next one hundred.' Kent, of course, was correct in his analysis. Many of the problems which surfaced in the Agency's early years continued to plague it. This was exactly why the Agency needed to document them, but no one saw the connection. The staff would be, according to Jackson, better employed for the time being in assembling and systematizing materials for later histories and filling the gaps left in the work already done.

Moreover, Jackson, with the consent of Grogan and DCI Dulles, began to move the program away from critically interpretative works. He suggested that the type of history that contained historical evaluation was not advisable in CIA because historians would never have access to all the evidence, especially intelligence community records (still a problem today). He also questioned the extent to which historians working for the CIA should be permitted to be evaluative or critical. For Jackson, they were Agency officers first, and historians second.

At the same time, forces outside the Agency also played a role in limiting substantive historical evaluation of the CIA and the intelligence community. The Hoover Commission, established in 1954 to examine the structure of the executive branch with a view toward reforming and reorganizing it, set up the Clark Task Force under General Mark W. Clark to survey the intelligence community. In addition, President Eisenhower created the Doolittle Committee chaired by General James H. Doolittle to examine the Clandestine Service. The CIA Inspector General, Lyman Kirkpatrick, supervised all internally prepared reports on CIA activities for the two groups. Kirkpatrick wanted no competition from the History Staff. He, therefore, pressured Dulles to issue a directive to the History Staff that its historical work 'will in no way impinge on the work of the Inspector General's Office.'

Given Dulles' directive and his own inclinations, Jackson carefully outlined guidelines for future historical studies that would not be controversial. They were to follow the general direction of his own study of Smith. That is, they were to put emphasis on a factual recital and a historical explanation of the organizational changes in each of the offices that made up the Directorate for Intelligence (DDI) and the Directorate for Support (DDS). (This later became the Directorate of Administration (DDA). What Jackson was advocating was administrative history. Excluded would be the organizational history of the Directorate for Plans and the Clandestine Service (DDP) and the Agency's overseas components. In fact, DDP officials opposed any mention of their activities. Given the Agency's strong security concerns and deep commitment to protecting sources and methods, Jackson believed he had little choice but to agree. DDP operations and activities would be too sensitive to write about.

As part of Jackson's plan, the History Staff would also prepare a series of informal office 'genealogies' and a series of individual historical projects relating primarily to organizational structure and the administrative process; perhaps important, but certainly non-controversial. Under Jackson's leadership the CIA History Program was becoming less and less analytical and less important to CIA senior leaders.

Although agreeing with Jackson's overall plan, Sherman Kent, the Director of the National Estimates Office and a trained historian in his own right, took issue with Jackson's basic premise. Jackson's plan, according to Kent, did not address the hard questions of history. For Kent, the historian had to be both a reporter and an archivist. He had to ferret out the real story from not only the official records which were often misleading and incomplete, but from interviews with the participants and, if possible, access to high level decision-making meetings. The major purpose of agency historians, Kent argued, was to further the operational efficiency of that agency. The historian had to be analytical and had to inject himself into the major decision-making process in order to record an accurate picture of the intelligence process.

Dulles seemed to allow the Historical Staff a great deal of leeway in choosing the direction it should take. He directed Jackson to keep under constant review the history of central intelligence and the CIA in order to produce a chronological history or histories and individual historical studies related to problems the Agency considered of sufficient importance to merit historical analysis. He also granted the historian full access to all CIA documentation 'within certain limits as he might from time to time impose'. Jackson, however, failed to take full advantage of this opening. Instead, he began producing organizational, administrative studies of the DDI, DDS, and DDC. Even these studies received only very limited distribution. In accordance with the Director's instructions, these new histories were not to be circulated but could be reviewed in the office of the Assistant to the Director, Colonel Grogan. Under this direction, the History Staff produced such studies as *The Organizational History of the Central Intelligence Agency 1950–1953, CIA Support Functions, A History of the Office of Reports and Estimates 1946–1951*, and a variety of guides and reference tools.

Given its basic work plan, the History Staff caused few bureaucratic problems and seemed to disappear into the expanding CIA bureaucracy. It tackled few hard questions and stayed away from the Directorate of Plans entirely. It had few major advocates among major CIA decision makers. Only Sherman Kent seemed to follow its progress and he remained extremely busy with the Office of National Estimates. Rather symptomatic of the program's status during the late 1950s, the CIA Telephone Directory listed the History Staff as a service or a housekeeping unit. By 1963 it had disappeared from the telephone directory as a separate entity altogether.

In 1958 Dulles transferred the history staff to the Public Affairs Office. This raised serious questions over whether the history staff could continue to produce objective historical studies or whether the emphasis would shift to products designed to project a positive public image of Agency activities. In November 1963 DCI John McCone transferred the history staff back to OIC. The transfer did not, however, reflect a renewed interest on the part of top management. Under DCI's John McCone and William Raborn, the history program continued to suffer benign neglect. The Agency's institutional culture provided little space for a history program. From 1954 to 1966 there were never more than two historians on the staff at any one time. The program languished. It received little high level support and CIA policy makers, in general, appeared uninterested and unconcerned with the small program and its activities. The historians themselves did little to promote an active program. They seemed content to have very little visibility within the Agency.

A RENEWED EFFORT

Upset with the general Agency attitude toward history, in 1966 Sherman Kent addressed a strong memorandum to DCI William Raborn. Entitled "The Agency and the Business of Its History", Kent's memorandum pictured the present neglected condition of the Agency's history program as short-sighted and ill-advised. The creation of a solid Agency historical program, for Kent, seemed essential if the Agency was to understand and profit from its past. Kent argued that history provided policy makers with the necessary background and analysis to enhance their decision-making capabilities. Good history promoted the efficiency of the Agency and the intelligence process. According to Kent, 'there was a good deal of catching up to be done given the present dodgy state of historical work in the Agency'. Kent urged Raborn to revise the current history program.

Praising the early work of Arthur Darling, Kent recommended that the Agency hire a professional historian who would be responsible directly to the Director, Deputy Director, or Executive Director. Kent also urged the creation of a board of senior officers to provide guidance and support to the program. He stressed that the historian would need such high-powered advocates since he 'inevitably tangles with recalcitrants down the line, especially those in the Clandestine Service who believed the activities of the service and those of a historian were in direct conflict'.

Raborn took no action on Kent's memorandum, but new DCI Richard Helms asked his Executive Director/Comptroller, Lawrence K. 'Red' White, to look into the matter. Helms made White directly responsible for the history program. White then solicited Agency suggestions and proposals for an on-going active history program. In the fall of 1967, White, on the advice of Sherman Kent, hired another Yale alumnus and retired history professor from the University of Michigan, Howard M. Ehrmann, as an Agency consultant. Ehrmann was to advise on the establishment of a permanent professional history staff for CIA. Located in the Office of the DCI, Ehrmann was literally across the hall from Helms and next door to Colonel White. Finding no history program *per se* at the Agency and only scattered histories being written in the Directorates, Ehrmann prepared a major report for White and Helms.

Submitting his study in April 1968, Ehrmann proposed a historical program for CIA of a substantial nature with adequate staffing and support. The new program would produce a top-level professional history of CIA, Ehrmann predicted. Ehrmann's proposal included the production of: (a) an overall account of the role and position of the DCI and the Agency in the Intelligence Community, (b) histories of the directorates, offices, staffs, and services, and (c) historical accounts of CIA activities and operations. In Ehrmann's plan the histories would be the work of a History Staff assisted by Historical Boards and writers from the four directorates. Ehrmann recommended a professional historian as chief, a deputy, and four Historical Officers one for each of the directorates. The Historical Officers, according to Ehrmann's proposal, need not be professional historians, but should be senior members of the Agency. They would be responsible for supervising the historical program of their directorates. They would work closely with the Historical Boards and writers, giving guidance in the planning of papers and serving as editors of the histories written in the directorates. Officers in the directorates and retired annuitants would write the individual studies.

While Ehrmann prepared his far reaching study, White moved the existing Historical Staff out of Headquarters. In order to make room for a rapidly-expanding Far East Division and the Vietnam problem, White moved the History Staff, now headed by long-time staffer, Philip Edwards, to the Key Building in Rosslyn, Virginia. White, pressed for space, justified his action to Edwards as having very little effect upon the history operation. White was mistaken. The move removed the staff from easy and direct contact with the majority of the Agency and top management officials. It isolated the history operation even more from Agency activities.

A MAJOR EXPANSION

DCI Helms liked Ehrmann's report and hired Ehrmann to implement it. Named Chief of the History Staff on 1 January 1969, Ehrmann retained his office next to Helms as well as the office space in Rosslyn. Ehrmann reported directly to Colonel White. Determined to carry out his ambitious program, Ehrmann pushed his concept of writing the histories of the CIA components. Of special concern was the Directorate for Plans and the Clandestine Service, where little history had been written since the creation of the Agency. These 'component histories' as they came to be known, were to record for the use of present and future Deputy Directors and other senior officers the circumstances which led to the establishment of each component, office or staff. The objective was to record organizational developments, changing requirements, and major decisions from the time of their establishment until 1965. Ehrmann's plan was intended to eliminate the 20-year gap in the Agency's history.

For his deputy Ehrmann selected a veteran CIA officer Bernard Drell. Under Ehrmann and Drell the CIA history program exploded. Although 'Red' White wrote to the Deputy Directors that the History Program 'is not the most urgent or important thing on your platter', he asked them to cooperate fully with Dr Ehrmann by appointing History Officers and History Boards for their directorates in order to bring the CIA history program up-to-date. He stipulated that writers for all directorate histories (there were over 500 identified projects) be chosen. He wanted the catch-up program completed by 31 December 1971.

The overall guidance and direction for this catch-up program became the principal activity of Drell and the History Staff located in Rosslyn. Ehrmann, although he reviewed most of the work, preferred to remain at headquarters and seldom ventured down to Rosslyn. By 7 January 1970, the History Staff, in addition to the chief and deputy chief, included documents officers, senior editors, copy editors, and clericals. All were kept busy drafting guides, aids, and reference works for the benefit of the directorate historical officers and writers. They reviewed and edited manuscripts and maintained a Master Index of Agency names, organizational changes, and events. They drafted a *Style Manual for Historical Writing* and *A Guide for Writing the History of a DDI Component*. In addition, Ehrmann brought aboard Ludwell Montague, a member of the Board of Estimates, to supplement the early histories of the Agency by bringing out the activities of the Clandestine Service and its place in CIA and offering an interpretation and evaluation of the role of General Smith as DCI. Wayne G. Jackson began a draft of the history of the Dulles period. In all, the Historical Staff expanded to a total of ten permanent positions and numerous loan-ins and part-timers. The concentration of personnel was clearly in the directorates, however. By 1970 there were a total of 468 history projects proposed in the directorates. Each directorate had appointed a History Officer and a History Board. In all 191 full or part-time writers worked on history projects. The Clandestine Service program alone called for 396 specific chronological histories or operational monographs and employed 50 full-time officers and 12 retired annuitants as writers.

The year 1970 proved to be the high point of the program as the directorates completed over 180 studies. Ehrmann kept continually busy giving training seminars on how to go about preparing a history and just what was to be included. He stressed he 'wanted facts' rather than 'free theory' and outlined how to construct a major research project. Despite Ehrmann's and Drell's efforts, however, the results were very uneven. The writers in the directorates were simply not trained historians. Most published histories were narrative, story telling monographs, rather than insightful, interpretative histories. Their length ranged from a few pages to several volumes and their quality varied enormously from excellent to mediocre and pedestrian.

PROBLEMS

By the time James Schlesinger replaced Richard Helms as DCI in February 1973 the program was under attack from the directorates as difficult and costly to maintain. Facing budgetary retrenchment with the end of the US involvement in Vietnam, the directorates questioned the overall value of the program and the commitment of resources which offered little perceived return. Even Ehrmann was forced to admit that most of the histories produced in the directorates offered little in the way of historical interpretation, were poorly researched, and poorly written. The concept of assigning the writing of histories to persons unfamiliar with research techniques and with historical writing styles was generally a failure. Moreover, for security reasons these histories were produced in such limited copies (one to three) and possessively squirreled away, that they were rarely used and practically forgotten by the Agency population in general.

Seeing the direction the program was taking, Ehrmann left CIA in early 1973. Bernard Drell, his deputy, became chief. His main duty was to complete the catch-up phase. At the time, although some 350 histories had been completed, over 150 projects remained and over 42 people continued working on historical projects in the directorates. Despite its short comings – the large size of the program as originally conceived, the modest allocation of resources committed to its achievement, its dependence, principally upon non-historians for research and writing, and the low priority it received, it did manage to produce a large body of historical literature and to document and preserve the early history of the Agency which otherwise might have been lost.

ABOLISHED

William Colby, Deputy Director for Operations and designated DCI, having little interest in the program and faced with budgetary restraints and growing opposition to the history program in the directorates, terminated the massive catch-up effort in mid-1973. Colby dropped the requirement for the writing of component histories and directed that a series of annual reports be prepared by the components as part of CIA's Annual Report to the President's Foreign Intelligence Advisory Board (PFIAB). The six-page reports which resulted proved quite disappointing as history. They showed little historical perspective and even less analysis.

A major reorientation of the entire program occurred with the retirement of Drell in the fall of 1973. Almost the entire History Staff either retired or was reassigned overnight. After Colby officially ended the component 'catch-up' history program, there were only two historians left on the history staff – Walter Elder, who had been McCone's Executive Assistant and was at the time without an assignment, and Jack Pfieffer, a University of Chicago history PhD. The rest of the staff returned to their home offices. The history component projects not projected to be completed by 30 June 1974 were simply dropped or canceled. Colby then appointed Walter Elder to head the History Staff.

Under Elder the history program became much smaller and more selective. It retreated once again into the background of the CIA bureaucracy. Colby's directive of 8 August 1973 still called for a CIA history program but a scaled back one which stressed the compilation of an accurate, comprehensive record of significant Agency activities suitable for inclusion in a government-wide declassification program that President Richard Nixon favored. In short, while there was still to be a history program, the staff, however, was to be discreet about what topics it wrote about. Greater emphasis was placed on complying with President Nixon's Executive Order 11652 which called for a renewed effort regarding the review and declassification of government records within the constraints imposed by security considerations. Colby placed the reduced History Staff under the Deputy Director for Management and Services, which had the responsibility for the new declassification program. Elder became little more than the general manager of the remaining classified histories.

Although not a trained historian, Elder held a Doctor of Philosophy degree from Oxford University, had been a Rhodes Scholar, and was, if not enthusiastic, at least sympathetic to the program. He suggested continuing the program with histories of the Helms and Schlesinger administrations and on selected topics such as Vietnam, Iran, Guatemala, Laos, the U-2 program, Cuba, the Cold War, and the Congo. He rejected proposals for studies on SALT, narcotics, and terrorism as 'not lending themselves to a full blown history anytime soon.' He, nevertheless, wanted to get the History Staff involved in current topics. He believed Colby strongly supported his efforts in this direction. He wrote that Colby suggested using mid-career officers on a rotational basis to complete the job. Both Elder and Colby firmly believed trained historians were not necessary for the writing of Agency history. Both believed experienced CIA officers were better able to understand and relate the Agency's story, having witnessed the events first hand.

Elder also believed Colby supported his other objectives of instituting an oral interview program of retiring CIA officials, relocating the staff to headquarters, and getting the staff reinstated in the DCI Office. He aggressively pursued his plans, but to little avail. The history program floundered. Although Colby approved the continuation of an Agency history program shortly after appointing Elder as Chief and actually approved its move back to headquarters to accommodate Elder, his busy schedule and opposition from the directorates soon put the entire program in jeopardy. John Blake, the Deputy Director for Administration (DDA), for example, vetoed the move back to headquarters. 'It was', he wrote, 'best to continue having the History Staff report to DDA.' Elder never protested to Colby.

In fact, Elder and the History Staff began to take on a variety of other historical related functions at the request of Colby and Blake. Colby asked Elder to take custody of all the Agency files relating to Watergate and to take charge of creating an Agency portrait gallery of selected officials, for example. When Colby abolished the Intelligence Museum Commission, he transferred its responsibilities to the History Staff. Blake also asked Elder to lecture at the Agency training courses on the Agency's history. Ironically, as the production of solid monographs and manuscripts declined, Elder and the small history staff took on a whole series of history related activities. Their main function, however, soon became related to the Agency's declassification and review effort. They wrote little Agency history.

The Watergate crisis of 1974 and the Senate investigation by the Church Committee into CIA activities in 1975–76 brought further problems to the history staff. A Senate request for over 50 of the component histories produced during Operation 'Catch Up' caused massive resentment in the Directorate of Operations (DCI Scheslinger renamed the Directorate for Plans the Directorate of Operations) to any further historical research. Rightly or wrongly, many in the Agency blamed the histories for the Agency's problems and poor public image. If the Senate Select Committee did not have these CIA histories, they reasoned, the Agency would not have been crucified.

Seeing little benefit from a separate history program and desiring additional positions for his declassification review efforts, John Blake informed Elder on 17 September 1974 that as of 30 June 1975 the History Staff must be down to two people, Elder and a secretary. Elder had to remove or relocate every one else. Not consulted on the decision, Elder, nevertheless, did little to protest. He wrote, 'If I were the Director, given budgetary constraints, I would give the history program a low priority.' Elder saw little benefit in continuing to compile histories that nobody used and dutifully went about reducing the staff. He terminated the contracts of three annuitant historians, Wayne G. Jackson, Paul Borel, and James Cooley and asked the secretaries to find new jobs. When approached by remaining members of the staff to protest to Colby, he responded angrily, 'Now is not the time to badger Colby about Histories.' (Colby was in the midst of the Congressional investigations of illegal CIA activities.) Elder did, however, write to Colby on 7 November 1974 with a prospectus that presented the CIA history program as of 1 July 1975, as 'consisting of one historian, one secretary, and some 350 cubic feet of documents, including some 400 alleged histories.' It was a 'one man band operation', according to Elder. There was no recorded response from the Director. Elder did manage to have Jack Pfeiffer retained in order to finish his study of the Bay of Pigs.

By 14 April 1975 Elder held out little hope for the retention in CIA of any history program. After returning from a meeting with Blake, Elder recorded that the Directorate of Administration (DDA) would not provide the history program with any further funds or slots. Not interested in running a History Staff under such arrangements nor in fighting a bureaucratic battle to preserve it, Elder now spent most of his time dealing with requests for CIA documents, including CIA component histories, from the Church Committee. The program was once again in limbo. Although the Church Committee requested, received, and used many of the CIA histories, the CIA history staff itself received little credit or attention from any of the investigative committees or commissions. Illustrative of its low status was the Rockefeller Commission report. When the Rockefeller Commission issued its report on agency operations, it called for a buildup of the Inspector General's and the General Counsel's staffs. It was silent, however, on the Agency's history program. No one, in fact, seemed concerned. There appeared to be little understanding of any historical function within the Agency.

The legacy of neglect continued. By the spring of 1976, when Jack Pfeiffer appointed himself acting chief, all that remained of the staff was one researcher and one secretary. Pfeiffer, nevertheless, continued to work on his Bay of Pigs study and the staff continued to maintain the Historical Documents Index file. According to Pfeiffer, following the release of the Church Committee Report, bitter, outspoken opposition, especially from the DO to any further CIA historical effort solidified. The other Directorates shared the feeling. Even in DDA, Pfeiffer wrote, 'the staff was merely tolerated and the interest was less than minimal.' Bitter, Pfeiffer was not even invited to DDA staff meetings.

Undeterred, Pfeiffer continued to put forward proposals for an expanded history program. He strongly believed that a professional, well documented history of CIA and its fundamental role in national security matters was absolutely essential for understanding US foreign policy and for preserving the institutional memory of the CIA. He called for the appointment of professionally trained historians and the transfer of the program from the DDA to the DCI. Only at the DCI level authority, Pfeiffer argued, could the program ensure the necessary cooperation and demonstrate its importance. Pfeiffer's immediate supervisor, Tom White, assistant for Information, DDA, simply ignored Pfeiffer's requests. Pfeiffer continued to work on his history and to develop a liaison with other government historians. These historians pressed Pfeiffer for CIA cooperation in declassifying and releasing CIA documents for publication. Department of State historians, for example, were especially concerned with keeping their *Foreign Relations* series up-to-date.

DCI Admiral Stansfield Turner first became aware that there might be a problem with the CIA history program when Secretary of State Cyrus Vance wrote to Turner in May 1979 requesting that the CIA history office work more closely with the Department's history office to ensure that its famous *Foreign Relations* series truly reflect the formulation of American foreign policy including US intelligence activities. Turner replied to Vance on 6 June 1979 and assured the secretary that the CIA history office would cooperate fully with State Department historians. In his letter Turner praised the close working relationship of the two staffs.

Despite Turner's letter to Secretary of State Vance, assuring him of close cooperation between the two history offices, DDA Blake decided to abolish the history program altogether. There were no funds for a CIA history program in the FY 1980 proposed budget. On 3 July 1979 White convened the entire History Staff in his office and informed them of the decision to abolish the program. He added that the three staff members were free to seek other positions, resign, or retire. Stunned, Pfeiffer got the termination date postponed until 31 December 1979 to help everyone find a position. At the meeting, White also informed Pfeiffer that the responsibility for responding to other government historians' requests for document review would be transferred to the Office of Training and Education (OTE) as of 10 October 1979 and he was to aid the transfer.

Determined to save his job and preserve the program, Pfeiffer alerted other government historians of his plight. At a Society for History in the Federal Government meeting in September 1979, Pfeiffer informed Richard Hewlett, head of the Department of Energy's History Office, David Trask, Chief Historian of the Department of State, and Paul Scheips of the Army's Center for Military History, of the proposal to abolish the CIA history office. All were appalled. Alen Weinstein, the author of *Perjury: His Chambers Affair,* publicly declared that the CIA was making a serious mistake and the society unanimously passed a resolution opposing the termination of the CIA's history staff. Others such as Mack Thompson of the American Historical Association (AHA) and Richard Kirkendall of the Organization of American Historians (OAH) urged historians all over the country to write to CIA in protest.

At the same time, Pfeiffer met with staff from the Senate Select Committee on Intelligence to answer questions concerning the abolishing of the CIA history program. His immediate supervisor Tom White also appeared. The committee staffers asked White the rationale for the termination of the program and staff. White responded by claiming that 'everyone from the DCI down was in favor of history', the problem was the Office of Management and Budget. History was simply too low a priority. Pfeiffer took issue with White's contention. He concluded his remarks by stating that most officials at CIA simply did not appreciate nor understand history or how important a professionally produced history of the Agency might be to Agency seniors. The committee seemed to side with Pfeiffer. Senator Birch Bayh, along with Congressmen Richardson Preyer and Thomas Kindness, wrote to DCI Turner to protest the elimination of the CIA history program. The DDA, however, did not take kindly to Pfeiffer's activities. Pfeiffer received a letter of reprimand for contacting

Congressional committees without getting official approval from the Office of Congressional Relations and was reassigned to the Classification Review Division on 31 December 1979.

A RENEWED INTEREST

With the Congressional letters in hand, Turner wanted to know what the flap was all about. He asked the new DDA, Don Wortman to investigate. Wortman assured the Director that the history function would 'in some form or other be preserved' and that the revised FY 1980 budget included funds for a CIA history program. He added in his note to the Director that future plans called for an expanded history staff.

External pressure on CIA officials to retain a history program also continued to mount in early 1980. In fact, as early as January 1980, David (Doc) O. Cooke, Assistant Secretary of Defense, upon the urging of the Office of the Secretary of Defense Historian, Alfred Goldberg, wrote to Admiral Turner expressing his deep concern over the state of the CIA history program. Turner, formerly head of the Naval War College and a strong advocate of history, asked his DDCI Frank Carlucci and James King, the Coordinator for Academic Affairs, to look into the matter further. King reported on 12 January 1980 that the program was a mere remnant of what it was formerly and even the remnant was scheduled for elimination. King concluded his report by stating that basically the program had been in liquidation since 1974. Upon receipt of King's memorandum, Turner acted quickly. He did not want to see the program abolished.

Turner replied to Senator Bayh and Congressmen Pryor and Kindness stating that the CIA history staff was to be retained and expanded from its 'present narrow focus'. Turner also set up a high-level Advisory Committee on Agency History (ACAH) headed by Hal Bean and James King to develop proposals for a serious historical program for the Agency.

At the same time, Thomas Troy, an intelligence analyst in the CIA's Center for the Study of Intelligence, also wrote a ringing endorsement for the preservation and strengthening of the CIA history program. After reviewing the past history of the program, Troy's report proclaimed that history as a function in the Agency was an absolute necessity. According to the report, the Agency could not afford to ignore its past. It could not be indifferent to its background and its place in the development of American foreign policy. Troy believed that the Agency had virtually abandoned its own history while over 125 other government agencies had established on-going historical programs. Arguing that ultimately the Agency was accountable to posterity for its actions and that its activities had to be portrayed and transmitted to future generations, Troy advocated not only the development of a long-term CIA history program but also its placement in the DCI's Office. Only by having the prestige and influence of the DCI behind it could the history office overcome hardcore internal opposition. Drawing on the committee's recommendations, Troy's report, and his own Naval War College experience, Turner suggested that Dr Martin Blumenson, a former colleague at the War College and editor of the General George S. Patton papers, be hired as a consultant to the committee to study the history program and make suggestions for strengthening it.

Blumenson accepted the appointment and set to work studying the CIA history program. He found the existing situation discouraging, 'Two ladies', he wrote, 'one a GS 08 and the other a GS 06, presently comprise the entire Historical Activity at CIA.' After examining the 360 'histories' written during the catch-up period, Blumenson declared them 'embarrassing'. They ranged from poor to excellent but 'should have been labeled "Preliminary studies" instead of being dignified by the term "histories".' The holding operation of the present staff, Blumenson believed, was unworthy of the status, dignity, and importance of the Agency and its well recognized and accepted place in the governmental structure. In his report of 15 June 1980 he wrote that a history program for the Agency was 'not a luxury but rather a legitimate tool' that could and should facilitate the Agency's work. While recognizing the extreme sensitivity of much of the Agency's production and the reluctance, particularly on the part of the Directorate of Operations, to record actions and events, Blumenson recommended a significant expansion of the history program. A well-defined historical program should, Blumenson believed, create and preserve the institutional memory of the Agency. It could provide insight into past operations, processes, methods, changing organizational structures and personnel. For Blumenson, the Agency could not deny its historical accountability. Deliberately overlooking this obligation left it to be fulfilled by groups, organizations, and individuals outside the CIA establishment – the press, disgruntled employees, and fiction writers. Their descriptions resulted in a more or less distorted picture of what the Agency did and denied the American public a true picture of its achievements. Moreover, Blumenson argued, a strong, professional history program would relieve the Agency components in large part from having to 'act as their own historians'. Blumenson set forth a compelling argument.

In addressing the question of organizational placement, Blumenson rejected suggestions that the History Staff be located in the Public Affairs Office or in the Directorate of Administration. For Blumenson, they performed altogether different functions and had interests and concerns wholly different from those of historians. He recommended the program be located at the top, as a separate entity immediately under the Director. This, he believed, was necessary in order to break down compartmentation control and to indicate to the Directorates that the program enjoyed the fullest support and confidence at the highest level. He further recommended that although the historians should take no active part in records management, they should have some advisory role with the records collecting and preservation process and to the extent possible, have full access to all Agency records and officials.

Blumenson recommended a small professional staff to carry out his proposed program. Heading it would be a senior, high level professional as Chief Historian, who would be given the opportunity to create and direct a meaningful historical program. Such an individual would be invited to attend as an observer the regular and important meetings and conferences at the highest Agency levels. He would be exempt from rotational assignments and his professional staff would have a special career track to ensure promotions and rewards. Blumenson thought the Deputy Historian should come from within the Agency but should have proper historical credentials. The Chief and the Deputy could then develop the program as they saw fit. Blumenson added that it might be helpful to have a Historical Advisory Committee of Agency seniors to discuss periodically the direction of the history program and it problems.

In its report to the Director of 15 July 1980, the CIA's History Advisory Committee relied heavily on Professor Blumenson's study and strongly supported his recommendations. The committee called for the establishment of an Office of the CIA Historian as an independent office under the DCI and for the CIA Historian to occupy an upper level Senior Intelligence Service (SIS) slot. The historian would 'sit at the Director's left hand' and enjoy DCI level access to programs and documents.

In its own investigations into the status of history in the Agency, the committee reported it found widespread support within the Agency for a program which would provide an accessible record of Agency activity, a teaching resource, a means of more easily and reliably providing data to the Congress and the public, and a way to respond to the requirements of other agencies involved in the maintaining and documenting of government histories. The committee attributed this change in Agency perception to the new Congressional and Executive Branch oversight requirements and the corresponding demands for accounting of past Agency activities which consumed an enormous amount of the directorates time and effort and often resulted in not always successful attempts to recapture knowledge of facts and events from the past. (The Senate established the Senate Select Committee on Intelligence (SSCI) in 1978 and the House created the House Permanent Select Intelligence Committee (HPSCI) in 1979.)

With his Advisory Committee's report in hand, DCI Turner, on 5 November 1980, transferred the Historical Staff from the Directorate of

Administration to the Office of the Director and attached it to the Executive Secretariat. He also announced that a new Chief Historian, not yet selected, would be responsible to the Director for the development and implementation of the Agency's Historical Program. In the same announcement, Turner also granted the Historical Staff access to all Agency personnel and records subject to the approval of the Deputy Director concerned and the Executive Secretary, provided that the Historical Staff could appeal a refusal to the Director. In addition, Turner directed the Advisory Committee to begin a nation wide search for a CIA Chief Historian and appointed Roberta Knapp, a former DDI Historical Officer and a Bryn Mawr history PhD, as Acting Chief and permanent Deputy. Before the committee completed its search for a new Chief Historian, however, William Casey replaced Turner as DCI on 28 January 1981. The future of the program seemed once again in doubt.

Casey, however, was a history buff and encouraged the committee to complete its search. He even suggested that the committee consider his New York neighbor, historian David Kahn, whose *The Codebreakers* (1967) was a well received book on cryptology, for the position. After an extensive search, the committee selected J. Kenneth McDonald, a military historian teaching at the Naval War College, for the position in March 1981. Casey approved the appointment and McDonald became the Agency historian in August 1981.

In October McDonald outlined his proposal for a new historical program before the Executive Committee. Stating that the CIA could not plan or act without being influenced by its historical experience and that it was, therefore, not a question of whether or not the Agency used history, but rather what kind of history it used and how well, McDonald proposed to build an entirely new program. Unlike past efforts, McDonald stressed his intention to use professionally trained historians to research and write Agency history. Moreover, he intended to place the Agency's experience in its overall historical context. The new histories would not only be useful to Agency employees but would clearly set forth the role of the Agency in the overall context of US policy. With a beginning staff of four professional historians and two support personnel, McDonald proposed to produce four categories of histories: (1) a short survey history of the Agency to be widely available within the Agency for training, reference, and general knowledge purposes; (2) a series on the leadership of the individual DCIs; (3) a historical monograph series to treat such topics as CIA's relations with Congress, its role in the intelligence community, technical developments such as overhead reconnaissance, and crisis such as the Vietnam War; and finally (4) a multi-volume long-term general history of the Agency which would stress the evolution of the Agency within a broad historical synthesis.

In addition to its writing responsibilities, McDonald suggested that the History Staff be CIA's point of contact with other government history programs that used CIA documents, provide an internal reference service on historical matters, and conduct an oral history program in order to ensure that the institutional memory be preserved. He also supported the idea of an in-house, senior History Review Board to help in setting priorities and reviewing manuscripts.

It was an ambitious program. The Executive Committee and DCI Casey approved of the new start nevertheless, and McDonald began to build a new program. Although the staff itself was located in the Ames Building at Rosslyn, McDonald, as some of his predecessors had, maintained an office at Headquarters. Casey strongly supported the new historical effort and often called McDonald personally for answers to reference questions. Although McDonald had access to the Director, however, he was never invited to sit in on high policy decisions or high level conferences or meetings, nor did he press the matter. Casey did reissue Turner's directive giving the History Staff full access to all Agency personnel and records subject to the approval of the Deputy Director or Head of the Independent Office concerned and the Executive Secretary. Working with Casey, McDonald also secured the declassification and release of old Office of Strategic Service (OSS) records to the National Archives. (This was part of a deal Casey made with Congress. In return for the exemption of most CIA operational records from the Freedom of Information Act, Casey agreed to release the OSS records.) Despite McDonald's best efforts, however, the history program never became an effective policymaking tool for decision makers in the Agency. The accepted belief was that history was nice to have but non-essential to the intelligence process.

During Casey's tenure and under McDonald's leadership, young historians and retired annuitants labored to produce professional quality histories. They started major projects on such topics as CIA/Congressional relations, the overhead reconnaissance program, and histories of McCone, Helms, Schlesinger, and Colby. Because the staff suffered a high turnover ratio and hiring problems, however, unfinished research and draft manuscripts became the norm. McDonald, a careful, cautious man, with no previous intelligence background, was reluctant to press too hard. McDonald had little direct evidence to show high-level Agency officials that history did, in fact, matter to the Agency.

PROBLEMS AGAIN

With the death of William Casey in 1987 the program lost a staunch advocate. Under the new DCI, William Webster, McDonald lost his seventh floor office at Headquarters and moved to Rosslyn. He also lost the easy direct access he had enjoyed with Casey.

Facing major cutbacks and attempting to streamline the organization structure of CIA, DCI Webster, over McDonald's protests, moved the History Staff to the Office of Training and Education in 1992. Once again, the CIA History Staff appeared to be exiled.

REVITALIZED

Like the old silent film series, 'The Perils of Pauline', the History Staff was once again snatched from disaster by the appointment of Robert Gates as DCI in November 1991. Gates strongly advocated a new openness policy for the Agency. He also believed in the value of history and getting as much of the Agency's story out to the general public as possible. Gates publicly admitted CIA involvement in 11 covert operations and declared the Agency would review the records for declassification and release. Gates wanted the history staff to take the lead in this effort.

After some discussion about the placement of the History Staff, Gates in 1992 moved the history program close to top management. He placed it in the revitalized Center for the Study of Intelligence (CSI) which reported to the Executive Director. David Gries, a senior CIA officer became the Director of CSI. Working closely with McDonald, Gries was determined to stress the Agency's history program and its value to the Agency. He added several positions to the history staff, called for an increased publication schedule, and worked to increase the visibility of the history program. Under this renewed effort a whole series of history publications began to appear, both internally and externally, and the History Staff and CSI sponsored historical conferences on the Cuban Missile Crisis and the Teaching of Intelligence. Gries also insisted the Agency's professional historians become involved in the complex John F. Kennedy assassination reinvestigation. In addition, McDonald and Gries began a seminar series for senior officials on the history of the Agency and promoted the teaching of Agency history within the Intelligence Community. When Congress mandated a strengthening of the Department of State's effort on the traditional *Foreign Relations* series, McDonald and Gries worked to ensure full CIA cooperation with Department of State historians in ferreting out intelligence documents for inclusion in the series. This surge of activity in 1992–93 set the stage for the modern structure of the Agency's history program. Although R. James Woolsey replaced Gates as DCI in February 1993 and both Gries and McDonald had retired by 1995, the program was on solid ground.

It remains to be seen how long the new focus on history will last.

Whether it will atrophy once more will depend not only on the attitudes of high-level Agency officials, but also on the ability of the historians themselves to sell their product and the quality of the histories and monographs produced and their effective distribution. The historians must demonstrate the utility of their work, enlist senior management allies to testify to its value, and find ways to remind the Agency of history's importance and utility. Only in this way will history and the CIA History Staff play any role in helping to document and preserve the Agency's past.

SUMMARY

From the time Walter Bedell Smith appointed Dr Arthur Darling as CIA's first historian in 1952, the role and size of the Agency history program varied greatly. With most Agency officials exhibiting little overall understanding of the value of history to the Agency's mission and function, and few aggressive History Staff directors, the history program suffered through peaks and valleys of DCI and organizational interest. Under Smith, the program flourished as Darling and his colleagues produced carefully documented studies of the origins and early years of the Agency and of the development of its organizational structure. Under Allen Dulles, John McCone, and William Raborn, the program suffered benign neglect. Of the senior managers, only Sherman Kent expressed concern. On a reduced scale, however, it continued to draft professionally researched and well written monographs. Upon the urgings of Sherman Kent and Executive Director/Comptroller 'Red' White, in 1968 the Agency initiated a major catch-up program designed to bring the overall history of the Agency up-to-date. Under DCI Richard Helms the History Staff rapidly expanded as it strove to produce historical studies of virtually all of the Agency's activities. operations, and components. The staff itself, however, served primarily in a supervisory, editing, and review role. CIA officers detached from their regular duties and retired annuitants undertook the writing of most of the over 500 projected history projects. Trained historians neither researched nor wrote the monographs. At its peak in 1970 the program had a central history staff of ten, four directorate Historical Officers, and over 190 writers and researchers. Component support for the effort varied from grudging tolerance to lethal opposition.

As competition for space, funds, and personnel increased and the Agency became caught up in Watergate and the Senate and House investigations into its activities, DCI William Colby abruptly halted the program in mid-1973. Although Colby supported a reduced program, by mid-1974 only one professional historian and two support staff remained and the program was transferred from the DCI to the Directorate of

Administration. It progressively declined until 1979 when DDA John Blake proposed to abolish it altogether. External and internal protests over this proposal prompted Admiral Stansfield Turner to re-establish the CIA history program on a new and more solid basis in 1980. When William Casey replaced Turner as DCI in 1981 the new history program with professional historians reporting directly to the DCI office emerged. It floundered again after Casey's death, only to be revitalized once more under DCI Robert Gates and activist David Gries. Despite its current strengthened position, there is little to suggest that Agency policy makers are using history insightfully. Whether or not the Agency has learned its history lesson remains to be seen.

NOTES

I relied almost exclusively on internal CIA History Staff records and personal interviews of some of the major participants in researching and writing this article. Unfortunately, although the information presented is entirely unclassified, the sources from which it is derived, including the interviews, remain classified. I, therefore, was forced to present the article without the accompanying footnotes.

1. This article covers the CIA history program only through the tenure of Kenneth McDonald as Chief Historian. It does not attempt an assessment of the current history program or its leadership.
2. A government history program may include a wide-variety of functions. Most are not restricted to the research and writing of major historical manuscripts. Their duties and responsibilities include writing policy papers for senior officials, organizing documentary collections, conducting oral history interviews, acting as an Agency reference source, both internally and externally, providing educational lectures and briefings, and, at times, becoming involved in records preservation issues and declassification questions. I focus primarily on the traditional responsibility of a government history program here; the production of solidly-researched historical monographs and articles which illustrate the evolution and activities of the Agency.

12

Conclusion:
An Agenda for Future Research

CHRISTOPHER ANDREW

In addition to revising previous interpretations of various aspects of CIA history, the essays in this volume help to set an agenda for future research. Most illustrate in different ways the new research opportunities generated by the continuing programme of declassification conducted by the CIA Center for the Study of Intelligence. Rhodri Jeffreys-Jones's reassessment of the foundation of the Agency is one of several contributions which cite documents declassified as recently as 1996. Bradley Smith, Helen Laville, Bob de Graaff and Cees Wiebes also identify some of the important source-material on CIA history now available in foreign and non-intelligence archives.

The history of CIA liaison with foreign intelligence agencies, on which de Graaff and Wiebes provide a pioneering case study based on Dutch archives, deserves to be followed by studies of other bilateral relationships.[1] Intelligence liaison is one important area in which the historical record remains highly relevant to current and future policy. The Presidential Commission on the Roles and Capabilities of the United States Intelligence Community (the Brown Commission) concluded in 1996, after visits to Britain and other intelligence allies: 'In general, ... the United States is deriving great benefit from these cooperative relationships'.[2] The 1996 report of the Twentieth Century Fund Task Force on the Future of US Intelligence reached a similar conclusion and called for greater intelligence sharing with foreign agencies.[3]

Though belief in the desirability of intelligence liaison has remained fairly constant during the CIA's first 50 years, awareness in Washington that there is anything worthy of imitation in the experience of foreign intelligence communities has clearly declined. The report of the Brown Commission duly acknowledges that, as a result of the Aldrich Ames case, ten of the CIA's most important Russian agents were executed and others imprisoned.[4] Yet the report also states as a self-evident truth: 'Without question, the United States has the most capable intelligence apparatus of any country in the world'.[5] At no point does the Commission point to anything that American intelligence operations might *learn* from the experience of the rest of the human race. Such breath-taking self-belief ('the Middle Kingdom complex', as it used to be called) has always been a defining characteristic of superpower – or almost superpower – status. It is crucial, for example, in understanding the mindset of the old *Pax Britannica* or the French *mission civilisatrice*. But it is a serious impediment to understanding the past record and future prospects of the American intelligence community.

US technical collection capability is, of course, in a class by itself. But the assumption that the 'intelligence apparatus' as a whole is unquestionably the best in the world lends some support to Gerald Haines's contention that 'Most CIA officers and decision-makers, although they use historical analogies every day, are basically ahistorical. They believe they have no time or need for history.'[6] In fact, with the development of the Agency's History Program in recent years, the CIA as an institution (though not, of course, all CIA officers) now shows greater awareness of the importance of the historical record than most of the federal government.

The current relevance of American intelligence history is only fully apparent if it is seen in comparative perspective. Even the Brown report briefly acknowledges that the relationship between intelligence agencies and policy-makers works less well in the United States than in several of its allies. For the past 50 years the British Joint Intelligence Committee (JIC) has proved better than the NSC or any other American body at resolving turf battles, setting intelligence priorities, coordinating assessment by Intelligence, Foreign Office, Defence and Treasury representatives, and gaining the confidence of policy-makers.[7] The JIC Red Book almost certainly attracts greater attention from consumers than US National Intelligence Estimates, which some policy-makers do not read at all. The Twentieth Century Fund Task Force on the Future of US Intelligence found that, outside the Defense Department, most government officials 'do not much value the [intelligence] analysis they receive'. The Task Force, like the Brown Commission, concluded that Washington could profit from the example of the JIC.[8] There is much more in the experience of outside world which has been ignored in the curiously parochial media and congressional debate on the future of the American intelligence community.

Defining exactly what the historical record contributes to present understanding is, of course, never easy. Those who understand the past are perfectly capable of losing their way in the present. Those who fail to understand the past, however, are virtually certain to do so. The lessons of experience, critically examined and reflected on, are as important to institutions as they are to individuals. Intelligence agencies which ignore their history are as vulnerable as individuals who have lost their memories. Winston Churchill was so much better than any other war leader during the first half of the twentieth century in his understanding and use of intelligence (which does not, of course, mean that he made no mistakes) because he drew on a lifetime's experience and had learned from his errors as well as from his successes. The unprecedented measures taken to preserve the wartime Ultra secret, for example, derived from an acute awareness of his own share of responsibility for revealing in 1927 that Soviet ciphers had been broken and for the subsequent inability of British codebreakers to decrypt Soviet diplomatic traffic.[9] Had Franklin D. Roosevelt, closely involved in naval intelligence as Assistant Secretary of the Navy from 1913 to 1920, learned as much as Churchill from the role of Sigint in naval operations during the First World War, the outcome of the Japanese attack on Pearl Harbor would probably have been very different.[10]

Some of the CIA's more notorious errors, like Roosevelt's failings before Pearl Harbor, have been closely related to misunderstandings of intelligence history. The disastrous overestimation of the efficacy of covert action by Allen Dulles and his senior operations officers during the 1950s, culminating in the débâcle of the Bay of Pigs, derived from a false comparison between wartime special operations behind enemy lines and paramilitary operations in peacetime. That false comparison was reinforced by superficial analysis of the apparently easy overthrow of the Iranian prime minister, Muhammad Mossadeq, in 1953 and of the Guatemalan president, Jacobo Arbenz Guzmán, a year later. More careful study of such successes would have shown that they would not be easily replicable in future. But the covert action enthusiasts in the Directorate of Plans did not wish their enthusiasm to be subjected to critical scrutiny by the analysts of the Directorate of Intelligence, which was kept in ignorance by Allen Dulles of preparations for Operation 'Zapata' against Castro's Cuba in 1961.

The woeful overestimation of the scale and success of Soviet deception during the 1960s and early 1970s by James Angleton, head of the CIA Counterintelligence Staff, similarly derived, at least in part, from a misreading of intelligence history. The prototype for this allegedly massive deception, Angleton believed, was the Trust operation of the 1920s based on what purported to be an underground opposition to the Bolshevik regime but was in reality entirely run by the OGPU. A critical history of the Trust would have revealed that, successful though it was, its victories were achieved against disorganized, second-rate opposition. Its most celebrated victims, Boris Savinkov and Sidney Reilly, both lured across the Russian frontier to imprisonment and later execution, had become fantasists prey to a variety of delusions.[11] Nothing in the history of the Trust provided any precedent for Angleton's extraordinary claims that both the Sino-Soviet split and the Prague Spring of 1968 were mere playacting – part of a grand strategic deception designed to mislead the West. Study of both the limitations of conspiracy theory and the history of actual conspiracy within open societies should be a compulsory part of the training of every counter-intelligence officer. Once contracted, conspiracy theory is an incurable condition.

One field in which the United States has unquestionably led the world during the last half-century has been in the application of science and technology to the business of intelligence. The path-breaking studies by Jeffrey T. Richelson, Allan A. Needell and Ronald E. Doel establish the importance of further work in this still under-researched area. The most important of the CIA's scientific and technological initiatives, the Imint revolution brought about by the development of the spy plane and the spy satellite, played a crucial role in stabilizing the Cold War. Had the United States remained as ignorant about the Soviet nuclear strike force as it had been up to the mid-1950s, there would have been more and worse 'bomber gap' and 'missile gap' controversies. Had the Soviet missile sites in Cuba been discovered, as Khrushchev had intended, only when they became operational, the Cold War might well have ended in hot war.[12]

The acquisition of all spy satellite photos from 1960 to 1972, together with supporting documents, by the National Archives at College Park, Maryland, will make possible for the first time detailed scholarly analysis of the Imint revolution.[13] The CIA has transferred the Metadata (index) of the 'Corona' spy satellite program, together with 'browse imagery', to the Geological Survey's EROS Data Center (EDC) in Sioux Falls, South Dakota, where they will be available via the Internet on the Global Land Information System (GLIS).

The current programme by the CIA's Center for the Study of Intelligence for the declassification of National Intelligence Estimates (NIEs) on the Soviet Union and International Communism from 1947 to 1991 will also make it possible to extend Lawrence Freedman's pioneering work in the field.[14] Preliminary analysis of these NIEs and other declassified documents has partially demolished the sweeping claims made in the early 1990s that the CIA had failed to predict the collapse of the Soviet Union.[15] Much further research is needed.

Another major area for future research is the hitherto neglected field of economic intelligence, outlined by Philip Zelikow. The database on the Soviet economy assembled by the CIA in the 1950s became of major importance in assessing the Soviet threat. It is at least arguable that the

Agency came to understand the true scale of Soviet defence spending rather better than the Kremlin. Nowadays, one third of the CIA's analysts are concerned with economic issues. Indeed the Agency probably contains as much expertise on international economic problems as all the other departments of the US government combined.[16] But, despite some studies of commercial and technological espionage, there is still no book which provides a reliable assessment, based on adequate documentary evidence, of the past successes and failures of either the CIA or any other major intelligence agency in the field of economic intelligence as a whole. There has also been little attempt so far to explore precisely what secret intelligence can add to the immense volume of open-source data on international economic trends.

The current limitations of economic intelligence were graphically illustrated during the 1995 Mexican financial crisis, aptly described by the managing director of the International Monetary Fund, Michel Camdessus, as the 'first financial crisis of the twenty-first century'. CIA assessments of Mexico's ability to maintain its exchange rate appear to have been more accurate than those of the US Treasury. That, at least, was the conclusion of the Senate Intelligence Committee, which reported after a review of CIA assessments: 'We were frankly impressed by their quality'.[17] What the experience of the Mexican crisis shows most clearly, however, is that no-one inside or outside the intelligence community had yet come to terms with the new era of massive financial transfers across national boundaries. As the last deputy head of the US National Intelligence Council, Gregory Treverton, acknowledged, 'The US government has no way of keeping tabs on the movements of its currency, not to mention less tangible money'.[18] Whether the intelligence community can or should monitor these movements remains an open question.

In addition to the topics covered in this volume, there are at least two other major aspects of the history of the CIA and the US intelligence community which represent major priorities for future research. The first is Sigint, the intelligence derived from the interception and analysis of communications and other signals. Though Sigint is the primary responsibility of the National Security Agency, the CIA contains a rarely-mentioned Sigint office which collects, *inter alia*, intelligence on foreign cipher systems. Sigint also represents a substantial part of the raw intelligence analyzed by the Agency's Directorate of Intelligence.

The biggest gap in our knowledge of United States intelligence collection during the Cold War concerns the role of Sigint. No history of the Second World War nowadays fails to mention the role of Anglo-American codebreakers in hastening victory over Germany and Japan. By contrast, most histories of the Cold War make no reference to Sigint at all. The secret

1948 UKUSA Sigint-sharing agreement, which is still in force, is conspicuous by its absence from textbooks on international relations.[19] No President referred publicly to Sigint until George Bush in 1991.

Studies of intelligence collection and analysis during the Cold War which discuss Humint and Imint but ignore Sigint are bound to suffer from some degree of distortion. In some instances the omission is critical. According to the CIA head of station in Seoul at the end of the Korean War, John L. Hart, 'Sigint was almost the only intelligence worth having in Korea.'[20]

Though the highest-grade cipher systems of the Cold War were far less vulnerable to attack than those of the Second World War, the total volume of Sigint greatly increased in both East and West. It tends to be forgotten that the KGB, like the GRU, was a Sigint as well as a Humint agency. In 1960, for example, the Sigint directorate of the KGB decrypted 209,000 diplomatic cables sent by representatives of 51 states. No less than 133,200 of these intercepts were forwarded to the Central Committee.[21] The volume of KGB and GRU Sigint seems subsequently to have increased still further.

Both the United States and Britain have been far slower to release Sigint records for the early Cold War than for the Second World War. Declassification did not begin until the release in 1995–96 of the 'Venona' decrypts of approximately 3,000 intercepted Soviet intelligence and other telegrams for the period 1939–48, mostly decrypted in the late 1940s and early 1950s.[22] In addition to providing information on several hundred Soviet agents, the material now available on the 'Venona' operation casts important new light on the development of the American intelligence community in the earlier years of the Cold War and on its relations with the White House. One of the most remarkable revelations of the joint NSA/CIA Washington conference held in October 1996 to mark the completion of the declassification of the decrypts was that 'Venona', the most important American intelligence on the Soviet Union acquired during the Truman administration, was – in all probability – never revealed to Truman himself.

In 1948 the Army Security [Sigint] Agency called in the FBI to help track down the many agents identified only by codename in the 'Venona' telegrams. J. Edgar Hoover, the long-serving and autocratic FBI director, was determined to keep personal control of the investigation, even if it meant not telling the White House or the Attorney General. Hoover was engaged in a war on two fronts against both the MGB (predecessor of the KGB) and the CIA, which threatened to challenge his monopoly of counterintelligence and operations in Latin America. 'Venona' showed that OSS, the CIA's wartime predecessor, had been heavily penetrated by Soviet agents, and Hoover also suspected – wrongly – that the same was true of the CIA. So the 'Venona' secret was kept from the CIA until Eisenhower was elected to succeed Truman in November 1952.[23]

The MGB, however, learned in 1947 – even before Hoover – that its telegrams were being decrypted from an agent in the Army Security Agency, William Weisband. The MGB received further intelligence on 'Venona', including the contents of some decrypts, from Kim Philby during his period as SIS liaison officer in Washington from 1949 to 1951.[24] Thus it was that the 'Venona secret' was communicated to Moscow almost six years before it reached either the President or the CIA.

By the standards of the Cold War, 'Venona'was a rather small-scale Sigint operation, never involving as many as a hundred people. Many much larger operations still remain to be revealed. When the Sigint records of, for example, the Korean War, the Suez crisis, the Cuban Missile Crisis and the Vietnam War are finally declassified, they are likely to have important implications for the history of the CIA as well as of the NSA. President Bush declared in 1991:

> ... Over the years I've come to appreciate more and more the full value of Sigint. As President and Commander-in-Chief, I can assure you, signals intelligence is a prime factor in the decision-making process by which we chart the course of this nation's foreign affairs.[25]

Perhaps the most important priority for future research on the CIA and the intelligence community concerns their influence on policy. On present evidence it seems likely that the weakest link in the American intelligence process has not been intelligence collection or analysis but the use made of it. The first of the measures proposed in 1996 by the Brown Commission to improve 'the performance of US intelligence' was directed at policy makers rather than the intelligence agencies:

> Intelligence needs better direction from the policy level, regarding both the roles they perform and what they collect and analyze. Policy makers need to appreciate to a greater extent what intelligence can offer them and be more involved in how intelligence capabilities are used.[26]

The Report of the Twentieth Century Fund Task Force on the Future of US Intelligence puts much of the onus for reform on policy makers, beginning with the President:

> Reshaping intelligence is not a task just for the director of central intelligence and the intelligence community ... The president, in partnership most especially with the secretary of state, must ensure that the intelligence community serves what he defines to be the nation's foreign policy priorities.[27]

Most presidents have not been very good either at managing the intelligence community or at understanding what it can – and cannot – do for them. Over the past two centuries, only four – Washington, Eisenhower, Kennedy (briefly) and Bush – have shown a real flair for intelligence. Unlike most presidents, Washington, Eisenhower and Bush all had extensive firsthand experience of intelligence before their election. Kennedy did not, despite a brief period in naval intelligence, but proved an unusually quick learner after the débâcle at the Bay of Pigs.[28] More detailed analysis of the use made by presidents of intelligence will require access to briefing records and documents such as the President's Daily Briefs (PDBs), of which very few have so far been declassified. On average, about 60 per cent of the topics covered in the PDB, arguably the world's most exclusive newspaper, receive no media coverage at all.

The pioneering study of presidential briefings published in 1996 by John Helgerson, Deputy Director for Intelligence from 1989 to 1993, marks a turning point in the study of relations between the President and the CIA. In addition to having full access to classified files, Dr Helgerson interviewed all surviving former presidents and most surviving Agency briefers. Though his book covers only the briefing of presidential candidates during the election campaign and of presidents-elect before their inauguration, it opens up an important new area of research in the history of every administration since Truman's.[29] Further research by historians outside the CIA, however, will require further declassification.

The wide-ranging programme of research which still remains to be completed on the CIA's first 50 years is only part of a much vaster global intelligence research agenda. The historical study of most of the world's intelligence agencies is still at a very early stage. How world leaders have used, misused or ignored the intelligence available to them remains one of the least understood aspects of the history of the twentieth century.

NOTES

1. 'When one explores the central place of liaison in the real world of intelligence and compares this with the slight emphasis it has had in the serious American literature of intelligence, liaison stands out as having been one of the least sufficiently studied aspects of the entire field.' H. Bradford Westerfield, 'America and the World of Intelligence Liaison', *Intelligence and National Security* 11/3 (July 1966) p.523.
2. *Preparing for the 21st Century: An Appraisal of U.S. Intelligence*, Report of the Commission on the Roles and Capabilities of the United States Intelligency Community, 1 March 1996, Ch.12.
3. *In from the Cold: The Report of the Twentieth Century Fund Task Force on the Future of U.S. Intelligence* (NY: Twentieth Century Fund Press 1996) p.9. The author was a member of the task force which produced this report.

4. The badly-mishandled Ames case was not typical of Agency operations. The Brown Commission concludes that, 'While the CIA has had too many operational and management failures, those failures do not represent the norm. Indeed, the Commission found that the CIA has had, and continues to have, important successes in what is a difficult and risky business'. *Preparing for the 21st Century* (note 2) pp.xx, 2.

5. Ibid. p.127.

6. See above, p.201. Even during the CIA's most ahistorical phases, there were always individuals who kept historical scholarship alive, chief among them Walter Pforzheimer, founder and first curator of the Agency's Historical Intelligence Collection from 1956 to 1974 and Washington's unofficial 'dean' of intelligence history ever since. Former DCI Robert Gates, himself a History PhD, wrote in 1995, 'DCIs come and go, and in 47 years there have been 16 of us. But there is only one Walter Pforzheimer . . . .' On Pforzheimer's career, see Hayden B.Peake and Samuel Halpern (eds) *In the Name of Intelligence: Essays in Honor of Walter Pforzheimer* (Washington DC: NIBC Press 1995).

7. *Preparing for the 21st Century* (note 2) p.32. On the current JIC, see *Central Intelligence Machinery* (London: HMSO 1993). The Brown Commission's conclusion that 'the concept embodied in the JIC can also be made to work in the United States' makes it the more extraordinary that it did not, apparently, find anything in the *operations* of foreign intelligence services which merited serious consideration by the American intelligence community.

8. *In from the Cold* (note 3) pp.7, 11.

9. Christopher Andrew, 'Churchill and Intelligence', *Intelligence and National Security* 3/2 (April 1988); repr. in Michael Handel (ed.), *Leaders and Intelligence* (London: Frank Cass 1988). See also the forthcoming book on Churchill and Intelligence by David Stafford.

10. Christopher Andrew, *For the President's Eyes Only: Secret Intelligence and the American Presidency from Washington to Bush* (London/NY: HarperCollins 1995) pp.104–22.

11. Christopher Andrew and Oleg Gordievsky, *KGB: The Inside Story of its Foreign Operations from Lenin to Gorbachev* (London: Hodder & Stoughton 1990; NY: HarperCollins 1990) Ch.3.

12. Andrew, *For The President's Eyes Only* (note 10) Chs.6, 7.

13. Kevin C. Ruffner, 'Declassification's Great Leap Forward: CORONA and the Intelligence Community', *Studies in Intelligence* 39/5 (unclassified ed.) (1996).

14. For a list of NIEs declassified up to 1996, available at the National Archives, see the brochure published by the Center for the Study of Intelligence in 1996, *Declassified National Intelligence Estimates on the Soviet Union and International Communism*. See also Donald P. Steury (ed.) *Intentions and Capabilities: Estimates on Soviet Strategic Forces, 1950–1983* (Washington DC: CIA Center for the Study of Intelligence 1996).

15. Bruce D. Berkowitz and Jeffrey T. Richelson, 'The CIA Vindicated: The Soviet Collapse *Was* Predicted', *The National Interest*, No.419 (Fall 1995) pp.36–47.

16. Philip Zelikow, 'American Intelligence and the World Economy', in *In from The Cold* (note 3) p.137.

17. See the forthcoming study of the Mexican crisis by Philip Zelikow.

18. Gregory F. Treverton, 'Intelligence since Cold War's End', p.119, in *In from The Cold* (note 3) p.119.

19. Even the few authors who refer to the UKUSA agreement sometimes wrongly date it as a 1947 accord. See Christopher Andrew, 'The Making of the Anglo-American SIGINT Alliance', in Peake and Halpern, *In the Name of Intelligence* (note 6) pp.95–110.

20. Andrew, *For the President's Eyes Only* (note 10) p.194.

21. KGB to Khrushchev, 'Report for 1961, 14 Feb. 1961, in the 'special dossiers' of the CPSU Central Committee; cited by Vladislav M. Zubok, 'Spy vs. Spy: The KGB vs. the CIA, 1960–1962', *Cold War International History Project Bulletin*, no.4 (Woodrow Wilson Center, Washington DC) (Fall 1994) p.23.

22. Robert Louis Benson and Michael Warner (eds) VENONA: *Soviet Espionage and the American Response, 1939–1957* (Washington DC: NSA/CIA 1996).

23. Interview with Dr Cleveland Cram, one of the first CIA officers given access to 'Venona' at the end of 1952; and address by Dr Cram to the NSA/CIA 'Venona' conference, 4 Oct. 1996.

24. Benson and Warner, VENONA (note 22) pp.xxvii–xxviii. SIS, unlike CIA, was promptly informed of 'Venona' by the British Sigint agency GCHQ.
25. Andrew, *For the President's Eyes Only* (note 10)
26. *Preparing for the 21st Century* (note 2) p.xv.
27. *In from the Cold* (note 3) p.4.
28. Andrew, *For the President's Eyes Only* (note 10) passim.
29. John L. Helgerson, *Getting to Know the President: CIA Briefings of Presidential Candidates, 1952–1992* (Washington DC: CIA Center for the Study of Intelligence 1996).

About the Contributors

Christopher Andrew is Professor of Modern and Contemporary History at Cambridge University and a founding editor of *Intelligence and National Security*. His books include *Secret Service: The Making of the British Intelligence Community* (1985), *KGB: The Inside Story* (with Oleg Gordievsky, 1990) and *For the President's Eyes Only: Secret Intelligence and the American Presidency from Washington to Bush* (1995).

Ronald E. Doel is Visiting Assistant Professor of the History of Science in the Department of History and the Geophysical Institute of the University of Alaska Fairbanks. He is the author of *Solar System Astronomy in America: Communities, Patronage, and Interdisciplinary Research, 1920–1960* (1996).

Michael Donovan is completing his University of Edinburgh PhD. on the history of US intelligence on Iran. He has taught at Strathclyde University and now lives in Washington DC.

Lawrence Freedman is Professor of War Studies at King's College, London. His books include *US Intelligence and the Soviet Strategic Threat* (2nd. ed. 1986), *Evolution of Nuclear Strategy* (2nd ed. 1989) and, with Efraim Karsh, *The Gulf War* (1993).

Bob de Graaff is employed at the Institute of Netherlands History at The Hague and is a lecturer at the Erasmus University in Rotterdam. With Dr Cees Wiebes (see below), he wrote *GLADIO der Vrije Jongens. Een particuliere geheime dienst in Koude Oorlogstijd* (1992), a study of postwar Dutch anti-communist private intelligence organizations, and edited *Hun crisis was de onze niet. Internationale Crises en*

Binnenlandse Veiligheid, 1945–1960 (1994), on international political crises and internal security.

Gerald K. Haines served in the CIA's history office and is now the National Reconnaissance Office historian. His books include *The Americanization of Brazil* (1989) and *Unlocking the Files of the FBI* (1993).

Rhodri Jeffreys-Jones is Professor of American History at the University of Edinburgh. His books include *The CIA and American Democracy* (1989) and *Changing Differences: Women and the Shaping of American Foreign Policy, 1917–1994* (1995).

Loch K. Johnson served as a senior staff member on the Senate Select Committee on Intelligence, on the House intelligence oversight committee, and on the Aspin-Brown Commission on Intelligence. He is Regents Professor of Political Science at the University of Georgia, and his books include *A Season of Inquiry: Congress and Intelligence* (1988) and *Secret Agencies: US Intelligence in a Hostile World* (1996).

Helen Laville is researching American women's organizations and the Cold War for a PhD at the University of Nottingham. She is a part-time lecturer in American and Canadian Studies at the University of Birmingham and is the author, with Scott Lucas, of 'Edith Sampson, the NAACP, and African American Identity', *Diplomatic History* 20 (Fall 1996).

Allan A. Needell is Curator in the Space History Department of the Smithsonian Institution's National Air and Space Museum. He is responsible for the museum's manned space-flight collections (Mercury, Gemini and Apollo). He edited *The First 25 Years in Space: A Symposium* (1983; 1989) and is working on a biography of the American science administrator, Lloyd V. Berkner.

Jeffrey T. Richelson is a Senior Fellow of the National Security Archive in Washington DC. His books include *America's Secret Eyes in Space: The US Keyhole Spy Satellite Program* (1990) and *A Century of Spies: Intelligence in the Twentieth Century* (1995).

Bradley F. Smith has taught at Cabrillo College, California. His books include *The Shadow Warriors: OSS and the Origins of the CIA* (1983) and *Sharing Secrets with Stalin. How The Allies Traded Intelligence, 1941–1945* (1996).

Cees Wiebes is a Senior Lecturer at the Department of International Relations and International Law, University of Amsterdam. With Bob de Graaff (see above), he is the author of *Villa Maarheeze 1946–1994*, a history of the Netherlands foreign intelligence service to be published in autumn 1997 by the Dutch Printing Office.

Philip Zelikow served as Director for European Security Affairs on the staff of the National Security Council, and is an Associate Professor of Public Policy at the John F. Kennedy School of Government, Harvard University. With Condoleezza Rice, he co-authored *Germany Unified and Europe Transformed* (1995), and he supplied one of the three background papers included in the Report of the Twentieth Century Fund on the Future of US Intelligence, *In from the Cold* (1996).

Index

Note: agencies etc. are indexed by their acronyms/abbreviations with full titles in brackets. The suffix n indicates a chapter endnote of interest.

Printed in the United States
89899LV00002B/169/A